Automobile Politics

The car – and the range of social and political institutions which sustains its dominance – plays an important role in many of the environmental problems faced by contemporary society. But in order to understand the possibilities for moving towards sustainability and 'greening cars', it is first necessary to understand the political forces that have made the car so dominant. This book identifies these forces as a combination of political economy and cultural politics. From the early twentieth century, the car became central to the organisation of capitalism and deeply embedded in individual identities, providing people with a source of value and meaning, but in a way which was broadly consistent with social imperatives for mobility. Projects for sustainability to reduce the environmental impacts of cars are therefore constrained by these forces, but must deal with them in order to shape and achieve their goals.

Matthew Paterson is Professor of Political Science in the School of Political Studies at the University of Ottawa. He is the author of *Understanding Global Environmental Politics: Domination, Accumulation, Resistance* (2000), *Energy Exporters and Climate Change* (with Peter Kassler, 1997) and *Global Warming and Global Politics* (1996).

Automobile Politics

Ecology and Cultural Political Economy

MATTHEW PATERSON

CAMBRIDGE
UNIVERSITY PRESS

CAMBRIDGE UNIVERSITY PRESS
Cambridge, New York, Melbourne, Madrid, Cape Town, Singapore, São Paulo

Cambridge University Press
The Edinburgh Building, Cambridge CB2 8RU, UK

Published in the United States of America by Cambridge University Press, New York

www.cambridge.org
Information on this title: www.cambridge.org/9780521691307

First published 2007

Printed in the United Kingdom at the University Press, Cambridge

A catalogue record for this book is available from the British Library

ISBN 978-0-521-87080-1 hardback
ISBN 978-0-521-69130-7 paperback

Contents

List of figures   *page* vi

Preface   vii

Acknowledgements   ix

List of acronyms   xi

  1 Introduction: (auto)mobility, ecology and global politics   1

  2 Automobility and its discontents   32

  3 Don't stop movin': the pro-car backlash   61

  4 Automobile political economy   91

  5 The car's cultural politics: producing the (auto)mobile subject   121

  6 Swampy fever, Mondeo Man   166

  7 Greening automobility?   192

  8 Conclusions   225

References   236

Index   267

Figures

1 'China opens up'   *page* 2
2 'No stumps 4 oil'   55
3 'So it's massively over-engineered for the school run'   150
4 'Unlimited access'   156
5 'Something under your skin'   161
6 'Swampy in Armani'   174

Preface

At the personal level, this book is perhaps the outcome of attempts to think more thoroughly about things which have occupied me on a daily basis since I started cycling to school at around the age of seven. At some point in time, I'm not clear when, I realised that this daily act of cycling had helped to form my political consciousness. I think that as an undergraduate in politics, with a number of feminist friends helping make the 'personal is political' connection, I started to realise that what I had taken for granted as just 'how I get about' had both political consequences and shaped how I experienced the political world. I realised that the simultaneous exhilaration of cycling in cities, with the constant potential for violence produced by, well, those bloody cars, and the sense of tension or anger that this engendered, helped me come to see that there was a daily, infrastructural, organisation of movement both by myself and by forces beyond my immediate control, even as I helped to produce them (from which I was thus definitely 'alienated' in the proper sense – I was reading Marx on 'estrangement' at around this time). So while the environmental benefits in the narrow technical sense were always there, as arguments to be produced when necessary to persuade, it was the visceral, experiential side that in an important sense produced in me a politics of automobility. It is precisely the strange realisation (for a white, middle-class man, in particular) that something I took for granted actually placed me in a marginal situation – relegated to the gutters, my needs neglected by the planning system, my safety constantly threatened – which produced a politicisation out of a banal act.

But cycling has also served as a key test case in distinguishing a properly Green politics from other sorts of transport politics. As I articulated this sense, mostly internally to myself or in the pub with friends, over the next decade or so, it became increasingly clear to me that if you spoke to someone who didn't like cars but came from the 'traditional left', for want of a better phrase, their contrast would always be with public transport. For me, while promoting public transport is all well and good it never excites in the way that a bike does, and for me this speaks to the way that Green ideology makes the personal–political connection in a way that social democracy does not, as well as the way that Greens tend to resolve an individual/community tension in very different, more libertarian ways than do social democrats. The bike requires you to be active, to be an agent, in the way that you produce your own life and contribute to the production of a particular kind of world around you. The bus or the train solves the transport/environment problem through collectivisation, while the bike solves it through personal responsibility for reducing one's wants. Now it matters little for the argument of this book which of these you prefer, but it does show that how we experience transport helps to shape (and be shaped by) our overall political orientation.

Acknowledgements

This book is the product of work on cars and environmental politics which began in around 1996. During the course of time I have thus accumulated an enormous number of debts. Perhaps the one most important to acknowledge is the ten years I spent at Keele University, with some of the most enjoyable colleagues one could wish to be around and, for the work that I do, perhaps still the best combination of interesting scholars in both environmental politics and critical International Relations to be found anywhere in the world. John Barry, Brian Doherty, Andrew Linklater, John Macmillan, Kara Shaw, Jill Steans, Hidemi Suganami, John Vogler and Rob Walker all deserve a particular mention.

Papers which have become part of this book have been presented to audiences at Keele University, Warwick University, the University of Ottawa, the British International Studies Association Annual Conference (1998), the AUTO21 conference in Ottawa (2003) and Carleton University. I am grateful to the attention given by all of those audiences. I benefited from a two-month stay at the Norman Paterson School of International Affairs at Carleton University during 2001 and in particular from the hospitality of Maureen Molot. Parts of the book have also been read variously by John Barry, Simon Dalby, Andy Dobson, Brian Doherty, Steve Hinchliffe, Deborah Mantle, Pete Newell, Paul Saurette, Julian Saurin, Ben Seel, Kara Shaw, Hidemi Suganami, Rob Walker, two anonymous reviewers for Cambridge University Press – and I am certain others whom I am unable to remember and to whom I can only apologise. Thank you to all for your critical comments and enthusiastic support. Thank you also to Jo VanEvery, Andreas Krebs and especially Chris Green for suggestions of appropriate songs to discuss in chapter 5. My thoughts on cars and global environmental politics have also been sustained by the parti-cipants in several years of my 'Car trouble: globalisation, hegemony and resistance' final-year seminar course at Keele University and the

MA course I taught on 'The political economy of the automobile' in the Winter semester 2004 at Carleton University's Institute of Political Economy. Paul Evans, Andreas Janz, Susan Kenyon and Emre Uckardesler stand out in particular for their engagement with this material. Finally, my thoughts on the subject have also been enriched enormously through working with Steffen Böhm, Campbell Jones and Chris Land as we co-organised the Automobility conference at Keele in 2002, and then as we co-edited the book *Against Automobility* which came out of the papers from that conference.

Some of the material in this book has already been published. For the most part, it has been heavily reworked. A few paragraphs which appear in each of chapters 2 and 4 first appeared in 'Car Culture and Global Environmental Politics', *Review of International Studies*, 26, 2000: 253–70 and are reproduced by permission of Cambridge University Press. Several paragraphs in chapter 5 first appeared in chapter 5 of my *Understanding Global Environmental Politics* (London: Palgrave, 2000) and are reproduced by permission of Palgrave. The passage discussing adverts from the BMW advert onwards in chapter 5 first appeared in Matthew Paterson and Simon Dalby, 'Empire's Ecological Tyreprints', *Environmental Politics*, 15, 1, 2006: 1–22 and thanks are due to Simon Dalby and to Taylor & Francis for permission to reproduce it. The material on 'Swampy fever' in chapter 6 was first published as 'Swampy Fever', in Benjamin Seel, Matthew Paterson and Brian Doherty (eds.), *Direct Action in British Environmentalism* (London: Routledge, 2000) and thanks are due to Ben, Brian and Routledge, for permission to re-use it. An earlier paper which became the basis for chapter 7 was presented to the AUTO21 conference in Ottawa (2003) and published as part of the proceedings of that conference and thanks are due to Maureen Molot for permission to reproduce the passages which remain as traces from it.

Thanks are also owed to those who granted permission to reproduce the images in the book. These are: *The Economist* (figure 1), thewhitehouse.org (figure 2), Daimler Chrysler UK Ltd (figure 3), Peugeot Motor Company plc (figure 4), Northern Rock plc (figure 5) and the *Daily Express* (figure 6). Finally, I wish to thank John Haslam and Carrie Cheek at Cambridge University Press for their enthusiasm and work on the book.

Acronyms

AA	Automobile Association
ABD	Association of British Drivers
AEI	American Enterprise Institute
BRF	British Roads Federation
CEI	Competitive Enterprise Institute
CIT	Commission for Integrated Transport
CJA	Criminal Justice and Public Order Act 1994
CNG	compressed natural gas
CVC	Coalition for Vehicle Choice
DBFO	Design, Build, Finance, Operate
DETR	Department for the Environment, Transport and the Regions, now
DEFRA	Department for Environment, Food and Rural Affairs
DfT	Department for Transport
EPA	Environmental Protection Agency
EU	European Union
FCCC	Framework Convention on Climate Change
FIA	Fédération Internationale de l'Automobile
FoE	Friends of the Earth
GCC	Global Climate Coalition
GDP	gross domestic product
ghg	greenhouse gas
GM	General Motors
I&M	Inspection and Maintenance
ICE	internal combustion engine
IPCC	International Panel on Climate Change
IPE	International Political Economy
IR	International Relations
IT	information technologies
JIT	just-in-time
LNG	liquified natural gas

LPG	liquified petroleum gas
MAD	Motorists Against Detection
NAFTA	North American Free Trade Agreement
NCC	National Consumer Council
NGO	non-governmental organisation
NICs	Newly Industrialising Countries
NIMBY	Not In My Back Yard
NMAA	National Motorists Association of Australia
NOPE	Not on Planet Earth
OPEC	Organisation of Petroleum-Exporting States
PEM	Proton Exchange Membrane
PFI	Private Finance Initiative
R&D	research and development
RTS	Reclaim the Streets
SACTRA	Standing Advisory Committee on Trunk Road Assessment
SMMT	Society of Motor Manufacturers and Traders
SUV	sports utility vehicle
VOCs	Volatile Organic Compounds
WCC	World Council of Churches
WMD	weapons of mass destruction
WRI	World Resources Institute

1 | Introduction: (auto)mobility, ecology and global politics

> I get around just as nature intended – in a car.
>
> (Meg Ryan, in *French Kiss*)[1]

> Roads girdle the globe
> We all safe in your concrete robe
> Hail mother motor
> Hail piston rotor
> Hail wheel.
>
> (XTC, 'Roads Girdle the Globe', *Drums and Wires*,
> Virgin Music, 1979)

The problems of movement

In November 1999, *The Economist* had a striking front cover announcing a story about the opening up of the Chinese economy (see figure 1).[2] The image used to convey the sense of the story was a superimposition of a six-lane freeway on the Great Wall of China. A number of juxtapositions, with a multitude of meanings, can be discerned in this image. The new is contrasted with the ancient. The straight lines and flat spaces of modernity, with a modernist domination of nature and landscape, are imposed on the curves involved in an ancient accommodation with

---

[1] The irony of this statement in the context of this book is that it is made while Ryan's character is on a plane about to take off. She contrasts the car as natural to the aeroplane of which she is terrified, while of course air travel (for rich Westerners at least) has become naturalised in the same manner as the car.

[2] 'China opens up', *The Economist* (20–26 November 1999). As Hooper shows in detail (Hooper 2001, esp. chapters 4 and 5), *The Economist* is a key publication articulating the interests and values of a largely Anglo-American business elite (Hooper 2001: 117) and one of the key proponents of 'globalisation' (*ibid.*: 118), representing it as the new 'frontier' (*ibid.*: 160–3).

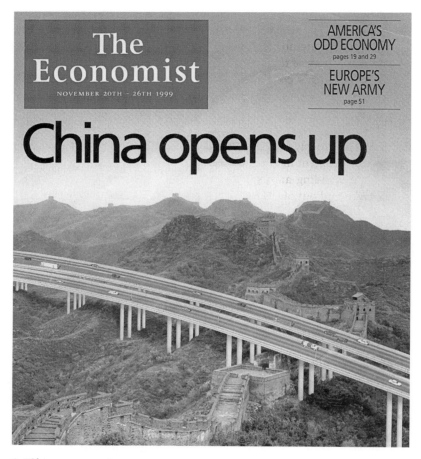

1 'China opens up'
Source: Reproduced by permission of *The Economist*.

physical–geographical features.[3] The physical flows, of both goods and people in general, and across borders in particular, which characterise contemporary political life are displayed transgressing the rigid spatial

---

[3] This is not the first time *The Economist* has used such an image. The cover of one of its periodic surveys, 'a survey on living with the car', entitled 'Taming the beast' (20 June 1996), similarly superimposed an image of the M25 London Orbital motorway on a painting of a bucolic scene from the Italian renaissance. The geopolitics of the China cover is missing but otherwise the juxtaposition of ancient–modern, 'nature'– 'technology' and so on, is strikingly similar.

separations of empire and nation-state invoked by the Wall. The Wall was, of course, built in the Early Han dynasty to keep out invading hordes (the Hsiung-nu), defined by their mobility in opposition to the stability and fixity of the Empire (Lattimore 1962).

The Economist's cover thus constructs a particular sense of a set of connections between what 'progress' is widely seen to entail and mobility or movement. But it is also more specific: it is the mass mobility of the car which is invoked as the image of progress, opening up spaces previously closed to trade. China's 'opening up' is depicted as the precise moment in which cars, and the mobility they (in the dominant understanding at least) make possible, are allowed to cross the border into and out of China, while by (probably inadvertent) contrast America has an 'odd economy' (whatever that means) and Europe focuses on developing an army. The fact that the Wall is on the ancient northern border of (Han-dynasty) China in an area where the nearest Chinese border (now further to the north) is with Mongolia is perhaps ironic, but tangential to the purposes here. The 'real' freeway being planned which will realise the image in the cover, is perhaps the 60 km bridge being planned to cross the South China Sea between Hong Kong and Zhuhai (Castells 2000: 439), the principal location of China's actual 'opening'. Nevertheless, as part of such an opening, the Wall has been rebranded, a monument laid beside it in 1989 declaring: 'once intended to ward off enemy attacks, today it brings together the peoples of the world. The Great Wall, may it continue to act as a symbol of friendship for future generations' (quoted in Mattelart 2000: 121).

For those with an interest in the 'classics' of western thought, it conjures up Marx and Engels' statement that 'the cheap prices of its [the bourgeoisie's] commodities are the heavy artillery with which it batters down all Chinese Walls' (Marx and Engels 1848/1967: 84). For the ecologically inclined, the immediate connection is to the question of 'what happens if the Chinese all have cars?', often invoked (always highly problematically, in terms of its ethics and politics) in western debates surrounding consumption levels, climate change, or environmental politics more generally (Brown and Flavin 1996; Tunali 1996; Richard Smith 1997). The Chinese state clearly recognises the symbolism here, and how it is intertwined with economic strategy, since it has started to ban bicycles from certain Beijing streets in favour of cars, in part 'to promote the country's fledgling automobile industry' (Chu 1998). Cars at the same time symbolised for some the downside of

China's 'opening'. One of the touchstones for hostility to China's new rich, made so by the 'opening', has been what is known as the 'BMW collision affair'. A BMW driver escaped punishment for killing a pedestrian, which symbolised for many the inequalities inherent in the 'opening' to the global economy (e.g. Bodeen 2004; Engler 2004).

However we read *The Economist* cover, at its heart is the question of movement. The transgression of boundaries is taken as the key to 'modernisation', and that transgression is represented through the freeway. This symbolism is not an accident. Movement is at the heart of all contemporary political practices, whether or not articulated through the buzzword of 'globalisation': the physical movement of people, goods, missiles, animals, or occasionally territory, as well as the virtual movement of electrons, images, information and ideas. Movement or mobility has also been a symbolic or discursive force underpinning modern political practices, although its importance is usually unacknowledged, taken for granted, in discussions of the dynamics of global politics in either academic debates or public discourse. Where movement appears explicitly it usually appears in one of two forms. At times it appears as a question of how 'we' (the character of the 'we' here varies according to the context) prevent certain forms of movement – migrants in nationalist discourse, elephant tusks in conservationist discourse, CFCs in environmentalist discourse. More commonly it appears as a question of how the movement – of fruit, car components, images, dollars, explosives, etc. – can be accelerated. The imperatives of contemporary political economy – for firms to improve their competitiveness, for states to improve their position in a global political–economic hierarchy, or for individuals to meet their workplace performance targets – all require continuous investment in a variety of technologies of movement.

We can perhaps start with conventional accounts of international politics. Warfare has been fundamentally transformed by technologies of movement: one of the most famous (but, of course, highly contested) accounts of the First World War's origins is that it was caused by train timetables (Taylor 1969). Since train systems require a high degree of co-ordination and logistical precision, once a decision to mobilise troops was made a war was inevitable (*ibid.*). The emergence of armoured vehicles powered by internal combustion engines (ICEs) is also conventionally thought of as being one of the decisive elements in precipitating the end of the First World War (Virilio 1986). The emergence of aeroplanes by the 1930s is similarly thought to have shaped the strategic possibilities available to military planners in the Second World War, facilitating both the fast overwhelming attack of '*Blitzkrieg*' and the ongoing attrition-at-a-distance of strategic bombing campaigns. In contemporary warfare, the crucial strategic advantage is with those able to penetrate air forces well into 'enemy' territory, to move troops at speed and to use virtual mobility – through surveillance and communications technologies – to full effect (Der Derian 1992, 2001).

The system of multilateral regimes currently in place to govern politics between states in the interstate system is, of course, highly dependent on extensive physical movement of diplomats, advisors, negotiators and lobbyists around the world, between their capital cities and the sites of negotiations. The irony of virtually continual dialogue between officials from many countries on climate change, moving from site to site as different governments host meetings,[4] at the same time contributing significant amounts of CO_2 to the atmosphere, is lost on few commentators.

Movement has perhaps been most obviously demonstrated in economic flows: those of food, raw materials, component parts and finished goods are all highly visible. The flow of people as tourists now constitutes the largest industry in the world (at least, according to the rhetoric of the tourist trade). But at the same time they are taken for granted, premised on the assumptions of classical economics which renders them the natural result of laws of comparative advantage. Only recently has it begun to be questioned whether it is rational for apples to be imported from Chile and New Zealand to the United Kingdom while apples growing on trees in Herefordshire, Suffolk, Somerset or Kent are left rotting on the ground (Monbiot 2004).

We can thus say, with Virilio (1986), that contemporary societies can be defined as *dromocratic*: ruled by movement and acceleration. Movement is not only *central* to contemporary politics – in the sense that many things would not happen without it – it is a *ruling principle* of contemporary life. If the Chinese state is to become a full member of the 'international community' it must subject itself unhindered

---

[4] For example, after the collapse of the formal negotiations in the Hague in November 2000 negotiators from OECD countries moved straight to Ottawa and then to Oslo for more meetings to try to resolve US–EU differences.

mobility. The central tension underlying what Virilio terms 'dromocratic' politics is that between the impulses of the masses for revolutionary action and the strategies undertaken by the military, the bourgeoisie and state builders (all closely interlinked) to repress the revolution while channelling the energy of the 'mobile mass' (the title of his opening chapter is 'From street fight to State right'). These impulses and strategies are all interpreted as principally orientations to *movement* – hence 'dromocratic' – which becomes simultaneously the rule *of* movement (mobility becomes an 'obligation'), *over* movement (it needs to be controlled and channelled) and *through* movement (it is through organising people's mobility that rulers pursue their particular projects and the maintenance of their power in general). In Virilio's words:

> The State's political power ... is the polis, the police, in other words highway surveillance ... since the dawn of the bourgeois revolution, the political discourse has been no more than a series of more or less conscious repetitions of the old communal poliorcetics [siegecraft], confusing social order with the control of traffic (of people, of goods), and revolution, revolt, with traffic jams, illegal parking, multiple crashes, collisions. (Virilio 1986: 14)

But 'dromocracy' is at the same time highly problematic, and does not go uncontested. We might problematise contemporary movement and mobility in global politics in several ways. The most prevalent is through debates about migration. For much of the twentieth century, the most widespread restrictions on movement were on capital (understood as finance). In the Bretton Woods period (post-1945) through to the early 1970s the movement of things and people was facilitated and accelerated while there were significant controls on the movements of money. But since the collapse of Bretton Woods and the onset of 'globalisation' the places of money and people in this scheme have been reversed. We are now faced with a securitisation of the movement of people where the contradictions in neoliberal globalisation are at their most extreme. Restrictions on the movements of people are increasing everywhere, and with them an intensification of the policing of borders on more or less obviously racialised lines (Bigo 2002; Walters 2002; Salter 2004).

In neoliberal globalisation's boost to the acceleration of global flows of dollars, microchips and so on, but also in the critical debates about the 'securitisation of movement', the unacknowledged ecology of these movements of both things and people is something that should be highlighted. Embedded in globalising processes, and necessary for their reproduction, is a set of movements which are irreducibly physical and as such represent and enact flows of soil, water, food, minerals, energy, toxic waste and so on. For the most part, these represent an appropriation by a 'global middle class' of the subsistence potential of many of the world's poorest regions, and thus have both an ecological and a global justice dimension. The majority of these ecologically significant movements are daily and local yet are also intertwined with globalising processes: as a means to access consumption items produced and distributed transnationally; as consumption items (cars) with a high degree of transnational production and global symbolism; and as a potential for national integration into a global economy (transport infrastructure).

Such movements are thus simultaneously three things:

- First, they are necessary conditions of the reproduction of a globalising capitalism. They represent precisely the site where M–M' cycles (those from investment, to production, to distribution, sale and consumption, to profit, to further investment) of various sorts are intensifying: the sites of both basic commodification (the bringing of new things – from genes to exotic fruits – to the marketplace) and heightened extraction of surplus value as low-wage labour is exploited in the name of 'comparative advantage'.

- Second, they are celebrated in terms of the 'freedom' of consumers, associated with progress and so on. This is most obvious in the term 'automobility' – the conjoining of 'autonomy' and 'mobility' in such a way as to legitimise the imperatives for movement that underpin modernity in general and globalisation in particular (a concept we shall develop later). Cars, the principal (although not the only) artefact of automobility, are the main daily form of movement for the world's upper-middle class, a significant element in a globalising economy and a signifier of global cultural convergence (as in Friedman's (2000) paean, which begins with the Lexus as the signifier of globalisation) and have particularly intensive ecological impacts and implications for global justice.

- Third, such movements are the very things that are accelerating the twin crises of ecological degradation and global injustice, especially famines. The throughput of energy embedded in cars (and, increasingly, aeroplanes) but also in the various commodities transported round the world to satisfy the consumer 'desires' of the global middle class, combined with relentless corporate attempts to drive down costs (where energy is itself underpriced), is a principal 'driver' of world-wide climate change, acid rain, urban air pollution and so on. The movement of foods (and cut flowers, etc.) and the embedded water and (degraded) soil they spring from makes a significant contribution to famines and starvation in many parts of the world – and, of course, the energy question provides, for many at least, a principal explanation for geopolitical adventures in Iraq, Afghanistan and elsewhere.

Movement is thus at the heart of *political economy*, *cultural politics* and *environmental politics*, the intersection of three themes or fields which inform the basic points of departure for this book. Movement is thus fundamentally problematic, by contrast with proponents of neoliberal globalisation who seek to accelerate all movement, with nationalists–racists who wish to restrict movements of people across borders but accept many other forms of movement, or with traditional leftists who wish to restrict movements of capital but resist the racism in anti-migrant discourse. At the same time as contemporary forms of movement are fundamental to current political practice they operate on an (ever-increasing) scale which cannot be continued indefinitely. 'Carboniferous capitalism' (Mumford 1934; Dalby 2002), and the automobility which gives it expression in daily life, requires continually increasing consumption of fuels which have both a limited lifespan and are at the heart of contemporary environmental change which threatens radically to alter the conditions of existence of the large majority of humanity and the other organisms which inhabit the planet.

The particular way that the focus on movement in many discourses across the social sciences is framed, however, tends to obscure this aspect. As Urry (2004) suggests in the context of sociology, 'the car is rarely discussed in the "globalization literature", although its specific character of domination is more systemic and awesome in its consequences than what are normally viewed as constitutive technologies of the global' (2004: 25). This is partly because the focus on mobility has tended to undermine the notion of fixed, clearly bounded societies, economies, cultures, or polities and has thus been on those movements which transgress borders (trade, migrants and so on). It is partly also because of a general tendency to analyse and focus on the extraordinary, the spectacular, or the novel and innovative at the expense of the mundane, the quotidian. The weakness Urry identifies in sociological discourse is similar in much contemporary debate in politics. As we shall see, the recent emphasis on movement in International Relations (IR) has similar weaknesses – concerned principally with undermining a statist conception of global politics, it ends up as a consequence uncritically celebrating movement. But the principal movements carried out on a daily basis are just as important in the reproduction of particular sorts of social and political order, and just because they do not physically cross established borders it does not mean that they are not in an important sense 'globally' organised.

Cars are globally the predominant daily form of mobility. Even for those who do not use a car, the conditions under which we move around are shaped fundamentally by car-led development strategies. Focusing on cars also demonstrates the ecological dimension to contemporary obsessions with mobility, with mass car use being at the root of a spectrum of ecological problems including urban air pollution, resource depletion for a wide range of materials (oil, iron, platinum, rubber, among others), climate change, soil degradation and loss of agricultural land. Such problems have significant impacts on human health but also present a substantial element in the fundamental unsustainability of contemporary societies.

This unsustainability of automobility is not uncontested. I discuss many of the arguments in chapter 2 in particular, but also elsewhere in this book. The initial stimulus for my interest in the questions I explore here is still a good illustration of the contested arena; in the early 1990s automobility was contested in the United Kingdom (in particular) in a most radical manner and in ways highly suggestive of precisely what is at stake in the politics of automobility.[5] From 1992 onwards,

---

[5] I should acknowledge that the material for the book comes predominantly from the United Kingdom and the United States. This is in part because I come from the United Kingdom and was living and working there while most of the research for the book was carried out, and because most of the literature on cars is American in orientation. There are obvious limitations of this focus. However, while all countries will have their specific nature in terms of car cultures, public policy, patterns of economic development, forms of political resistance and so on, I would argue that the striking similarities across countries, especially in terms of the political forces 'driving' car-dominated development, suggest that to talk of a 'global politics of automobility' is legitimate. It is not the aim of this book to provide a comparative analysis of different countries, but to suggest that a focus on the similarities is illuminating.

stimulated by the UK government's roads building programme and the perceived weakness of traditional environmental non-governmental organisations (NGOs), a new generation of activists adopted direct action methods, first to oppose road building projects, then to reclaim urban space from the car and promote alternative forms of urban living. These protests involved a range of strategies, from physical occupation of construction sites, occupation of offices of companies involved in the projects, construction and habitation of protest camps, destruction of machinery, through to, in the most high-profile (and for many inspiring) cases, the construction of elaborate walkways between trees to protect woodland to be cleared for road construction (as at the Newbury Bypass and elsewhere), recreation of houses to be demolished as art work (in the M11 protest) and creation of networks of fragile tunnels under proposed construction sites (as in Fairmile at the A30 protest) (on the roads protests generally, see Seel *et al.* 2000).

The roads protests provide an important illustration of what is at stake in contesting automobility. They gradually moved from objections to particular impacts of car-led development – such as loss of forests or other ecosystems or valued countryside, loss of community and collective space in cities – to a total critique of automobility itself as implicated in a whole range of problems and contradictions intrinsic to modern society. The protests widened from objecting to road building, to objecting to the dominance of cars in cities, to mobilisation against neoliberal globalisation (one of the trajectories of Reclaim the Streets, a major network involved in anti-car activism, was towards 'Reclaim the summit' direct action at the Birmingham G8 summit in 1998) and to providing alternative models of modern urban life centred around community rather than commuting, place rather than mobility. They thus suggest that what is at stake in contesting automobility is precisely the need to question modern societies and polities themselves. They are also suggestive at times of re-articulations of global politics. UK anti-globalisation activism is one example, and the articulation by some of anti-roads actions in terms of global obligations concerning climate change (see, for example, www.risingtide.org.uk) is another. More unexpected forms of international solidarity and politics have also arisen. Protesters from Colombia visited the Newbury Bypass protest; while the Newbury protesters were amazed that the Colombians had actually managed to stop the Pan American Highway going through their territory, and that they had not been beaten by security guards and police, or imprisoned by the state, as in the United Kingdom, the Colombians were equally amazed that the Newbury protesters had not been supported by the UK Department of the Environment. Both groups performed an indigenous identity in opposition to 'progress' (Vidal 1996).

But these contestations operate as much at the level of everyday life as at the level of heroic politics. Take, for example, an 'ordinary' suburb in a western city. Kings Heath in Birmingham exhibits many of the chronic transport-related crises pervasive in many European, Asian and some North American cities, which are rapidly being globalised around the world (Freund and Martin 1999).[6] Transport is one of the overwhelming and omnipresent conflicts in local politics; there are organisations representing single streets ('Action for Addison Road') whose identity is defined by their relation to particular aspects of the local transport question.[7] The city council was (and continues to be) involved over several years in massive planning and consultation exercises in response to the range of issues thrown up both locally and city-wide.

Kings Heath exemplifies the problems of mobility and modernity endemic in western urban settings which can be traced back at least to Haussman's attempts to accelerate movement in the construction of planned arterial roads in Paris in the 1850s (Berman 1982: 158).[8] It is a densely built, turn-of-the-twentieth-century suburb, which is simultaneously a residential area, the second or third biggest shopping area in the city, thus bringing in many to the area from across South Birmingham, and also contains one of the ten large arterial roads heading into the city centre. In common with many similar districts it

---

[6] I lived in Kings Heath between 1997 and 2003, and this account is based mostly on (inevitably partial) observations of and participation in local transport politics during this time. The formal consultations over the schemes discussed here were mostly during 2000–2. For a more general account of transport policy and politics in Birmingham during this period, focused on city-wide developments and on policy documents and debates, but broadly in line with the analysis here, see Vigar (2001: chapter 6). Thanks are due to Steve Hinchliffe for comments and updates on the local situation.

[7] Action for Addison Road even had their own website (actionforaddisonroad.org), now unfortunately offline.

[8] Berman (1982) quotes David Pinkney to the effect that Haussman's boulevards 'were from the start burdened with a dual function: to carry the main streams of traffic across the city and to serve as major shopping and business streets; and as the volume of traffic increased, the two proved to be ill-compatible' (Pinkney 1972: 214–15; Berman 1982: 158). As we shall see, the tensions in Kings Heath are even more pronounced.

started as a suburb organised around trains and tram services, both of which were lost in the post-Second World War years. It has four primary schools and four secondary schools in or close to its core and thus has all the problems of the 'school run'. The roadspace is caught up in competition for a great mix of uses, most of which conflict with each other. The main road is only 11 m wide along the High Street (where all the shops are) and from a transport planner's point of view is thus too narrow for four lanes which might make bus lanes possible, or provide simultaneously for parking and continuous traffic flow.

These technical aspects produce a proliferation of discourses about what the 'problem' is, and of course what any consequent 'solutions' are. What follows is a tentative attempt to map the complexity of these discourses.

For the traffic planners in Birmingham City Council, the overriding concern seems to have been to improve flow into the city centre. Reflecting a fairly traditional modernisation perspective, the imperative behind the Council's plans and consultation was to free up roadspace along the High Street to improve the 'flow' of traffic. The whole panoply of circulation metaphors – flow, friction and so forth – was in place to service these proposals rhetorically (see chapter 5). But at the same time, the planners' rhetoric was overlaid with a variety of discourses within transport planning that emerged during the 1970s. The simplest overlay has been that of emphasising flow for public transport rather than simply for cars.[9] One part of the High Street scheme is thus the introduction of a new 'showcase' bus route, with service 50x departing every 10 minutes but stopping only in some four places between its park and ride terminus 2 miles south of Kings Heath and the city centre, with electronic signs informing passengers when the next 50x is coming – thus enabling both an increasing flow of people down the High Street and a reduction in the flow of vehicles. (The regular service 50 departs every 3–4 minutes, so passengers can 'choose' to lower their mobility levels by taking the slower bus, at least at certain stops).

---

[9] As Vigar (2001: 127) notes, concerning Birmingham City Council in general: 'its approach to transportation policy by 2001 was one that reflected an economic realism to keep traffic moving while also trying to shape the modal split rather than the demand for movement *per se*.' 'Modal split' is a transport planner's term which refers to the share of journeys made by different transport modes (car, bus, etc.).

But there is a host of other overlays in planners' discourse which complicate the simple focus on an imperative to improve mobility. The planners proposed traffic-calming schemes, pavement-widening/ improvements for pedestrians, some cycling improvements (selective streets shut off except for cyclists). These reflect changes within planning discourse towards notions of 'liveable cities' (e.g. Newman and Kenworthy 1999; for Birmingham, see Birmingham City Council 2000). All of these developments were also legitimised and organised through 'participatory' processes (focus groups, neighbourhood forum meetings, consultation documents, roadshows, etc.) aimed at legitimising (even co-opting, local residents into) the suggested schemes. Such legitimisation broadly failed, but was nevertheless attempted.

Most conflict occurred over proposals for parking. This had two aspects to it: the regulation of parking on the High Street to make way for increased flow and the proposals for a residents'-only parking scheme. The 11m-wide road meant that, as we have seen, four lanes were impractical, so there was little sense (from a planner's point of view) in attempting to ban parking totally as it still would not make space for bus lanes.[10] The scheme adopted meant that there was no parking at any point on both sides of the High Street. This was very controversial, with protest from local businesses fearful of loss of trade (especially the 'mobile' trade – those on their way home from the city centre, who now don't stop on the High Street) and from those residents addicted to being able to park anywhere.[11]

The residents'-only parking scheme was even more controversial. It was to operate in the area close to the High Street to limit parking on residential streets to their residents. Car-owning residents tended to support the scheme, but not that they would have to pay for its

---

[10] Cycle lanes did not come up in discussions in the focus groups I participated in, even with a group weighted towards cyclists, including me, and led by a transport planner who 'outed' himself as a cyclist.

[11] Addiction as a metaphor comes up frequently in relation to car use (e.g. Alvord 2000: chapter 5). Castells (2000) suggests that 'In those cities, particularly in Europe, where a radioconcentric pattern still dominates daily commuting ... commuting time is sharply up, particularly for stubborn automobile addicts' (2000: 426). Even George W. Bush adopted the 'addiction' metaphor in relation to oil, in his 2006 State of the Union address. Pro-car backlash writers, such as those discussed in chapter 3, object to the addiction metaphor (e.g. Kazman 2001).

implementation. Those on streets outside the scheme complained vigorously that they would be swamped by displacement effects.

These complex discourses surrounding movement in Kings Heath all reflect the general problematisation of automobility in the last three decades of the twentieth century. Many of the regulatory changes developed in response to social movement activism since the 1960s in both the United Kingdom and transnationally about the way that car-led development had shaped and destroyed city forms and the forms of urban life they had enabled. The 'new' transport management was created by discursive shifts in planning (after Jane Jacobs, see Jacobs 1961) emphasising community, etc. over more 'high-modernist' visions of urban life going back to Le Corbusier. Le Corbusier had provided the vision of urban life that dominated planning and architectural philosophies for much of the middle part of the twentieth century, with his uncompromising image of progress through high-rise buildings, large open spaces and freeways. This explicitly involved the destruction of nineteenth-century city forms; as one of Le Corbusier's most famous followers, Robert Moses, stated: 'when you live in an over-built metropolis, you have to hack your way through with a meat ax' (quoted in Berman 1982: 290, Moses was the chief planner of a range of modernist projects in New York). In her classic work on the death and life of great American cities, Jacobs (1961) provided a radically alternative vision of city life which rejected Le Corbusier's heroic modernist vision of a planned, designed, city in favour of attention to the small detail of how cities actually work. By the early 1990s it had become impossible in most UK cities to engage in a strategy such as Moses had articulated – building large freeways that destroyed older neighbourhoods. In Birmingham's case, this point was reached in the defeat in 1991 of proposals to build a new road, or expand existing ones, to connect the newly completed M40 to the city centre (Vigar 2001: 128–30). The proposed new road would have gone to the east of Kings Heath High Street, but would have displaced much traffic from it, thus simplifying the area's problems (assuming, of course – which is generally regarded as a bad assumption – that such a motorway would not simply create traffic rather than displace it).

Departure points

These preliminary comments are suggestive of my points of departure and intended destination for this book. The first is a range of debates and concerns in environmental politics. At the most general level, the study of environmental politics addresses the politics of sustainability and unsustainability. It asks, on the one hand, what is it about contemporary political institutions, actors, systems, discourses, ideologies, identities and so on which contributes to the unsustainable character of the way which humanity collectively (but very unequally) interacts with the physical world around it. It asks, on the other, what the political conditions are under which humanity might behave in a manner which in principle can be sustained indefinitely. This general set of questions then prompts a myriad of specific issues and avenues of research – into political theory, international politics, social movements, public policy and the like. Many of these fields, of course, reflect pre-existing disciplinary boundaries already set up more generally within the study of politics.

I would make two principal points in relation to contemporary environmental politics. First, if we want to address the two general questions just posed, my answer would be something like this. The world is principally on an unsustainable path because, on the one hand, of the particular organisation of society as *capitalist*, with associated patterns of class conflict, global inequalities, market competition, growthmania and state economic management, which engender continually increased throughput of resources, production of pollution and disruption of ecosystems and, on the other, the existence of specific sorts of subjectivities, ways of being in the world, which means that people attach positive value to precisely those objects and practices which produce widespread environmental degradation. The politics of producing sustainability therefore lies in both transforming capitalism (by which I mean both projects to transform capitalism from within and attempts to find alternatives to capitalism) and in cultural change to produce new sorts of human subjectivity and sociality. In terms of academic debates, environmental politics should thus be understood through accounts of political economy, on the one hand, and cultural politics, on the other, and through attempts to think critically and productively within these fields and perspectives.

Second, I would argue that the academic literature in environmental politics tends to start with an account of individual and collective subjects, and the political institutions, structures and discourses within which they act and which they are occasionally able to transform, which is abstracted from the material practices of their everyday lives

which are the principal immediate sources of environmental change.[12]
A couple of examples can help to illustrate this. In international environmental politics the tendency is to study the actions of states in
relationship to others to mitigate this or that environmental 'problem'.
But the models of agency attributed to states are drawn from theories
of IR which regard states either as rational actors in the sense used by
rational choice theory (with perspectives divided into so-called
'realists' who assume that states aim to maximise relative gains, and
liberal institutionalists who assume that the purpose is to maximise
absolute gains, see Baldwin 1993; Paterson 1996) or as 'reflexive'
agents, where states act 'towards objects, including other actors, on
the basis of the meanings that the objects have for them' (Wendt 1992:
396–7). While there is plenty of nuance and opportunity for debate
between them, nowhere do these models permit analysts of environmental politics to consider the throughput of resources, and consequent generation of environmental change, which sustain modern
states as a condition of possibility of their action. In political theory,
there has been considerable debate on 'environmental citizenship' (e.g.
Dobson 2003; Haugestad and Wulfhorst 2004). This debate focuses
broadly on how the bundle of rights and obligations that defines the
core of particular ways that make individuals members of specific
societies (perhaps including an emerging 'global' society, and perhaps
a conception of society which extends beyond the limits of simply a
human society) is and/or can be reshaped along ecological lines. But
again, while there is an occasional discussion which might lead us to
think materially about citizenship (particularly the 'consumerisation of
citizenship' in neoliberal societies) this is not taken as the basic starting
point. Environmental/ecological citizenship becomes thought of as a set
of abstract obligations to others within society, overlooking the ways
that such sorts of membership in society are sustained and made possible
by specific sorts of ecological flows. To conceptualise a 'global' citizenship without envisaging the socio-technical systems – air travel, the
internet and so on – and thus the energy, materials and toxic chemicals
to sustain such a form of citizenship, for example, seems to me highly
problematic. I would rather start with with specific sorts of material
practices that engender environmental change, and then ask how these
practices are connected to, structured by (but at the same time

---

[12] This point is also made by Horton (2006), focusing on social movement analysis.

influence) patterns of state action in the international sphere, citizenship, or any other political concept. My point would be that this reinforces the focus on political economy and cultural politics as outlined above, since these are the sites in which these material practices are principally *organised* and *interpreted*.

Robyn Eckersley's book *The Green State* (2004) is a good illustration of how the study of environmental politics tends to operate, and what for me are its weaknesses. I highlight her book because it is in my view the best book about environmental politics to appear for a long time, a wonderfully rich and broad-ranging, synthetic work. I am also struck by the way Eckersley develops an account of a critical environmental politics as an 'immanent critique' – an attempt to analyse not only what is ecologically problematic about contemporary politics but to analyse how that politics is changing in ways which offer opportunities for environmentalists/Greens to intervene, promote particular tendencies and move towards more ecologically viable types of politics. My intention in this book is to interrogate the politics of cars in a similar light: to suggest that while there are dominant forces which structure the world in an unsustainable fashion, this dominant organisation of society is contradictory and contains elements which prefigure and suggest the possibility of an alternative, and the social forces which might push for it.

Eckersley argues that there have been three principal elements in global politics which have engendered ecological unsustainability. These are the competitive interstate system, global capitalism and the weak character of liberal democracy. These have both generated patterns of development which are unsustainable and also provided significant constraints to responding to the social and ecological disruptions generated by the unsustainable development. But at the same time one can discern tensions or contradictions within these systems of power and processes operating within and beyond them which serve to show the possibilities of *both* 'greening' them *and* developing new forms of politics beyond them. Thus within the anarchic interstate system a set of processes Eckersley calls 'environmental multilateralism' is emerging, entailing a transformation of interstate anarchy from a 'Hobbesian' logic (of unremitting conflict) to a 'Kantian' logic (of peaceful co-existence), capitalism is being 'greened' by processes of 'ecological modernisation' and experiments in discursive, deliberative and transnational democratic practice are emerging to make up for the weaknesses of liberal democracy. The pursuit of sustainability entails principally pushing at these three doors to develop politics into a set of overlapping 'ecological democracies'.

But while this is an attractive programme, and a useful way to understand the current situation regarding environmental politics and the potential for transforming them in the direction of sustainability, it still in my view suffers from the problems suggested above. The 'greening of democratic institutions', in Eckersley's vision, posits mechanisms to 'represent' non-humans, to take account of transboundary effects and so on, but this is abstracted from the material daily life of those who might participate politically. It thus, in effect, from the point of view of the material I detail in this book, overlooks the fact that liberal democracy is 'anaemic' in the ways Eckersley (and other ecological democrats) discusses at least in part *because of* the co-evolution of liberal societies and automobility. The reproduction of the hyper-individualist version of liberalism, where the 'individual' is posited as pre-social and pre-discursive, has become reproduced in the twentieth century principally through the daily use and hegemony of the car (Rajan 2006). Automobility serves to underscore the separation of individuals from each other, driving in their little private universes with no regard for the consequences of the actions in which they have the fundamental right to engage, just as they vote in their private worlds of liberal consumerist democracy. To envisage an alternative democracy, based on recognition of the discursive constitution of individuals and their relation both to each other and to political and social institutions, thus entails thinking also in terms of alternative daily practices which might recognise and reinvigorate the senses of self which recognise obligations to others, communality and so on.

Eckersley does have an explicit political economy since she makes globalising capitalism one of the principal forces which engenders unsustainability. One of the implications of thinking about political economy and cultural politics *in relation to each other* would, however, be to emphasise that capitalism is not only reproduced at the level of state and interstate management, the strategies of multinational firms and so on, but at the level of everyday life. The daily practices of drivers (and myriad other producers and consumers) serve as crucial links in reproducing both particular patterns of capital accumulation and accumulation in general. Ecological modernisation needs to be understood not only in terms of the capacity of states and 'progressive' firms to reorient patterns of investment towards the range of economic sectors which need to develop to reshape societies in the direction of sustainability and away from unsustainable economic forms, but also in terms of the cultural conditions under which these investments might be realised. So to take a relatively trivial (but instructively so) example, one of the principal obstacles to electric cars has been the way that they were feminised through early twentieth-century discourses that emphasised the importance of power (as brute strength), so that such cars were consistently undervalued (Scharff 1992). Sustainability from this perspective becomes a fundamental question of what sort of people we want to be.

My second departure point is the contemporary debates between political economy and poststructuralist perspectives. While these range across the social sciences, I come to them (for reasons of historical accident as much as anything) principally through debates between these perspectives about global politics. So I take as specific points of departure those writing about contemporary developments in global capitalism, broadly in relation to the theoretical framing of 'neo-Gramscian' International Political Economy (IPE), and those in broadly critical IR who read contemporary global politics in terms of Foucault's notion of governmentality.

The former provide the most prominent current account of how we might think about the dynamics of contemporary capitalism – focusing, for example, on the dynamics of specifically neoliberal globalisation (Rupert and Smith 2002), the emergence of a transnational capitalist class (van der Pijl 1998; Sklair 2000), the privatisation of governance (Lipschutz with Rowe 2005), the embedding of global capitalism in 'new constitutional' forms of authority (Gill 2000) and, most recently, through revisiting the notions of empire and imperialism (Hardt and Negri 2000; Nederveen Pieterse 2004).

I take the latter perspective here as a point of departure for two principal reasons. One is that it has across the social sciences since the 1970s provided one of the most significant lines of critical enquiry against the Marxism which informs the political economy account. It questions (among other things) the discussion in Marxism concerning the existence of objectively given class interests, the reduction of ideology to the hegemonic presentation of class interests and the teleology of universal emancipation underpinning the Marxian account of history (Laclau and Mouffe 1985). It has provided one of the principal sites at which various authors have attempted to articulate a specifically *cultural* political economy (Ray and Sayer 1999; du Gay and Pryke 2002; in IPE, see de Goede 2006) – not to reject out of hand the utility of classical political economy accounts based on Marx, Gramsci and so on but to insist on the importance of cultural components to capitalism: its dependence on shared (and contested) meanings, identity and so on, and the historically contingent and constructed relationship between those identities and cultures with the 'core' of capitalist development.

The second reason for taking poststructuralism specifically in IR as a starting point is that it makes movement one of its prominent themes. Movement in much of this literature becomes understood as a transgressive act, which both practically disrupts established political orders and in academic (and political–discursive) terms undermines traditional accounts of politics centred on allegedly sovereign states. The movement, of peoples (migrants, refugees, diasporas, in particular – tourists or globe-trotting western academics are less frequently discussed) is effectively celebrated (as opposed to critically analysed) in much of this literature, since it sounds the death knell of institutions, practices and theories which assume that the principal forms of political life go on within the bounded territories of states.

Several of the essays in a special issue of *Millennium* on 'Territories, Identities and Movement in International Relations' (1999) are instructive here.[13] In his introductory essay, Brock emphasises that one of the main points of researching the triad of 'territories, identities and movements' is to reject conventional accounts of the relationship between 'order and movement around the world' (Brock 1999: 485). For conventional accounts of IR, the movement of 'migrants, refugees, asylum seekers and others would … constitute disorder' (*ibid.*). By contrast, to approach territoriality, identities and movement from a critical perspective means for Brock to view 'these people as expressing the very order of things' (*ibid.*). So far, so reasonable – the global order is constituted by the range of movements across borders in ways that realists have no conceptual tools to grasp. But in several of the chapters (the main exception is that by Agnew 1999) this quickly becomes a celebration of those movements in an uncritical manner. Soguk and

---

[13] For other collections on this theme that display similar problems to those outlined here, see for example, Shapiro and Alker (1996) or Albert *et al.* (2001).

Whitehall (1999) are the most breathlessly gushing, concluding their chapter:

> In the exhilarations of the contemporary world, more than ever the territorial universe of statist boundedness has given way to a socio-cultural, political–economic and geographic state of linkages, opening, expanding, contracting, closing, displacing and replacing, 'submarine-pooling', affirming identity differences across small distances, but also creating 'zones of proximity' spanning vast space that nevertheless sweep identities into one another's shores. The inexorable transversality is an embarrassment to the state of modern territoriality, a permanent reminder that the transversal is not the territorial's constitutive other, its governmental residue or its postmodern after-effects, but instead its wandering ground … transversality is an affirmation … through which people recover their multiple peoplehoods from the stranglehold of 'the state/nation/territory trinity'. (Soguk and Whitehall 1999: 697–8, the closing quote is from Agamben 1995: 118)

So keen are these authors to undermine both statist IR theory and statist–racist political practice, and so all-consuming is the attention to identity, that the conditions of possibility of all this movement are never questioned. Brock vaguely raises a question here, however, and Agnew alludes to an answer. Brock prompts us to identify shifts from 'old' to 'new' migration so as to 'find out in which way[s] migration does change' (1999: 495). Agnew then offers a quick response: the rise in migration, combined with shifts in its character, in particular the emergence of 'translocal' communities on which Mandaville (1999) nicely elaborates later in the issue,[14] 'ow[es] something to the increased ease of international movement in the age of the jumbo jet but also related to massive international economic differences' (Agnew 1999: 513). Suddenly the celebration of transversal connections needs to be seen in a new light: the production of intensified global inequalities and a set of material practices which cannot, under any plausible ecological scenario, be sustained on a mass basis. Thus, while this literature gives us a useful focus on the theme of movement in world politics, and resistance to the racism involved in statist or nationalist attempts to

---

[14] Mandaville (1999: 665) emphasises that what is now distinctive is 'transmigration', which entails 'constant movement between multiple spaces and communities rather than permanent or semi-permanent settlement'. This, of course, is the condition that intensifies precisely the sort of movement I seek to problematise here.

restrict migration is to be welcomed (e.g. Doty 1999; Bigo 2002), the manner in which it does this remains problematic.

Two final things about both these kinds of debates about world politics are worth making. The first is to emphasise that people in both traditions make considerable effort to connect global politics to 'everyday life', and thus create possible openings for understanding much of the material I discuss later in the book. In the debates in IPE, this tends to involve attempts to engage in productive dialogue with Foucauldian approaches. Gill's 'The Global Panopticon' (1995) is a useful example here. The article shows how the reproduction of contemporary capitalism entails the development of a range of surveillance measures that create self-discipline by subjects themselves. Consumer credit practices are particularly significant here; the creation of consumer debt becomes simultaneously a site at which individuals have to monitor themselves to manage their debt levels and a means by which people's relationship to the workplace is then structured, as debt constrains their ability to leave workplaces, negotiate with employers and so on. Langley (2003) develops this interrelation of credit and other financial practices with global politics in more detail. He focuses on how the expansion of consumer credit to finance house purchases and consumption activities since the 1980s, particularly in the United States, has sustained both economic expansion and its skewed distribution and consequences, as it drives diplomatic and economic negotiations surrounding the US trade deficit, protectionism and more recently the dispute over the value of the yuan. Langley also shows how the recent shifts in pension provision, broadly from collectivist final-salary 'pay-as-you-go' schemes (whether public or private) towards 'defined-contribution' schemes, are produced by discourses about the appropriate division of financial risks between firms and workers but creates conflicting consequences in terms of people's interests as workers (in higher salaries) and as pension holders and by extension investors (in higher profitability). Davies and Niemann (2002) similarly argue that 'everyday life' is central to the production of global politics. They develop their account in conceptual terms using Henri Lefebvre's (e.g. 1971) notion of everyday life as the site where struggles to overcome the alienation and contradictions of modern life meet the ideological representations organised to legitimise that life. Davies and Niemann emphasise Lefebvre's attention to space as a socially produced dimension to everyday life in order to undermine orthodox IR's account of space as an objective 'container', a representation which permits the focus on diplomats and politicians as the place where IR 'occurs'. Recognising the socially produced character of such spatialities is one means to open up conceptually to the production of global politics by practices beyond those of diplomats and the like. Davies and Niemann then develop the aspects of everyday life central to the production of global politics, which they take to be work, leisure/consumption and the family.

The second is that, while writers in both traditions have alluded to ecological questions (in particular Litfin 1994; Kuehls 1996; Dalby 2002; Levy and Newell 2005) it would be fair to say that much more work could be done on how they might think ecologically and what tensions exist between their basic conceptual and normative presumptions and those of environmental politics. In neo-Gramscian accounts, references to ecology are at times incorporated in a relatively crude manner into the framework in terms of capitalism's basic limits on the one hand, and as an element in anti-corporate or anti-globalisation activism, on the other.[15] When treated more fully (Levy and Newell 2005) ecology is discussed in terms of the debate within neo-Gramscian IPE about a transnational capitalist class (van der Pijl 1998; Sklair 2000) and about the restructuring of the hegemony of this class at the global level. In effect, the environment becomes a case study in how capital pursues its interests globally, with occasionally a more ambitious claim that the environment is one of the principal sites where this restructuring of global politics is occurring. But even here the specificities of ecological politics are not discussed particularly fully. In poststructuralism, more attention is usually given to ecology's specificities, in particular because of the power/knowledge focus deriving from Foucault (1980), which draws attention to the way in which scientific knowledge and its production intertwine with the reproduction of political orders. But beyond the occasional reference to biopolitics, work in this vein has not yet dealt particularly fully with the socio-political processes driving ecological change – Litfin (1994) focuses on the power–knowledge dimensions to ozone politics, Kuehls (1996) on debates about sovereignty and ecology and Dalby (2002) on the discourse of environmental security.

---

[15] See for example Cox (1997); Gill (1997, 2002); van der Pijl (1998); Rupert (2000). The fullest treatment within this group of writers is in Mittelman (1998).

In the context of this political economy–poststructural conversation, cars act as a 'vehicle' for developing these arguments and how they may be brought into fruitful relationships with each other; the two perspectives can be seen to be in some sort of tension. Certainly there has in the social sciences since at least the late 1980s a form of inter-action between them where the former is regarded as irredeemably reductionist, committed to 'base–superstructure' models which reduce everything to a logic of either capital accumulation and/or class conflict and leave little space for interrogating why specific changes in political discourse or organisation occur when and how they do and the latter is deemed to suffer irretrievably from 'relativism' (a lazy charge if ever there was one), unable to interrogate critically the ethico-political differences between different discourses or to root an interpretation of such discourses in concrete social forces. But a premise of this book is that a much more fruitful engagement between the two is possible, and the emerging debates about a 'cultural political economy' are a useful example of a site where such engagement is being pursued.

But my point is also stronger. Part of the aim here is to establish both the centrality of ecological questions in the production of contemporary global politics (in other words, if you are not thinking ecologically, you are not really accounting adequately for global politics *at all*), and that the nature of critical thought about such politics is radically transformed if one takes ecological questions seriously. My concern then is also to show how when one thinks through cars/automobility in this way the concreteness of the analysis and the materiality of the subject matter, if you like, also disrupts the abstract nature of both arguments in critical IR–IPE, and in environmental politics.

The third departure point is the emerging debates in the social sciences around the concept of automobility, a term necessarily used a number of times already but which now needs to be elaborated. It is useful to start with conventional accounts which focus in some way or other on 'the car'. Consider this statement from a well-known business studies book on the state of the car industry. After discussing the 'benefits and disbenefits' of the car over the last hundred years (focus-ing primarily on air pollution), Maxton and Wormald (1995: 12–19) conclude the discussion with a short section beginning 'It is too easy to blame the car manufacturers ... This is not strictly fair. While it is true that car manufacturers produce such polluting machines, it is the consumers who own and drive them' (1995: 19). We can also see this juxtaposition of interests and responsibility elsewhere – to promote fuel efficiency, car owners' groups argue for fuel economy standards to be imposed on manufacturers (such as Corporate Average Fuel Economy, or CAFÉ, in the United States and Canada) while manufacturers argue for use of fuel taxation measures. But ultimately this understanding, which separates out the different actors, their interests, responsibilities and so on, is a mistake. In attempting to assign responsibility between producers and consumers, Maxton and Wormald overlook that *both* are part of a complex system or regime within which such assignations of responsibility may be made (and argued over) but which nevertheless are an integrated whole. To take another example, Loren Lomasky (whose views are discussed in detail in chapter 3), in his argument defending unrestrained car use, argues that the 'costs of marginal automobile usage' must be weighed against the fundamental freedom produced by car use on the ethico-political scale (1997: 8). In other words, in ethical (and, by implication, empirical) terms only *each individual* journey by an individual driver counts. But it is the aggregated, iterated, cumulative, systemic, nature of 'the car' which generates both the benefits and the disbenefits of cars to individuals, and to society. We thus need some sort of systemic account to understand the complicated politics of cars. Automobility is emerging as the term which can encapsulate this understanding (Rajan 1996; Shove 1998; Urry 2000, 2004; Böhm *et al.* 2006). The original use of automobility in the early twentieth century referred to the fact and experience of being auto-mobile, of driving a car, and was thus connected to another noun, 'automobilist' – the person who is auto-mobile (the word '*automobiliste*' is still used in French – in English, we have the less ambiguous 'motorist') and some still use it in this individualist sense (as does Lomasky, for example). But it is now more common, and conceptually more useful, to treat it as referring to the overall 'system' which makes the act of driving a car – and more specifically the act of driving a car as an act of 'autonomous mobility' – *possible*.

John Urry (2000) provides a useful overview of the principal elements of this system. Automobility involves: 'the quintessential *manufactured object* produced by the leading industrial sectors and the iconic firms within twentieth-century capitalism'; the industry which developed the 'key *concepts* … employed in understanding the development of … the trajectory of contemporary capitalism'; 'the major item of *individual consumption*', producing status through the sign-values it is

associated with; 'a *machinic complex*' involving the complex socio-
technical linkages between the car and a range of other industries and
technologies; 'the single most important *environmental issue*' because of
the intensity of resource use and production of pollutants; 'the predominant form of quasi-private *mobility*'; and 'the dominant *culture*'
which 'sustains major discourses of what constitutes the good life' (Urry
2000: 57–8).

Two points are worth making about this emerging literature on
automobility. One is that despite the turn to regarding automobility
as a socio-technical system, assemblage, regime, or other such conceptual vocabulary calling attention to the complex interrelation of the
practices, technologies, etc. which make it up, there is at times a
tendency to fall back on a phenomenological account of automobility,
to focus on automobility as a feature of individual daily lives (see, for
example, most of the contributions to Featherstone *et al.* 2004). This
is partly because of a resistance to the 'grand theorising' prevalent in
much contemporary social theory, including that represented by Urry's
attempt to account for automobility as a system. But while there is
much of use and interest in this phenomenological account of automobility to explain how automobiles produce modern mobile subjects,
the individualisation entailed inevitably concedes, for me at least, too
much ground to that with which the car is conventionally and ideologically associated – for example, paying attention to cars as a performance of individual identity can come close to celebrating them as an
extension of 'human freedom'.

The second point, however, is perhaps more important for the argument of the book as a whole. In Urry's account of how automobility
becomes dominant, in particular, there is a lack of politics (see also
Böhm *et al.* 2006). I shall elaborate this point in chapters 4 and 5 in
particular, but for the moment it suffices to suggest that the account
which Urry offers portrays the expansion of automobility as the result
of a complex interaction of a number of technological and social trends
but without conveying the sense of the concrete decisions and the
struggles over them which favoured automobility over its alternatives.
Just to give one initial well-known example, the construction of the
bridges over the parkways to Jones Beach in New York by Robert
Moses (Winner 1980), where the deliberate construction of bridges too
low to allow buses to use the parkway was a conscious act of engineering
to exclude those on low incomes (and, in particular, African Americans)

from gaining access to the beach which at the same time created powerful incentives for expanded car use. While automobility can certainly be regarded as 'systemic' in the manner that Urry suggests, it is at the same time composed of concrete decisions to favour certain sorts of interests, normative visions, forms of power and so on, and is frequently contested and challenged in ways which shape its development as a 'system'.

A road map

The automobile is thus inherently political. But, just as importantly, so is being automobile. The term 'automobile' functions simultaneously as noun and adjective, and this book interrogates both the narrower sense of 'the politics of the car' and the broader sense of the politics of a specific way of being oriented around the twin, mutually intertwined, yet ultimately contradictory, values of autonomy and mobility.

But any book, and this one is no exception, needs to engage in this interrogation for a particular purpose. For me, the starting point is the manifest unsustainability of the current form that automobility takes and sympathy to a set of claims that it cannot be made sustainable. Given that sustainability is a condition of possibility of any other sort of politics, if this is the case we must entertain the possibility that automobility must go.

But a fundamentally political question immediately poses itself. We need to ask questions about how the current situation came about. If we are to understand how we might move to a more sustainable social form then we need to understand the political forces, discourses, meanings and imperatives which have brought the current situation about and which act as constraints on (and opportunities for) projects to make the way we move ourselves and various objects around, and the amount we do so, sustainable.

Arising out of these various concerns, the material which follows can be understood in terms of two levels. The first, most immediate of these, concerns the debates about the environmental politics of the car. Is the car – or, more coherently automobility – fundamentally unsustainable? Can it be greened? But, also, is contemporary society inevitably wedded to the car – is, if you like, automobility 'natural', as some of its proponents (along with Meg Ryan) claim? These questions are dealt with in a range of ways throughout the book. Chapters 2 and

3 discuss the ways in which cars and car-dominated societies have been contested throughout the twentieth and twenty-first centuries, and then the attempts in the 1990s to generate a backlash against anti-car sentiments. They have both the general purpose of destabilising the common-sense assumption that a car-based society is 'naturally' embedded in human ambitions and values and is essentially uncontested, but also the more specific purpose of presenting and analysing the range of discourses through which cars have been both legitimised and contested. They can be read at the most basic level in terms of a debate 'against and for cars'. Chapter 2 deals with a range of different critiques of cars and car-dominated societies and with the emergence of anti-car movements in many countries. It suggests that opposition to cars and automobility has come in varied forms, of which I focus on seven: a technocratic environmentalism; concerns about safety; opposition to the way that automobility has restructured urban space; the inequalities of car-dominated societies; the atomistic nature of automobility; resistance to obsessions with speed; and automobility's connection to oil geopolitics. Chapter 3 analyses what I suggest was a backlash against anti-car sentiments in the 1990s, principally through an analysis of its chief ideological manifestations – James Dunn's *Driving Forces* (1998) and Loren Lomasky's *Autonomy and Automobility* (1997). It suggests that, at its core, this backlash had to rely on a hyper-individualism which made hard assumptions that individuals (at least ethically speaking) *pre-exist* society, that their autonomy (understood negatively as the absence of state interference) is the *principal* ethico-political value which trumps all others and that this autonomy is intrinsically expressed through movement. All of these assumptions are interrogated critically in chapter 3, which argues they cannot be sustained. Chapter 6 also looks again at some of the discourses and politics underpinning anti-car activism and the attempt to contain it, principally through the lens of governmentality – which has by then been developed in chapter 5. Chapter 7 looks at current attempts to 'green' the car – or, more broadly, the system(s) of mobility across societies – suggesting at this level of analysis that significant greening is possible but that the fact of greening is significantly constrained and its specific character shaped by the two principal structuring forces of automobility – political economy and cultural politics. The concluding chapter 8 then revisits more generally the points made above about environmental politics to discuss how the analysis of the

car's politics affects these debates, principally in terms of the potential for ecological transformations of politics in general.

The second level of analysis is raised by these environmental politics concerns. If automobility is to be understood as structuring environmental degradation then we have to pose the question: how and why did automobility come to be so dominant? In chapter 3 we see that a common answer to this question is that automobility arises as a more or less 'natural' extension of the human urge for freedom and the connection of that freedom to movement. In other intellectual contexts, we see early in chapter 4 that another common answer is because transport growth is necessarily connected to economic growth and cars enable the pursuit of growth better than other transport technologies: again, in effect, the growth of cars and automobility is rendered inevitable. In chapter 5 we see that the answer given in some of the emerging literature on automobility, in particular by John Urry, is couched in terms of systems theory; that a range of particular, contingent, socio-technical changes came together in the late nineteenth and early twentieth century (the internal combustion engine; pneumatic tyres; pressures (largely by cycling groups) to improve road surfaces; pressures to reduce the number of horses in towns and cities; resentment of monopoly practices by tram and bus companies; adoption of mass production practices and so on) which then reached a point where car manufacturers received rising returns to scale and a cycle of growth was set in train. Alternatives were then increasingly crowded out – literally, in the physical dominance of cars on streets, but also through the relative competitiveness of cars over alternative modes of transport because of the returns to scale the industry had. The continued dominance of the car can then be understood through the concept of path dependence – particular development paths favour those practices within them and make it difficult to promote alternatives.

The arguments that the rise of the car is either a 'natural' expression of human autonomy or simply an inevitable consequence of its economic advantages can be fairly quickly dismissed. The former should be read simply as an ideological effect of a libertarian insistence on a particular account of freedom as freedom from 'interference' from state control in all areas of life, and the priority (ethical and empirical) of individuals in relation to the state or any other form of social restraint. The latter mistakes the particularities of the way that cars were deployed and promoted in their early history and beyond for the general importance of mobility in modern societies. With the systems-theoretic account there is much of descriptive and heuristic value but I argue, principally in chapter 5, that it tends to present the emergence of the 'system of automobility' as a process without agents – that the notions of rising returns to scale, path dependence (and in relation to the possible 'greening of cars' discussed in chapter 7, tipping points) obscure the patterns of power which enable certain social forces (manufacturers, oil companies, road construction firms, state managers, military elites) which benefit disproportionately from automobility to promote it, and their own agency in pursuing these interests. Chapters 4, 5 and 6 between them then argue that the rise and reproduction of automobility should be understood principally in terms of the particular way in which capitalist development was secured in the early twentieth century, on the one hand, and the construction of particular sorts of mobile subjects, on the other. In other words, automobility has been so dominant and successful because of its ability to reproduce capitalist society – its *political economy* – and its ability to mobilise people as specific sorts of subject – its *cultural politics*. In the former (analysed in chapter 4), automobility was effective because it simultaneously provided a core role in the way that long-term patterns of production and consumption were stabilised – commonly termed a 'regime of accumulation' – from the 1920s onwards in what was known as Fordism, and provided a commodity around which a whole set of symbols, images and discourses could be constructed which served effectively to legitimise capitalist society. In automobility, the means of securing legitimation and the means of securing accumulation became one and the same. But the symbols and images cannot be reduced simply to an *effect* of this legitimation project and attention needs to be paid to the active manufacturing of an 'automobile subject'. Chapter 5 shows how this should be understood in relation to a more general importance of mobility in the construction of subjects by governors, who from the eighteenth century onwards needed to constrain and regularise movement but increasingly simultaneously to accelerate it (principally for economic and military purposes). In this view, for governors, automobility became highly useful, as it enabled movement again to be articulated as 'freedom' when it had become increasingly problematic to make this connection by the late nineteenth century. Chapter 6 continues this analysis by revisiting the notion of a 'backlash' against anti-car sentiments, but this time in terms of notions of governmentality, focusing on the way that attempts to rearticulate automobility in normative terms involve constructing the subjects of car drivers and also of those opposing automobility, in particular ways.

Conclusions

Exploring the politics of automobility is to interrogate one of the principal phenomena which structures daily life (both materially and normatively) across much of the planet, one of the most important aspects of the global economy and one of the foremost causes of global environmental degradation. If we take ecological challenges seriously we necessarily call into question and fundamentally problematise the forms of political authority, economic production and consumption and modes of subjectivity which currently prevail. At its heart, the argument which follows is that automobility is principally an *economic* form obsessed with accumulation and a *political* form of subjectivity constructed around mobility which structures environmental degradation and which must be challenged and resisted in order to restructure societies to pursue sustainability.

2 | Automobility and its discontents

> They paved paradise and put up a
> parking lot.
> (Joni Mitchell, 'Big Yellow Taxi', 1970)

> No cars, No people
> No food, No people
> Stopped, Short, Grinding halt
> Everything's coming to a grinding halt.
> (The Cure, 'Grinding Halt', *Three imaginary boys*,
> Fiction Records, 1979)

Chapter 1 suggested, among other things, the complex problems that automobility has thrown up for contemporary societies. For many, it is the organisation of societies around cars which has produced these chronic problems, and a range of movements and discourses opposing the domination of societies by the car.

Some of these contestations appear rather abstract and divorced from everyday life. But many are tangible; automobility not only has large-scale implications, it also engenders a range of immediate social and ecological dislocations, as the Kings Heath story in chapter 1 suggested, which themselves produce their own resistance. In relation to road building, in particular, against which there was much protest in the early 1970s in the United States as well as more recently in the United Kingdom and elsewhere, the resistance is against automobility's systemic disruptions of daily life, community, place and immediate livelihoods and identities. Berman vividly invokes one side of the reaction to automobility as modernisation: 'we hold back the tears, and step on the gas' (1982: 291). Such resistance goes to the heart of modernity's dynamics – what is being resisted is precisely a world where, in Berman's invocation of Marx and Engels, 'All that is solid melts into air' (1982; Marx and Engels 1848/1967: 83).

It is worth emphasising that this political contestation over the car is not new. Far from being the unproblematic technology which everyone until the early 1990s viewed as a promoter of human liberty and welfare, it has often been seen as both environmentally and socially damaging. For Wall (1999), there is even a prehistory to anti-roads politics – for example, the Iceni revolt against Roman rule led by Boudicca, which (in Wall's view) was produced in part by the roads which the Romans used to extend their rule across Britain (Wall 1999: 19–20). Certainly, later anti-roads protesters used the analogy with the Roman empire's road building projects as part of their rhetoric, with the production, for example, of a version of the *Asterix* comic entitled *Asterix and the Road Builders* (*ibid.*: 20). Two earlier periods can be identified when car culture came under particular challenge. The first was at the beginning of the car's existence: a classic expression of opposition to the car (e.g. McShane 1994: 144) is often taken to be Toad of Toad Hall in Kenneth Grahame's *The Wind in the Willows* (1908):

It is the motor car that overturns innocent stability, the golden age; aboard a car Toad becomes 'the terror, the traffic-queller, before whom all must give way or be smitten into nothingness and everlasting night'. (Overy 1990: 73, quoting from Grahame 1908)

Cars were widely seen in negative terms. In 1908, the then British Prime Minister Herbert Asquith, called them 'A luxury that is apt to degenerate into a nuisance' (quoted in McShane 1994: 113). They were associated with danger, noise and dirt, and threatened to disrupt established modes of urban life. For the most part, resistance to the car quickly foundered on its identification as a symbol of progress, as I show in more detail in chapter 4. But ambivalence nevertheless remained. As J. W. Gregory put it in 1931:

The future of the road is being contemplated with different feelings. The motorist looks forward hopefully to the whole country being covered by a network of straight 120ft wide thoroughfares, to the corners at all road junctions being rounded off and having a transparent wire fence instead of hedges, to the surface being so smooth that horse traction is impracticable, to the companionship of abundant high-speed motors, to by-pass roads that will avoid the villages and towns, and to the absence of any picturesque distractions except the milestones, direction posts, and the petrol pumps.

This prospect is regarded with dismay by those who admire British rural scenery and our country roads, with their graceful bends, the varied trees and avenues along them, their hedgerows sheltering song-birds and gay with flowers, their grass verges, and the infinite variety of views from their winding course, and who deplore each main road being altered into a straight black band of which the chief merit is that it can be left behind so quickly. (Gregory 1931: 277–8)

The second period of contestation was from the early 1960s through to the late 1970s. A large number of books detailing the development of automobility and the problems of a car-dominated society were produced, which discussed a much wider range of questions beyond the immediate violence and danger created by individual cars. Two of the earliest were John Keats' *The Insolent Chariots* (1958) and Lewis Mumford's *The Highway and the City* (1963).[1] Surveying the books produced in this period, it is useful to identify four strands of critique (inevitably overlapping in some writers). There was a strand focused on the urban form (Cadeau 1960; Jacobs 1961; Mumford 1963; Leavitt 1970; Owen 1972), on the way that car-led development, in particular (and in some cases exclusively, as in Leavitt's arguments) through road building, disrupted and destroyed particular urban forms and produced a range of social and economic problems.[2] There was a strand focused on questions of safety, consumers' rights and danger (Cadeau 1960; Nader 1965; Buel 1972). There was a strand focused on the problems specifically facing the US car *industry* (as opposed to the problems for US society from automobility *per se*), including critiques such as those concerning safety or pollution, but also including discussion of declining

---

[1] The list of these books is long, including Cadeau (1960), Renaud (1967), Groupe Lyonnais (1968); Sauvy (1968); Mowbray (1969), Leavitt (1970), Schneider (1971), Aird (1972) Buel (1972), Flink (1972, 1975), Jerome (1972), Owen (1972), Fabre and Michael (1973), Rothschild (1973), Davies (1975) and Brown, *et al*. (1979b). Cars were often discussed in general environmentalist texts of the period; see, for example, Dumont (1974: 52–6). For a smaller flurry of similar books in the 1990s, see Engwicht (1993), Zielinski and Laird (1995), Holtz Kay (1997), or Alvord (2000). Most of these books have a significantly more action-oriented approach than those of the 1970s; some, like Alvord, also betray the legacy of a hyper-individualist culture, focusing for the most part on the changes that individuals can make to their own lives.

[2] In the United Kingdom this was represented most by the activism led by John Tyme against motorway building, documented in his *Motorways versus Democracy* (1978). That activism opposed motorway construction *per se*, and destruction of both countryside and cities was a central part of his rhetoric (1978: 1–2). Also see Wall (1999: 24–33) on the opposition to motorway construction in the United Kingdom which started in the early 1960s.

profit rates and increasing overseas competition (Jerome 1972; Rothschild 1973).[3] Finally, there was a strand of what one might call 'total critique' – a collecting together of all the above specific arguments into something which suggested that the car as the dominant mode of mobility must go (Schneider 1971; Buel 1972; Jerome 1972; Flink 1975; Tyme 1978). This critical orientation is exemplified in the classic utopian novel of the 1970s, Ernst Callenbach's *Ecotopia* (1975), where one of the defining features of the Ecotopian society, which forms as Northern California, Oregon and Washington break away from the United States, is the absence of cars.

These elements in the arguments developed specifically in the late 1960s and early 1970s are unpacked further below. Many suggested that in this period US society in particular experienced 'disenchantment' with the car (Flink 1975: chapter 7) or that the car industry had lost the 'social support' mechanisms which had sustained its growth and favourable political climate in the previous decades (Rothschild 1973: 245; also Davies 1975 or Gordon 1991: 14). This is perhaps best exemplified by the Chair of GM, James Roche, who stated that 'America's romance with the automobile is not over. Instead it has blossomed into a marriage' (as quoted in Rothschild 1973: 7; see also Jerome 1972: 24). While Roche intended it as a restatement of the attachment of Americans to their cars, it was widely taken as a statement that 'the romance' was over (Flink 1975: 210) – as Jerome put it at the time, 'marriages, by comparison to love affairs ... are dull, dull, dull' (1972: 241).[4]

While there are many commonalities between these reflections on automobility's consequences, such contestations have had a variety of modes. I will discuss seven, although the list is not exclusive and the categories overlap significantly and are presented in no particular order of importance.[5]

---

[3] In effect Nader (1965) also falls into this category, since his analysis is focused on the way that the oligopoly within the industry is part of the problem.

[4] The logical conclusion of this is of course Alvord's anti-car book-cum-self-help manual *Divorce your Car!* (2000).

[5] Some are impossible to categorise except through their religious orientation, such as the project of the World Council of Churches (WCC) on 'motorised mobility, climate change and globalisation' (WCC 2000), or the more widely known campaign in the United States by the Evangelical Environmental Network with the slogan 'What would Jesus drive?', focused on the SUV (see the network's website at www.whatwouldjesusdrive.org). Their campaign focused on climate change and issues of peace and security.

Modes of critique and protest

Technocratic environmentalism

I will look first at the technocratic environmentalism exemplified in the early 1970s by the Club of Rome or The Worldwatch Institute and adopted by other mainstream environmental groups when discussing the car (e.g. Greenpeace 1991).[6] The predominant arguments surrounded the environmental implications of mass automobility in terms of resource use and pollution. Cars were implicated in general worries about resource scarcity thrown up, on the one hand, by the 'Limits to Growth' arguments of the early 1970s (Meadows *et al.* 1972) and, on the other, by the 1973 oil crisis, which appeared to confirm the importance of such resource scarcity. Such a technocentric account of the environmental impacts of automobility is also seen in much general air pollution campaigning against cars, and also in more recent debates such as those over the notion of food miles (see, for example, SAFE Alliance 1994).[7]

The central features of this sort of critique can be broadly recounted as follows. Cars are a major origin of the pollutants causing a number of the major air pollution problems which societies currently face. Concerning global warming in the OECD, road transport (of which cars are a substantial majority[8]) produce 23 per cent of the CO_2 emitted into the atmosphere. According to the IPCC (2001: 16) the principal gas responsible for global warming needs to be reduced to a 'small fraction of the current emission level' in order to stabilise CO_2 atmospheric concentrations and thus (after a time lag) climatic

---

[6] This is not a form of argument employed only by such mainstream organisations. See, for example, Trainer (1985: 23–4), who presents the problems of automobility in a similar way but from a Green/Marxist framework.

[7] The concept of food miles is intended to work as a heuristic device to capture the total environmental and social costs of food production and consumption through the miles the food travels from production to plate; see http://www.sustainweb.org/chain_fm_index.asp, viewed 15 August 2006.

[8] For Australia, the only country for which the IEA (1993: 222) gives a figure, cars contribute 65 per cent of total road transport emissions; because of its size, Australia has higher than average emissions from freight. For all OECD countries, Gordon (1991: 7) suggests that cars account for 85 per cent of all the energy used in transport (and therefore 85 per cent of the CO_2 emissions, since practically all the transport emissions come from oil).

conditions.[9] This, of course, includes only emissions directly from fuel use; the IEA estimate that this is only 60–65 per cent of total greenhouse gas emissions throughout the life of a car, the rest coming from fuel extraction, processing and transport (15–20 per cent), manufacturing (10 per cent) and tailpipe emissions other than CO_2 (1993: 37). Even this discounts the emissions involved in road construction (to say nothing of the deforestation that construction often either directly involves or indirectly promotes). They are also the major contributor to many of the gases known collectively as Volatile Organic Compounds (VOCs) and to about 90 per cent of total carbon monoxide (CO) emissions. Chemical reactions involving these compounds produce tropospheric ozone, another greenhouse gas. However, cars assume greater importance in the politics of global warming than even this suggests since, along with aviation, they are the only sector whose underlying emissions' trend in industrialised countries is one of growth. Emissions from domestic and industrial sources have been roughly stable or steadily declining since the mid-1970s. Dealing with cars thus becomes particularly important, as it is widely recognised that technical advances can easily be outstripped by growing car use (see chapter 7 for more on this).

Cars also are a significant cause of acid rain. Road transport accounts for between 33 and 50 per cent of Nitrous oxide and Nitrogen dioxide (NOx) emissions in industrialised countries (McCormick 1989: 62), averaging 48 per cent across the OECD as a whole (IEA 1989: 34). About 60 per cent of road transport NOx emissions come from cars.[10] These gases cause acid rain, which has already created substantial damage to lakes and fisheries, crops, buildings and human health throughout the industrialised world, and is starting to have a similar impact in other countries.

[9] The OECD 23 per cent figure is calculated from IEA (1993: 30–2). The global figure is lower, at about 14 per cent (Walsh 1993: 5). In its first report in 1990 (Houghton *et al.* 1990: xx), the IPCC stated that a 60 per cent reduction in CO_2 emissions was necessary to stabilise the climate. In the IPCC's Third Assessment Report (2001), since the complexity of the analysis had increased they hesitated to put a percentage figure on the necessary reductions. But the figures (e.g. IPCC 2001: 17) suggest that 'small fraction' is of the order of a reduction to around 10 per cent of current emission levels.

[10] For slightly differing figures, see Boehmer-Christiansen and Weidner (1995: 93) or Transnet (1990: 36). The 60 per cent figure cited in the text is midway between the figures given by these two sources.

Cars are also a significant cause of local air pollution problems. VOCs, benzene, lead, CO, particulates and other exhaust emissions have been associated with a wide range of health problems. These include brain damage, respiratory problems and infections, lung cancer, emphysema, headaches, aggravation in those with heart disease, low birth weights, leukaemia and stress (from noise levels) (Freund and Martin 1993: 29–33).

The second major class of environmental problems which relates to a car economy is resource depletion. Simply using a car consumes between 35 per cent of the oil used in Japan and up to 63 per cent of that in the United States. Oil is also a major resource in asphalt and therefore in road production. In the United States, car production consumes 13 per cent of the steel, 16 per cent of the aluminium, 69 per cent of the lead, 36 per cent of the iron, 36 per cent of the platinum and 58 per cent of the rubber (both natural and synthetic) (Freund and Martin 1993: 17–19).[11]

This technocratic form of environmentalism, as we have seen, became prevalent in the late 1960s and early 1970s. Cars played a key role in both the more general articulation of concerns about pollution and resource depletion in that period and a series of anti-car books was published, particularly in the United States, in which this dimension was one of the main problems of a car-dominated society (e.g. Jerome 1972; Nader 1972: 146–69; Rothschild 1973: 9; Flink 1975: 221–6; for a later example, see Zuckerman 1991: chapter 2). Later in the 1970s, after the oil crisis in particular, as we shall see, the technocratic elements become more pronounced in anti-car discourse. Brown *et al.*'s *Running on Empty* (1979b) was important here, showing that reactions against cars were not only populist but occurred in the realm of elite environmental NGOs such as The Worldwatch Institute where the authors worked (the book is in fact an extended version of a Worldwatch paper, Brown *et al.* 1979a). They suggested that while safety and pollution issues might be technologically resolvable, since the possible alternative ways of powering cars were only in their infancy and unlikely to be able fully to replace oil (chapter 4), and given the massive increases in car ownership and vehicle miles travelled (chapter 5) the possible increases in fuel efficiency were also inadequate, the emerging oil

---

[11] For the car industry and its supporters, the flip side of this is the extensive economic benefits created by the industry. See, for example, AAM (2001: 7).

shortages would be the central constraint on the car. They suggested that in an age of restricted oil supply its use for cars was unlikely to be given high priority,[12] and that alternatives to the car were thus necessary. The Worldwatch Institute became a steady source of papers on cars from this perspective (Flavin 1985; Renner 1988; Lowe 1989 (on bicycles), 1990, 1994 (on rail); Sheehan 2001 (on sprawl)), with most of the accounts being in this technocratic mode.[13]

Such arguments were less prevalent in the 1980s, partly in line with the general decline in interest in environmental problems, partly as the discourse moved away from notions of 'limits to growth' towards 'sustainable development' and partly because the predictions about the imminent collapse of oil supplies proved fallible and oil prices declined during the 1980s as OPEC collaboration weakened and alternative sources of oil came on stream. But they became transformed by the emerging interest in transnational and global pollution problems – in particular, acid rain and then climate change – and by the emerging crisis in many of the world's cities which (for some) engendered a technical response related to planning, transport modes and urban design. This mode of questioning automobility can be seen in diverse sites, including in the IEA (1993) and the World Resources Institute but also among environmentalist writers such as Newman and Kenworthy (1999) or Litman (2002, and more generally at www.vtpi.org), all of whom develop the concept of 'automobile dependency' as a concept to explain the problems of cars and a normative framework for approaching policy, and in the efforts to 'green' the production of cars through notions of industrial ecology (Graedel and Allenby 1998). It also underpins the strategies of many mainstream environmental organisations which sought to critique the car (or, in the case of the anti-SUV discourse, particular sorts of car)

---

[12] This is certainly implausible with hindsight, and arguably was so at the time. Most western countries had already switched electricity supply away from oil to coal or gas, but had rationed oil for use in cars only by using price mechanisms to stimulate efficiency gains and thereby reduce oil imports and had also attempted to limit it with speed restrictions. There was already a concerted effort to find alternative and diversified sources of oil – in Alaska and the North Sea, for example, both of which were developed in the 1970s at least in part because of the oil crises.

[13] See Luke (1997: chapter 4) on The Worldwatch Institute's brand of environmental politics.

from the point of view of its use of resources and its generation of pollution.

Many of the elements of what started out as a critique of automobility have thus become standard elements in policy practice of corporations and states which seek to 'redesign' the car to meet objectives such as reducing emissions which generate acid rain or climate change or to minimise urban congestion and sprawl. This in effect has generated the principal discourses underpinning efforts to 'ecologically modernise' automobility, discussed further in chapter 7.

Safety

Sooner or later, you're gonna listen to Ralph Nader
I don't wanna cause a fuss, but fast cars are so dangerous.
                                            (Buzzcocks, 'Fast Cars', 1977)

A second sort of reaction against automobility is based on concerns about safety. Although the first death from a car 'accident' (of Bridget Driscoll on 17 August 1896) sparked violent protests, in the car's early years their dangers were rapidly normalised (e.g. McShane 1994).[14] Cars are now one of the principal causes of early mortality across the world; in the United Kingdom, for example, more people have been killed on the roads since 1945 than were killed on active service in the Second World War (Hamer 1987: 2; for general figures on this, see Wolf 1996: 201–4). Across the OECD, 107,406 people were killed on the roads in 2001 (IRTAD/OECD 2003); global estimates put the figures at between 1.2 and 5 million annually,[15] with the International Federation of the Red Cross and Red Crescent rating road accidents the third highest cause of premature death and making road safety one of its principal humanitarian priorities (Tickell 1998).

---

[14] Nader (1972: 295) erroneously, or perhaps just parochially, has the first death as being that of H. H. Bliss in 1899 in New York. McShane (1994: 174) is clear that Bliss was the first American killed by a car. For a full account of this event, and the debates it provoked, see Dauvergne (2005: 40–1). For a more recent focus on safety questions, see Milton (1991).

[15] A joint report by the World Health Organisation (WHO) and the World Bank (2004: 3) gives the 1.2 million figure, with 50 million injured annually by cars (as cited in Dauvergne 2005: 41). Tickell (1998) cites figures of up to 5 million.

In the early 1960s, however, Ralph Nader initiated a range of campaigns against car manufacturers, showing that they had knowingly built a lack of care for safety into their designs (Nader 1965).[16] Since then many of the protests have been to do with cars' safety aspects, with the growth of organisations (e.g. Roadpeace or the Royal Society for the Prevention of Accidents (ROSPA) in the United Kingdom, or their equivalents elsewhere[17]) dedicated to reducing the dangers associated with a car-dominated mobility system. These have tended to operate as 'insider groups' in policy-making processes, with only occasional symbolic protests such as 'die-ins'. Many of the technological developments in car design have been to do with improving safety, mostly for those in the car (compulsory seat belts, crumple zones, roll bars, air bags and so on) but some also for those outside, and many of the developments in transport policy have been designed to reduce such dangers (traffic calming, 'home zones',[18] reduced speed limits, 'safe routes to school', etc.). One could suggest that safety has been the principal site around which states and firms have acted to legitimise car culture, seeing the threats to personal safety as the core issue which could serve to delegitimise automobility. Yet still, with all of these changes, rates of death and injury are still in absolute terms extremely high – there is no other area of social life where such constant attrition of human lives is tolerated.

A more recent but related set of arguments has concerned other health impacts of automobility. While such impacts were an important component of the 'technocratic environmentalist' arguments, movements have now emerged highlighting the health impacts of the lack of exercise which automobility engenders. Some argue, for example, that automobility has produced 'obesogenic' environments where physical activity is structured out of daily routines by long travel distances, sedentary jobs, fear of danger in streets and so on (e.g. The iWalk Club n.d.; Litman 2002: 9–10).

---

[16] For an account of US safety politics in this period, see Luger (2000: chapter 3).

[17] ROSPA gives a list of, and links to, many of these organisations, at http://www.rospa.org.uk/roadsafety/links.htm, viewed 22 August 2005.

[18] Home zones are ways of redesigning residential neighbourhoods to increase safety, reduce car use and speeds (radically – frequently a 10 mph speed limit) and increase community use of the streets. See http://www.homezones.org/concept/html for details.

Automobile space: continual road building[19]

Third, some have resisted the dislocation to urban infrastructure and the rural environment brought about by one of automobility's main features, continual road building. A car-based society has radically altered space; urban space, in particular, has been systematically reconstructed to make allowance for the space required to move people about in cars. Cars take up huge amounts of land which could be used for other purposes; the highest figure is for Los Angeles, where two-thirds of all land space is alleged to be devoted to car use – driving, parking (at shops, work, home, restaurants, etc.). For the United States as a whole, about half of urban space is devoted to car use, while 10 per cent of available arable land is taken up by roads and parking places (Freund and Martin 1993: 17–19).

Many of the works published in the 1960s and early 1970s already mentioned express this idea (Jacobs 1961; Mumford 1963; Leavitt 1970; Owen 1972). For Mumford, 'the right to have access to every building in the city by private motorcar, in an age where everyone possesses such a vehicle, is actually the right to destroy the city' (1963: 18). A range of specific problems results from this destruction, including increased crime, the soaring cost of infrastructure for road construction and suburbanisation, the degradation of peoples' aesthetic experience and the decline in a sense of community. Some make strong claims indeed: Leavitt argues that the Watts Riots in Los Angeles in 1967 resulted at least in part from freeway construction in the city (1970: 5).

Suburbanisation is one of the principal phenomena to which people writing in this mode have objected. Kunstler (1994) refers to the emergence of sprawling suburbs as a 'geography of nowhere'.[20] The

---

[19] Of course, it is not only anti-car writers who make the claim that automobility has transformed urban space, as the argument figures widely in more general analyses of urban change and development. See, for example, Banham (1971) or Bottles (1987) on the classic case of Los Angeles, or Graham and Marvin (2001), more generally. It is also not only the case that opposition to road building is wholly urban in character. Opposition to road building to protect countryside – or, in a North American context, 'wilderness' – has also been important in developing anti-car movements. On the interrelations between anti-car sentiment and the US wilderness movement, see Sutter (2002).

[20] Of course, others are unambivalent in the opposite direction, as in Baudrillard's rambly paean *America*, celebrating uncritically the 'Astral America: the lyrical nature of pure circulation' (1988: 27).

widespread adoption of the car co-evolved with a form of urban development which is very low density, thus increasing the distances between people and between people and their jobs, schools and services. Effective provision of public transport is rendered increasingly difficult, in some cases impossible. Many suggest that this has become a self-reproducing trend, as the reorganisation of towns and cities to make car-based mobility more possible has meant that increasingly a car has moved from being a luxury to a necessity (Illich 1974; Gorz 1980; Wolf 1996), undermining the uncritical claims that the car is an extension of human freedom.

In the United States in the late 1960s,[21] the challenges were rooted to a great extent in the effects of the Highway Aid Act 1956. This created a network of interstate freeways across the country but also provided support and finance for freeways within cities (Leavitt 1970; Davies 1975). Berman (1982) discusses the effects of such construction in New York. For him, the Federal Highway Program which the 1956 Act produced was a development of Robert Moses' grand schemes for reconstructing New York. Berman describes in great detail the destruction of the Bronx by the Moses' Cross-Bronx Expressway, and the resistance it engendered. His account of the experience of modernity centres on the complex politics of the development, where those in the Bronx widely predicted (correctly) the destruction of communities and the generation of slums which the road would produce, but at the same time felt very strongly the impulse to modernism which the road represented.

This reconstruction of cities to meet the expanding 'needs' of automobility is also one of the principal origins of social and political resistance to automobility itself. While the opposition to the Bronx Expressway failed, later resistance to expressway building in New York (such as to the Lower Manhattan Expressway), and to the use of Highway Trust money for expressway construction in other US cities, was more successful (Davies 1975; Berman 1982: 337). The Embarcadero Freeway in San Francisco became the lasting symbol of

---

[21] There were also challenges elsewhere, but compared to the challenges to car culture in the 1990s they were much more clearly developed in the United States. On UK opposition in this period, see Hamer (1987: chapters 5, 6), or Tyme (1978). The UK opposition centred around plans to build inner-city motorways in London and the expansion of the motorway programme in the early 1970s. Opposition was also expressed in books, although in smaller numbers than in the United States (see, for example, Aird 1972).

this resistance, stopped in mid-construction by such opposition (Davies 1975: 33).[22]

More recently, the UK roads protests (in particular) during the 1990s were either about the destruction of rural landscapes and amenities (Twyford Down, Newbury Bypass, A30) or about the destruction of communities and urban amenities (M11 Link Road, M77). This resistance to road building and the further development of a car-dependent economy was to a great extent local in character, in recognition of the way that construction necessarily destroyed city neighbourhoods and in many ways was designed deliberately to do so (e.g. Davies 1975). But it also took on an 'environmental' character in the more narrow understanding of that term, related to an emerging understanding of the car's role in resource consumption and pollution, prevalent themes in that wave of environmental concern.

One of the most important movements opposing automobility on this dimension has been Reclaim the Streets (RTS). RTS attempted to reclaim urban space as a public space, in this case for parties and community building. Arising out of the roads protests in the United Kingdom – in particular, the urban M11 Link Road campaign – RTS consciously re-articulated anti-road into anti-car (or even anti-automobility) protest. This loose organisation has organised parties in public streets, shutting them down to traffic, as a form of protest but also to show how public space has been transformed and destroyed by the car and the shift from the boulevard to the highway that Berman analysed. It also tries to suggest an alternative vision of urban life not dominated by cars and the imperatives of movement and flow, making explicit the link between a politics of resistance to the car and to the state and revealing the complicity of the state in reproducing the dominance of the car, as such street parties are themselves illegal.

Such movements are, if marginal in many places, widespread across the world, and not only in industrialised countries. The World Carfree Network, founded in 1993 as Carbusters (which still publishes a magazine with that name) has members in such countries as Bangladesh, Brazil, Colombia, the Czech Republic (its current base), Greece, Italy and the United States.[23] Most of these organisations, and

---

[22] See Low and Gleeson (2001) for evidence of similar opposition in Australia.
[23] See the organisation's website at http://www.worldcarfree.net, and that of *Carbusters* at http://www.carbusters.org.

the arguments in *Carbusters*, focus on the reaction to the impact of cars on urban life and attempts to reclaim cities from automobility. They also make connections to other issues such as climate change. In Canada in 2001, for example, the following organisations were in existence opposing the domination of cars: the Car free cities network, Auto Free Ottawa, the Green Modes Coalition, World without Cars, Transportation Alternatives, Transportation Options, the Centre for Sustainable Transport, Critical Mass (in a number of cities) and magazines from these movements such as *TransMission* and *Auto Free Zone*. In the United States, the Alliance for a Paving Moratorium was a co-ordinating organisation for such activism in the 1990s, especially through its magazine *Auto Free Times* whose principal focus was the ecological damage resulting from road construction. Its successor organisation, 'Culture change', still argues for 'depaving' of paved roads.[24]

In addition to resistance movements arising from this aspect of automobility, a large body of research and lobbying has been stimulated to promote forms of development which avoid the problems posed by continuous road building, suburbanisation, etc. This has focused on (among other things) policies in favour of public transport, new sorts of planning principles (liveable cities, new urbanism, smart growth, etc.), pedestrianised areas in cities, the promotion of cycling and so on (for more details, see chapter 7). Some of the analyses here concern specific issues such as the economic costs of suburbanisation (the discourse of 'smart growth', developed in chapter 7, is a good example here), while others (e.g. Newman and Kenworthy 1999) are more 'systemic' in character.

Unequal movements

Fourthly, some have highlighted the 'social justice' dimensions of cars. In Gorz's early classic article 'The Social Ideology of the Motor Car' (1980), automobility's basic contradiction was shown to be that the goods which cars can express (mobility, class status, individualism) lose their force once everyone owns a car (and is thus immobile, the same, a mass). The car's symbolic politics thus depend on a continual attempt to recreate (varied) forms of inequality within car

[24] It also maintains an archive online of *Auto Free Times*, at http://www.culturechange.org/about_sei.htm, viewed 21 July 2005.

consumption. Others have focused on the inequalities still expressed
in car-dominated societies, whether through differential ownership
of and access to cars, by class, gender and race (Buel 1972, chapter 7;
Jerome 1972: 14; Hamer 1987; Wajcman 1991; Freund and Martin
1993: chapter 3; Whitelegg 1997: chapter 9; Gilroy 2001); through the
way that suburbanisation enabled and then (driven by assumptions of
universal car ownership) created new forms of inequality (lack of
access to resources, social isolation) for those in suburbs without
cars; or through the way that the car/road as a specific technology
has been used to engineer certain inequalities (Winner 1980).

While initially a high-status object for the very affluent, the car was
quickly appropriated as something which could democratise society
and erase class barriers. Henry Ford was very clear that this was the
purpose of the Model T Ford, and that mass ownership of cars was a
direct substitute for class politics:

The time will not be far when our own workers will buy automobiles from
us ... I'm not saying our workers will ... govern the state. No, we can leave
such ravings to the European socialists. But our workers *will* buy automobiles. (Quoted in Wolf 1996: 72)

While the car has been sold as a democratising force, non-democratic
political leaders used a similar ideological effect. Hitler, in particular,
promoted the *ideology* of mass motorisation (no actual German civil-
ians drove 'people's cars' or Volksmobiles after the Second World War
(Virilio 1986: 25; Wolf 1996: 98–9)) and the first large-scale motorway
construction projects. In Hitler's case, this had distinctly military purposes – the design for the Volksmobile Beetle was such that it could be
put to both civilian and military uses and the motorways were constructed to make troop movement quicker and more flexible than by
using rail transport. But as an ideology it was also designed, as in Ford's
rhetoric, to help erase class differences and 'to meld the German people
into unity' (Sachs 1992: 53; Wolf 1996: 97–101): the very name
'people's car' was part of this. The Nazis used the metaphor of 'circulation' to promote motorisation, connecting car use to the ideology of
blood and soil (Sachs 1992: 47–50).[25]

---

[25] Chapter 6 discusses circulation metaphors in a little more detail. They operate as
'organic' metaphors tying the way the body works and the way 'nature' works
through a series of flows (of blood, oxygen, nutrients, etc.), to normative arguments about how society should work – as organised through structured flows

This rhetoric of the car as a democratising force endures and, as discussed in chapter 3, is emphasised in the 'backlash' against anti-car sentiments. Overy (1990), discussing the democratic pretensions of Ford and other car manufacturers, tends to reproduce their claims uncritically: 'There is a very real sense in which the democratization of motor-car ownership and motor transport matched the correspond-ing political shifts towards mass politics and greater equality' (1990: 62; see also Bayley 1998).[26] But gender, racial and class inequalities have been built into the promotion of cars, and perhaps into their nature as a technology: a car-centred economy has helped to reproduce such inequalities crucial in the reproduction of capitalist societies.

Cars are gendered in a number of ways, in the imagery of cars in adverts but also in the design of cars itself (Wajcman 1991; Wernick 1991: 72–5; Freund and Martin 1993: 90–3; McShane 1994: 132–40; Wolf 1996: 207–8). Cars are produced either as masculine, 'figured as rocket, bullet, or gun, that is as a sexual extension of the male', or as 'Woman . . . as flashy possession, mistress or wife' (Wernick 1991: 74). Prevailing patriarchal constructions of masculinity as dominance (where the car simply becomes an extension of the man) and femininity as submission ('she handles really well') are reinforced. Wajcman (1991: 134) suggests that the latter construction is dominant: 'Manufacturers encourage the male user to perceive his machine as a temperamental woman who needs to be regularly maintained and pampered for high performance' (Chambers 1987: 308, cited in *ibid.*). More prosaically, car adverts are predominantly aimed at men (although this is gradually shifting as the proportion of car buyers who are women increases) and use sex to sell cars (e.g. Marsh and Collett 1986; Baird 1998: 147–8). Even where cars are marketed at women, sexist portrayals of women are still commonplace (despite a common narrative of progress in eliminating sexism from public culture), as in the use in the United Kingdom in 1998 of 'supermodel' Claudia Schiffer disrobing before getting in her Citroën Xsara.

that bind the social body together and make it productive. In the Nazi context, of course, this operated crucially through their concept of race – the flows needed to be among those of the same 'race'; if not, then the 'impurities' would pollute the social body just as poisons in the blood would harm a body.

[26] I leave aside the more obviously ideological arguments of Lomasky (1997) or Dunn (1998) for chapter 3.

Occasionally, the car is presented as a liberator of women, a claim emphasised in a survey of the car in *The Economist* (25 January 1986; see Tiles and Oberdiek 1995: 135). Virginia Scharff (1991) gives the fullest account of the rise of the car in such terms. Analysing women's relationship to the car in early twentieth-century America she argues that the car made it possible for women to lead more independent lives, engage in a broader variety of work and break down established norms of femininity, as well as facilitating the organisation of the suffrage movement in rural areas. Apart from the consequences of the car for women developed below against which such benefits have to be weighed, a fatal weakness of Scharff's account is that the women who appear in her narrative are almost exclusively inordinately privileged. They come from the ranks not even just of the (upper) middle classes but the extremely wealthy. Generalising on the basis of their experience seems particularly unwise.[27]

For most writers, cars have been important technologies in buttressing male power. Connell (1987) argues that cars have been central technologies in tying working-class men to a notion of hegemonic masculinity which maintains male power in capitalist states, giving notions of masculinity tied to aggression, violence and technology a mass base (1987: 109–10). 'The gradual displacement of other transport systems by this uniquely violent and environmentally destructive technology is both a means and a measure of the tacit alliance between the state and corporate elite and working-class hegemonic masculinity' (1987: 110). In a similar vein, McShane (1994) shows how the emergence of the car occurred at a time when industrialisation was eroding traditional forms of masculinity, and that 'the motor car served as a battlefield in the wars over gender roles that were so important in early-twentieth-century America' (1994: 149; cf. Scharff 1991). In the United States, the late nineteenth century experienced a moral panic surrounding masculinity as industrialisation meant that many men were no longer using their 'brute strength' in their daily lives and women were making important inroads into a number of occupations. Masculinity was thus refigured to include notions of 'mechanical ability', in an attempt to maintain particular workplaces as male domains: 'Mechanical ability was becoming an attribute of gender, not social class' (McShane 1994: 153).

[27] The exception, of course, is the question of the suffrage, where the benefits can be claimed for a much broader group of women.

While cars have therefore been important symbolically and materially in reproducing male power, they have also been directly instrumental in the way that public space has been (re)masculinised in the
twentieth century. While cities and towns have been progressively
more organised spatially to serve the needs of car-centred transport,
the diversity of uses of public space has declined. Simultaneously, men
have been able to make cars predominantly theirs. Wolf (1991: 204–5)
gives figures for Germany concerning differential access to cars by men
and women: 79 per cent of eligible men have a driving licence, while
only 50 per cent of women have one; 47 per cent of German men have
'continuous' access to a car, while only 29 per cent of women do. Only
22 per cent of the cars registered in Germany are owned by women.

Public spaces in central cities have been increasingly masculinised,
and one of the predominant attitudes to city centres expressed by
women is now fear (Wajcman 1991: 131; Tiles and Oberdiek 1995:
136; Wolf 1996: 206–7). The process of suburbanisation has in many
cases involved a direct decrease in the mobility of women (at least those
in 'traditional' nuclear families with male breadwinners), moved out
to homes in suburbs, away from friends, shops, etc. Even where distances remain walkable, women's mobility has often been hit by urban
road building as dual carriageways and urban freeways make walking
across urban areas more difficult, dangerous and/or time-consuming
(Kramarae 1988: 121, quoted in Tiles and Oberdiek 1995: 136).[28]

Such spatial reorganisation has been predominantly organised
through social divisions around race and class. Suburbanisation was
founded initially on American rural anti-city ideology, at a time when
US cities were becoming more concentrated and the ethnic mix of
the cities more diverse. Suburbanisation allowed middle-class white
Americans the chance to revitalise a rural ideal and escape from the
working classes and those from other ethnic backgrounds in order to
maintain their privileged status (Freund and Martin 1993: 103–4;
McShane 1994: 123). Winner's (1980) analysis of the New York parkways built by Robert Moses is instructive here. Moses, as we saw in
chapter 1, explicitly created white middle-class spaces in the parkways

---

[28] Although it is always dubious to conflate women and children, children's independent mobility has also been reduced by the car, as parents increasingly
prevent children from going across towns and cities on their own because of
fears about their safety on the roads (Hillman *et al.* 1990, quoted in Tiles and
Oberdiek 1995: 135).

by engineering out public transport predominantly used by black and working-class Americans. The classic example is the construction of the Jones Beach Parkway, from Manhattan out to Long Island, where the bridges were deliberately constructed too low to allow buses, and thus working-class/African American New Yorkers, to reach the beaches (Winner 1980; Berman 1982).

The relationship between cars and class is more complex. As shown already, an ideology of cars promoting a blurring of class boundaries persists. But access to cars is highly differential. We have already seen this regarding gender-based inequalities, but it applies also to other forms of inequality. In the United Kingdom, in the richest 10 per cent of the population, 90 per cent of households have cars, while in the poorest 10 per cent, only 10 per cent do so (Hamer 1987: 2). Moreover, the car-centred economy has *reduced* mobility for many: those dependent on public transport or cyclists and pedestrians and those relocated by the suburbanisation produced by the car, but without access to one.[29]

This last point is one of the sites where forms of social exclusion have directly prompted social movements opposing automobility. Critical Mass has been a form of protest in a number of countries since the early 1970s (Doherty 1997: 10), involving regular mass cycle rides in towns and cities. More recently it has become a loose unorganised network of pro-cycling protests, where once a month cyclists in a number of towns and cities have met and cycled round the city centre during the Friday rush hour, clogging up the traffic. The point is to show how particular transport modes – and, through them, forms of mobility and subjectivity – dominate and to challenge that domination's reaction to the car's 'radical monopoly' (Illich 1974) and forms of exclusion.[30]

---

[29] Alongside the inequalities of ownership are inequalities of risk. Children in poor communities are at least three times as likely to be hit by a car than in richer neighbourhoods, as they are more likely to play unsupervised in the street, more likely to live near main roads with high levels of air pollution, more likely to walk to school, and have fewer resources devoted to traffic calming (Clark 2002a).

[30] One complication here is, of course, that some elements in an anti-car politics can also themselves further enhance inequality. Policies based on price mechanisms operate further to exclude those on low incomes from access to a car. Regulations to increase safety likewise increase the costs of cars. Jerome (1972) encapsulates the problem: 'the paradox of the automobile compounds itself: attempts to save lives and to save the planet become instruments of political repression' (1972: 242). This is at times emphasised by those in the backlash; see chapter 3.

Atomistic individualism

A fifth type has been opposition to the ideology of the car as the symbol
of atomistic individualism, with the car symbolising urban alienation
and loss of community. In many ways this sort of critique is simply
the flip side of precisely what is celebrated by the car's defenders
(see chapter 3). The car is promoted as an expression of individual
freedom; as a tool which enables individuals to extend their range of
freedoms through the flexible character of the mobility it provides,
through the way it enables that mobility to be solitary and exclusive
and through the way the car itself becomes an expression of individuality – from the choice of make, model and colour through to
individualised styling of the car itself. But for critics, this is a form of
freedom which denies dependence on others, which isolates people
from each other, which threatens family cohesion (Berger 1992),
which destroys community bonds and obligations and entrenches
a selfish, competitive, aggressive social form (e.g. Zuckerman 1991:
chapter 4).

Gorz's critique perhaps best represents this view:

Mass motoring effects an absolute triumph of bourgeois ideology on the level
of daily life. It gives and supports in everyone the illusion that each individual
can seek his or her own benefit at the expense of everyone else. Take the cruel
and aggressive selfishness of the driver who at any moment is figuratively
killing the 'others', who appear merely as physical obstacles to his or her
own speed. This aggressive and competitive selfishness marks the arrival of
universally bourgeois behaviour, and has come into being since driving
has become commonplace. ('You'll never have socialism with that kind of
people', an East German friend told me, upset by the spectacle of Paris
traffic). (Gorz 1980: 70).

With or without the Marxist reading of this dynamic in terms of both
its contradictions (the car is presented as furthering individual freedom
while the exigencies of mass motoring destroy the possibility of its
realisation) and its class specificities (individualism as bourgeois ideology), this view of automobility as an expression of liberal individualism
is widespread. While as Rajan (2006) points out, the silences of many
contemporary liberal political theorists on automobility is interesting,
the connection has been made very clearly and forcefully by the libertarian Lomasky in an article called 'Autonomy and Automobility'

(1997). For Lomasky this is a positive connection, and I will return to
him in chapter 3 concerning the backlash against anti-car politics, but
for many critics of car culture, automobility entails a form of individualism which emphasises the separation of people from each other and
the lack of responsibility for each other, in what Kunstler calls the
'freedom of a fourteen-year-old child' (1996: 60–1). Such a hyper-
individualism is for these critics both itself anti-social and directly the
source of widespread social problems. Putnam, in his analysis of the
decline in community and social capital in the United States, *Bowling
Alone* (2000), identifies the TV and the car as the 'two chief culprits in
the tide of civic disengagement sweeping across the USA' (as quoted in
Horton 2003). Others (e.g. Renaud 1967) express such concern specifically in relation to a claim that cars contribute to a decline in
Christian morality because of such individualising effects.

One of the problems for anti-car ideology arguments and activism is
the limitation imposed by the hegemony of individualism. Meaton and
Morrice (1996), for example, attempt to articulate an argument for
limiting car use starting from John Stuart Mill's well-known distinction
between self- and other-regarding actions. Having run through some of
the environmentalist and safety-oriented arguments discussed above,
they then attempt to conceptualise this in terms of the lack of a right of
individuals to impose harm on others. This 'other-regarding' character
of car use is then the ethical basis for regulating its use. While this has
some tactical use, perhaps, it rapidly encounters many of the same
problems which we shall see in more detail in the more aggressively
individualist, pro-car ideology of Lomasky in chapter 3.

Against speed

Sixthly, many critiques of the car focus on the notion of speed and
mobility, emphasising the fact that in many cities average speeds are
now often no faster than they were before the car's emergence, with
London averaging 7 mph, Tokyo 12 mph and Paris 17 mph in the
rush hour (Wajcman 1991: 127). The critiques in popular accounts,
such as Ben Elton's *Gridlock* (1991) focus, among other things, on
the irony and frustration produced by the car: the myth of the car is
centred around speed and mobility but since it simultaneously produces congestion on a scale never previously seen it is simple (at least
in Elton's fictional account) for political elites to manipulate this

and produce a total Gridlock of London, in order to justify further road building.[31]

A classic critique is in Ivan Illich's *Energy and Equity* (1974). Illich calculated that:

> The typical American male devotes more than 1,600 hours a year to his car. He sits in it while it goes and while it stands idling. He parks it and searches for it. He earns the money to put down on it and to meet the monthly instalments. He works to pay for petrol, tolls, insurance, taxes, and tickets. He spends four of his sixteen waking hours on the road or gathering his resources for it. (*Ibid.*: 30).

On this basis, Wolf suggests that speed is a myth, not in the sense of an organising social motif but as something false and to be debunked. He calculates that taking into account all these factors which Illich discusses the 'real' speed of car transport averages at approximately 20 kmh, about the same speed travelled by a 'very fit cyclist' (1996: 187).

Beyond this debunking of the myth of speed, critics focus on the articulation of the car as a social form which continuously accelerates – work rates, distances travelled, volumes consumed – and plays a central role in *compelling* people to adopt this accelerated way of life. The cost of cars compel people to work longer hours to pay for them, the dynamics of (sub)urban change compel people to drive more, the restricted remaining time compels people to increase consumption to meet needs (eating out rather than cooking, etc.). One of the main symbolisms of the counter-cultural movements was a valorisation of slow versus fast (Belasco 1989), while more recent social movements have similarly praised slowness as a self-conscious reaction to contemporary acceleration (as in the Italian-led 'slow food movement'). Sachs (1992) makes this explicit by articulating the bicycle as the symbol through which this reaction against speed can be manifested (1992: 196–203; see chapter 8 for more on bicycles).

---

[31] Elton (1991) also focuses on the inequalities produced by car-centred transport, with one of his two main characters having cerebral palsy and therefore being unable to drive and being disabled by the car-centred system and the other having lost her legs when hit by a car, but then being reliant on a car because of the inadequacies of London's public transport for those in wheelchairs. His other theme is the corrupt relations between government ministers and the roads lobby.

Consumerist geopolitics[32]

A final critique has been the way that various social movements have connected cars to oil imperialism and thus to opposition to US foreign policy. This has been seen most recently in the moral panic around the way that the development of the market for Sport Utility Vehicles (SUVs) is regarded to have driven up US oil imports and thus led to a more adventurist foreign policy (figure 2).[33]

Opposition to SUVs in the United States has come from a diverse range of actors. Friends of the Earth sells bumper stickers saying 'support OPEC, buy an SUV'. The 'What would Jesus drive?' campaign already mentioned focused, alongside climate change, on the way that the decline in fuel economy because of the rise of the SUV made the United States more dependent on Middle Eastern oil and that 'Christians should strive to lessen circumstances that could lead to violent conflicts by reducing our consumption of oil' (Evangelical Environmental Network n.d.). A substantial part of the reasoning behind these campaigns was that the rise of the SUV in the 1990s entailed a dramatic decrease in the overall fuel economy of the North American car fleet and thus an increase in imports, which drove up oil prices, exacerbated already strong tensions in oil-producing regions, especially the Middle East, and contributed to the apparent 'necessity' of US intervention in Iraq and Afghanistan to secure preferential control over supplies of oil.

Michael Klare perhaps most fully expresses this 'oil geopolitics' argument (2001, 2004).[34] Klare suggests that the defining moment was during the First World War when the British Navy switched fuels for their ships from coal to oil.[35] Securing access to oil, in a European

[32] For a fuller analysis of 'anti-SUV' and 'anti-oil imperialist' discourses, see Dalby and Paterson (2006).
[33] Anti-SUV activism has engaged in many of the elements of anti-car critiques already discussed – in particular safety questions, the technocratic environmentalism (mostly around climate change), and the critique of individualism. For analyses of these campaigns, see Gunster (2004) or Vanderheiden (2006). For an account of the oil/empire argument focusing on car (including SUV) advertising, see Paterson and Dalby (2006).
[34] See also Mayer (2002); Harvey (2003: chapter 1); McQuaig (2004); LeBillon and El Khatib (2004); Jaffe (2005).
[35] See also Sampson (1975: chapter 3). The literature on oil multinationals, epitomised by Sampson's *The Seven Sisters* (1975) and Yergin's *The Prize* (1993), routinely analyses this oil/empire connection as something uncontroversial and scarcely worthy of critical comment.

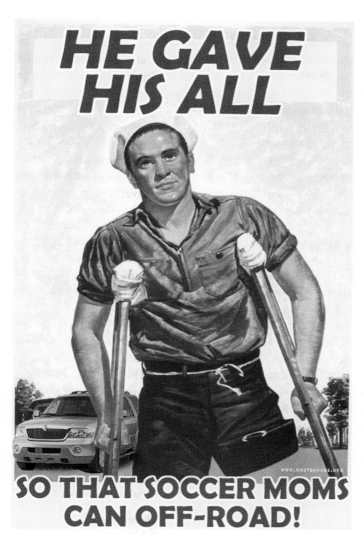

2 'No stumps 4 oil'
Source: from http://www.cafepress.com/thewhitehouse/32519. Reproduced by
permission of thewhitehouse.com.

context already dominated by supply from the Middle East, became a strategic objective and the emergence of tanks, armoured cars and aeroplanes cemented this objective. During both the First and Second World War both sides fought to gain and secure access to the main oil fields and the Middle East then became a key strategic area in peacetime and throughout the Cold War. The situation changed during the early 1970s when the producer countries began to use the 'oil weapon' for their own purposes and the withdrawal of supplies itself became a strategic weapon. This was the first time that the United States threatened military force to open up access to oil; since then, the dynamic has been the increased US dependence on imports and the continued increases in demand, which increased the pressure on US administrations to find access to (and control of) new and diversified sources. This is used by Klare as an explanation not only for US engagement in the Gulf in 1990–1 and 2003 but involvement in Central Asia, an interest in politics in Venezuela and so on (Klare 2001, 2004).[36]

The argument is sometimes couched in terms of the interests of the oil companies (many with very close ties to successive US administrations) (e.g. Gökay 2003; McQuaig 2004). In the case of the war against Iraq since 2003, the closeness of many senior US officials to oil companies is often noted (e.g. McQuaig 2004). The plans for an invasion of Iraq clearly long preceded either the 11 September attacks or the claims about weapons of mass destruction (WMD), which emerged as official (but ultimately unfounded) justifications for the war. Getting access to the oil resources in Iraq to prevent French, German and Russian control, to offset the increased risks after 11 September of overreliance on the Saudi Arabian regime and to ensure that trading in Iraqi oil continued to take place in US dollars thus appear as the most plausible explanations for the invasion.[37] The particular character of the

---

[36] For other arguments related to this, see Morse (1999) on the changing geopolitics of oil, or Campbell (2005) on associating this geopolitics with the driving of SUVs.

[37] McQuaig details the evidence for this claim very fully (2004: especially chapter 2). The Saudi regime became more clearly problematic for the US administration after 11 September 2001, both because many of the World Trade Center's attackers had come from Saudi Arabia (as does Osama bin Laden) and because of increased fears of attempts to overthrow the existing regime, the US' most loyal ally in the region. Of course, both of these increased risks are directly the result of the presence of US troops in Saudi Arabia since 1990.

reconstruction of Iraq after Saddam Hussein's regime had been over-thrown also supports this interpretation (*ibid.*: chapter 3).

But what is clear in the anti-SUV activism is that a broader connection is made: it is not only the interests of oil companies but the way that such interests gain broad legitimacy from the recognition of the dependence of daily life on such intervention.[38] For anti-SUV activists, this dependence has been critically affected by the rise of the vehicle in the 1990s as the cause of the decline in fuel economy and the increase in imports.

But the argument can be and has been made in a broader context than merely the current focus on SUVs. The argument was made in relation to the Gulf War of 1990–1 (both regarding the Iraqi invasion of Kuwait and in relation to the US-led military action against Iraq) before the rise of the SUV and when the fuel economy of American cars was at an all-time high.[39] And the argument was made during the 1970s – the United States became a net oil importer in 1970 and took an increasing strategic interest in the Middle East during the decade to protect sources of oil, threatening military retaliation over the Organisation of Petroleum-Exporting States (OPEC) action in 1973–4 which quadrupled prices and restricted supply, building up a strong relationship with the Saudi elite and so on.[40] Lovins and Lovins (1982)

---

[38] What is important is the successful rendition of such intervention as necessary to securing the conditions of continued SUV use (or, as in my argument below, car-driving more generally) – specifically, regular supplies and low prices. This is, of course, highly contradictory – the implicit consumerist underpinning of the legitimacy of, for example, the invasion of Iraq in 2003 is therefore the desire to secure low oil prices, while the trajectory of oil prices since the invasion (which were in fact declining immediately prior to it) has sky-rocketed to unprecedented levels. The contradiction here is that, in practice, oil companies, like oil-exporting countries, favour high oil prices (so long as consumption is not cut back, but short-term price elasticity of demand is notoriously low regarding oil) as it raises their overall profit levels. Nitzan and Bichler (1995; Bichler and Nitzan 2004) observe that the great majority of the wars in the Middle East since the late 1960s have been preceded by a period where oil companies performed less well than the Fortune 500 average, that oil companies outperform this average after such wars and that their profits are positively correlated with high oil prices.

[39] Such arguments were made during the 1990–1 Gulf War (e.g. Lovins and Lovins 1990; Brenner 1991). For some, this recognition had widespread cultural resonances, in films such as *The Big Lebowski* and more explicitly *Three Kings* (Martin-Jones 2006).

[40] Most of the 1970s literature on cars makes little mention of this, partly because most of it was published before the oil price hike of 1973–4. It is also partly because the connections between cars and oil are only relatively rarely made

refer to this as the 'brittle power' of what Amory B. Lovins had earlier (1977) termed 'hard energy paths', where the vulnerabilities to disruption of supply and the way it encourages military measures to defend that supply are considered one of the key frailties of the oil/automobility complex (Freund and Martin 1993: 130).

Conclusions

The strength of movements opposing automobility in various ways has varied but there has been a constant theme throughout western societies (at least) since the late 1960s which has emphasised automobility as a means of domination as opposed to liberation and accordingly resisted its projects. In addition, even where explicitly articulated movements have not arisen, automobility politics has been an ever-present element in many places, over issues as diverse as countryside (or so-called 'wilderness') destruction, road safety, congestion, sprawl and air pollution.

Bringing these critiques of, and resistances to, automobility together suggests a number of things. Some emphasise specific questions, inviting reformist responses, technological fixes, specific policies (electric cars to limit urban air pollution, safety features, lower speed limits and so on). But when we put all of them together, they are more suggestive of a total critique which argues that the specific problems engendered are contained inherently within automobility's logic. Thus critiques and resistances tend towards counter-hegemony in their form of argument and action.

Some of the political resistance against cars can help to illustrate this point. Resistance to road building in the United Kingdom has often been made up of an odd alliance of 'Not In My Back Yarders' (NIMBYs) wishing to protect their local sites of amenity and radical Green activists operating more on 'Not On Planet Earth' (NOPE) principles. There are many instances of movement from the former to the latter type, as involvement in protesting develops in protesters a deeper sense of the social changes necessary to create sustainable

(e.g. Buel 1972: chapter 6) and the critique is of the way that the US government has subsidised the oil industry as it has the car industry. 'National security' appears in the discourse at this point in terms of straightforward economic protectionism – protecting the US oil industry from 'cheap foreign imports' (Buel 1972: 125–6).

societies.[41] The awareness of the more deep-thinking Green activists of the way in which road building and car culture is embedded in a set of power structures is clearly evident in the way that they understand their own actions. This is perhaps shown most fully by Seel (1997) in his analysis of the Pollok Free State protest camp against the M77 extension in Glasgow, which he conceptualises as 'embryonic counter-hegemonic resistance'.[42]

At the same time a substantial element of these movements which started in the late 1960s has ended up in the 'long march through the institutions', engaging in reform projects – developing transport policy, urban planning and the like; some of this is elaborated in chapter 7. It is this development which enables Dunn (1998, see chapter 3) to suggest (if unpersuasively) that such anti-car forces are now dominant in the United States. My argument would nevertheless be that such reform projects remain contradictory and that the tendency of such policies and practices is to reveal further the basic contradictions of automobility itself.

This tendency is most clearly seen in those critiques which focus on automobility's restructuring of urban forms. First, automobility is seen to be inconsistent; having made people free to leave the city it makes it possible to overcome such spatial separation only by compulsory car driving. Having held out the possibility of universal mobility, the attempt to realise this results in *'le grand embouteillage'* (the great bottleneck/traffic jam) (Duteurtre 2002). As Jerome (1972) puts it: 'A hundred million passenger cars would seem to represent a substantial degree of realization of the dream of mobility. But the fascinating aspect of this exercise in industrial overkill has been the rapid diminution of the significance of mobility, per se' (1972: 15). Mobility ceases to be a freedom and becomes a necessity.

Second is the realisation that mass automobility, premised on *autonomous mobility*, has resulted in a society far more heavily planned than previously and far more regulated than can be regarded as consistent with the libertarian impulses of automobility's defenders discussed in

---

[41] For example, Mick Smith (1997: 350, n. 32) quoting *The Guardian*, 1 March 1996.

[42] For other analyses of roads protests in Britain see, for example, McKay (1996); Doherty (1997, 1999); Mick Smith (1997); Welsh and McLeish (1996). The analyses by McKay (1996) and Seel (1997), in particular, support the interpretation given here.

chapter 3. Schneider refers to this as *'tyrannus mobilitis'* (1971: 22),[43] while Jerome again expresses the dynamic well:

The planned society necessary to make an explosively expanding technology work is a frightening bargain ... The more complex the technology becomes, the more certain is the need that it be controlled and turned to socially ameliorative uses ... the more certain the need for that control, the more evident that that control must be from the top downwards. (Jerome 1972: 255–6)

Thus, for the most prescient of critics of the car since the 1960s (such as Jacobs, Rothschild, Jerome, or Schneider, Illich, in particular, or more recently Sachs), the solution to the problems of automobility is to restrict movement. But this conclusion is, as we shall see in chapter 3, fiercely contested.

---

[43] I leave aside for the moment Virilio's notion of 'dromocracy', which will be an obvious connection for some readers, in favour of keeping to those critics of a car-dominated society. I develop this concept in chapter 5.

3 | *Don't stop movin': the pro-car backlash*

> Have you noticed how most car orientated
> websites now have a section on the ubiqui-
> tous 'environment'? You could be forgiven
> for thinking it is a compulsory subject. It is in
> fact the latest form of political correctness.
> Green activists have succeeded in brain-
> washing most of the public into accepting
> that the 'environment' is the new god before
> whom we must all bow down in submission.
>   Well our environment page is different.
> Our page does not use the 'environment' as a
> weapon against drivers, our page tells the
> truth. Find out how emotive scaremongering
> about pollution and man-made 'global
> warming' are being used to intimidate you
> out of your car.
>
> (Association of British Drivers, heading paragraph to
> 'environment' page, at www.abd.org.uk, click on
> 'environment', viewed 21 March 2005)

> The breaking up of the dialectic of the human
> milieu in favor of automobiles ... masks its
> irrationality under pseudopractical justifica-
> tions. But it is practically necessary only in the
> context of a specific social set-up. Those who
> believe that the particulars of the problem
> are permanent want in fact to believe in the
> permanence of the present society.
>
> (Guy Debord, 'Situationist Theses on Traffic' 1959: thesis 8)

In the summer of 2002, a small network of activists in the United Kingdom started physically to destroy speed cameras. Calling themselves

'Motorists Against Detection' (MAD) their premise was that speed cameras were being used simply as money-making devices for police forces and local councils and that, more broadly, they were part of a 'war on motorists'. By November 2004 they had destroyed 750 cameras at a cost of £32,000 each (Wainwright 2004). MAD claimed that 'we represent an unheard band of motorists and bikers fed up with this continuing proliferation of speed cameras, specs cameras, bus lane [*sic*], parking and now congestion cameras' (MAD 2002). Within the discourse of groups opposed to speed cameras, the state agencies involved in administering the system (often called Safety Camera Partnerships) are known as the Talivan (e.g. at http://www.abd.org.uk/talivan.htm, viewed 27 March 2005). This particular campaign against speed cameras saw some success in reversing policy; the government agreed to paint them yellow so that they would be visible, 'to give motorists a chance to outwit them' (Bennett 2002).

This narrative about a 'war on motorists' and a range of political actions to 'defend motorists' rights' can be seen as part of a broad-based backlash against the arguments, movements and emergent policies discussed in chapter 2. It expresses a sense that the movements which oppose various aspects of automobility, or automobility as a whole, have become 'too' powerful and warrant some sort of resistance to defend the 'interests' of motorists. Similar hostility can be seen in the same period against traffic calming measures and other 'restrictions' on car users (on opposition to traffic calming, see Clark 2004). In response to many of these movements to limit, reorient, or fundamentally oppose automobility, as well as to its inherent contradictions – especially in the denser cities of western Europe and Asia – the movement's promoters, managers and ideologists have reacted in a variety of ways. Collectively, these operate as a set of attempts to 'recuperate' automobility from its critics. One element is a range of attempts to 'green' the car; I leave that discussion to chapter 7. This chapter suggests that another significant element has been a backlash against anti-car sentiments.

After detailing a little more fully the existence of a range of movements, networks, think tanks, academics and populist writers who can be regarded as part of this backlash, I analyse the nature of the anti-anti-car discourse, emphasising in particular that it rests both empirically and normatively on a *hyper-individualism*. The growth of cars is explained in terms of the individual agency of drivers and of politicians responding to such agency, while the car is defended in terms of its normative status as an (if not *the*) embodiment of human autonomy. I discuss this discourse in relation to two sustained arguments advancing the backlash agenda (Lomasky 1997 and Dunn 1998).

The chapter, combined with the analysis in chapter 2 in particular, also shows that, at a basic level, automobility is irredeemably contested. I emphasise this as those involved in the backlash take an opposing stance here; they stand as living proof of the contested character of automobility's politics while asserting that 'essentially' automobility is not contested. The opponents of the car are just 'elites' with no social base; within society at large, the car is taken for granted and valued in unambiguously positive terms.

The pro-car backlash

The actions of MAD against speed cameras are the extreme end of a spectrum of opposition to the 'war on motorists'; MAD is, if you like, the backlash's paramilitary wing.[1] Broadly, the backlash can be said to contain four distinct elements. The two principal ones are conservative think tanks and opinion formers, and populist 'grassroots' organisations. These are supported by some politicians, mostly but not exclusively conservative in ideological terms, and a small number of academics who serve to legitimise in particular the strategies of the think tanks.[2] I focus below on the first two elements as the most important politically, occasionally referring to politicians as supporting actors. I leave

---

[1] The imagery here is deliberate and deserved; MAD's spokesperson, Captain Gatso, stated happily that 'I don't get my hands dirty, I'm like Gerry Adams' (quoted in Wainwright 2004). The name 'Captain Gatso' comes from the main type of speed camera, known as a Gatsometer after its inventor, Maurice Gatsonides.

[2] Interestingly, given the nature of other aspects of the 'green backlash', groups explicitly representing corporations with interests in automobility have been fairly quiet, perhaps preferring to let populist groups work for them. See, for example, the British Roads Federation (BRF) (1999), which complains of cutbacks to road construction but with little by way of 'backlash' rhetoric; or an even more conciliatory response by the Society of Motor Manufacturers and Traders (SMMT) to the Labour government's 'New Deal for Transport' (SMMT 1998), seen in other circles as part of the 'war on motorists'; or an article by the Chief Executive of the BRF, Richard Diment, criticising the protesters against the Newbury Bypass in predictable but very moderate tones (Diment 1996). The Fédération Internationale de l'Automobile (FIA), the international body joining together national motorists' organisations, put together a highly 'constructive'

discussion of the academics for the second part of the chapter and focus on analysing their arguments, as they in effect contain the most sustained attempts to support the claims of backlash organisations. The backlash against anti-car ideologies is thus similar in structure, and contains indeed many of the same players and strategies, as those involved in a more general backlash against environmentalism in the 1990s and beyond (on which see Rowell 1996; Beder 1997; Switzer 1997; Paterson 1999).

At a broad level, the emergence of a backlash is in part the legacy of a long-standing strategy of resistance by car and oil firms against regulation along a number of dimensions.[3] There has been, since the 1950s at least, a significant lobbying effort by car industries, as well as funding for 'alternative' research programmes to dispute the claims made by scientists, social movements, or regulators, in order to resist lobbying on specific issues especially road safety, a range of pollution control questions and fuel efficiency (Rajan 1996; Doyle 2000; Luger 2000; see chapter 7 for more details). Most of this has remained at the level of the specific issues at hand (see e.g. Bruce-Briggs 1975), with perhaps the exception of the assault on Ralph Nader by General Motors (GM) during the 1960s (Scharff 1992). Overt feminisation of Nader, questioning his masculinity (and thus his authority to speak) was available, and used, as a strategy; in the 1990s backlash such feminisation of the car's critics was largely avoided, certainly in print. The backlash emerged specifically in the 1990s for a number of reasons, partly because of the radicalisation of the political right, in particular in the United States, which turned in this context on the intertwining of religious, corporate/economic and individualist/consumerist hostilities to environmentalism in general with the perceived failure of the car manufacturers adequately to defend the interests of motorists. Within the backlash, the car manufacturers are at times seen as having 'sold out' to environmentalists and so new organisations and strategies were needed. In one sense, the backlash arose in part out of the increasing

response to the climate change negotiations running up to Kyoto in 1997, in contrast to the Global Climate Coalition (GCC, on which see chapter 7) (AIT/FIA 1997), while defending the specific interests of motorists. There are some exceptions, notably the International Road Federation's 'Roads – Dispelling the Myths' which reproduced the GCC's ideas concerning climate change, and attacked anti-car/road activists (reprinted in Gamble 1998).

[3] Ward (1991: 29–31) gives earlier examples of backlash discourse, including the use of academics to legitimise road lobby interests. This is interpreted by Ward as an 'individualist backlash'.

contradictions between the interests of car manufacturers and car drivers, a tension born of the politics of distributing the costs of mitigating the car's various externalities.[4] As these costs increasingly shifted from the manufacturers to the users of cars (from safety belts and catalytic converters to congestion charging and inspection/maintenance regimes), the political organisation of pro-car politics also shifted.

This then produced the distinctive ideological twist to the backlash – rather than a series of specific interventions to deal with particular problems, a 'war on motorists' has been declared. We are told similarly that we are witnessing 'The Vanishing Automobile' (O'Toole 2000), or that the car's 'enemies' are winning. Dunn (1998) argues that policy coalitions favouring limits on car use have become dominant in the United States, writing about 'the anti-auto forces that are taking on an increasingly prominent role in the discussions about future transportation policy' (1998: 4).

The two principal elements of the backlash have, as outlined above, been conservative think tanks[5] and populist organisations. The US Competitive Enterprise Institute (CEI) has been the most prominent of the former.[6] From the mid-1990s onwards it promoted the 'Automobility and Freedom Project', deliberately designed to relegitimise

---

[4] The 1990s saw a split in the interests between car and oil firms over pollution control, with the former increasingly resenting the way that the oil companies had been able to avoid doing anything about the content of petrol to limit pollution, the costs falling on car companies. This was brought to a head by California's 'zero emissions' legislation which requires manufacturers to have a (rising) proportion of their vehicles sold classified as 'zero-emitting' in order to be able to sell at all in California. This legislation forces car manufacturers to plan post-oil cars and thus think about the differences between their interests and those of the oil companies. Consumer organisations, when discussing fuel economy measures, almost always favour fuel economy standards like CAFÉ, while car manufacturers' organisations prefer 'price mechanisms' such as fuel taxes (e.g. SMMT 1993; CAA 2001). Each in effect is attempting to shift the principal costs of efficiency measures on to the other.

[5] As always, there is an exception. In this case it is Karl Zinsmeister of the American Enterprise Institute (AEI), who has written critically about the role of cars and suburbanisation in creating 'inhospitable places for individualism and community life' and encouraging 'rootlessness' and the decline of the traditional family (Zinsmeister 1996).

[6] Others that have produced work on the car or automobility have included the AEI, the Independent Institute, the Heritage Foundation and the Thoreau Institute. I focus on the CEI partly because they have produced the most work in this area, but also because the themes are common across all the organisations concerned.

the car in relation to what it saw as threats. The CEI commissioned
a series of reports from academics and other writers; the most widely
discussed, and arguably the most fundamental to their project, was
Loren Lomasky's *Autonomy and Automobility* (1997), which I shall
discuss in detail later in the chapter. The others included papers called
'The Central Planning of Lifestyles: Automobility and the Illusion of Full-
Cost Pricing' (Cordato 1997) which focuses on the politics of using
pricing mechanisms to try to affect the behaviour of drivers; 'Engines of
Liberty' (Hanasz n.d.) which suggests that cars played an important
role in undermining Communism in Eastern Europe and 'Cars, Women
and Minorities: The Democratization of Mobility in America' (Pisarski
1999). A large volume of smaller publications – focused principally on
measures to limit sprawl or promote 'smart growth', promote public
transport, or generally plan to deal with automobility's problems – was
also produced. The ideological tone is broadly consistent with a stereotypical 'hostility to big government' prevalent in US neoconservatism,
and an opposition between such government, on the one hand, and both
individual consumers and firms, on the other.

These views have been popularised in the media, in conferences and
through the networks within which the CEI moves. One such event was
the conference on 'Preserving the American Dream of Mobility and
Homeownership', organised by the Thoreau Institute in February
2003.[7] The agenda is instructive of the concerns of these organisations –
focusing on strategies to oppose 'smart growth', land use planning
strategies (see chapter 7), the promotion of public transport, protecting
private property rights, 'selling the idea of autos and highways' and so
on (TI 2003). The General Counsel of the CEI, Sam Kazman, has
spoken regularly on 'Automobility and Freedom', including at the
first 'Preserving the American Dream' conference, as well as at 'The
Objectivist Center', an Ayn Rand-inspired think tank.[8]

The second element is a range of populist organisations attempting
to mobilise car drivers to oppose policies which might threaten their
interests. In the United States, the principal one has been the Coalition
for Vehicle Choice (CVC, now no longer operating[9]), which was the

[7] This has become a series of annual conferences with the same title.
[8] The talks are all close variants of each other, and draw heavily on the papers
commissioned by the CEI. See, for example, Kazman (2001).
[9] At the time of writing, its website, at www.vehiclechoice.org, no longer exists.

main means by which opposition – in particular, to enhanced fuel economy or enhanced safety standards and to US participation in the Kyoto Protocol – were articulated as a question of consumer's rights. In the *Washington Times*, Mike Anson wrote in an article reproduced on the CVC's website, that 'If the fuel economy standards are raised, cars and trucks will have to get smaller and less powerful. Based on the cars and trucks people are buying most, that is not what they want ... I'm letting my representatives know that I oppose the Global Warming Treaty [Kyoto] and that I support the CAFÉ fuel economy freeze ... I really want to be able to buy the pickup truck I want with the engine I want' (Anson 1997). The National Consumer Council (NCC) similarly lobbied on behalf of 'consumers' to resist increased fuel economy standards and similar measures. During the run-up to the 2000 US presidential election some in the Bush team claimed that ratifying Kyoto would mean that Americans might have to 'walk to work'.[10] In the United Kingdom, the Association of British Drivers (ABD) has operated as a quintessentially populist movement, articulating car politics as a constant threat by elites and the powerful against 'ordinary people'. It similarly presents itself as a marginal group in effect forced to establish itself because 'mainstream' groups such as the Automobile Association (AA) are not adequately defending drivers' rights.[11] Its statement of aims begins: 'The objective of the ABD is to provide an active, responsible voice to lobby for the beleaguered British car driver' (www.abd.org.uk[12]). The *raison d'être* of the National Motorists

---

[10] Other articulations of car driving clearly represent it in fundamentally cultural, rather than narrowly economic, terms. In debates about 'smart growth', a planning discourse in North America promoting urban reconcentration (to meet transportation planning needs and the economic needs of the 'new economy', as well as environmental and social justice goals) a commentator wrote in the *Globe and Mail* that 'we' could shift from cars to bicycles as a mode of transport, 'if we wanted to live like the Dutch'. Unless the commentator is to be regarded as monumentally ignorant, the most reasonable reading of this is that car driving is understood as a cultural right rather than a rational pursuit of specific ends.

[11] Mainstream organisations such as the AA have at times adopted similar populist rhetoric, as in the 'Fair Deal for Motorists' campaign in February 1999. This had classic populist sloganeering such as 'we cannot accept taxes collected under the cloak of environmentalism which do nothing to provide an alternative to the car' (AA 1999).

[12] The ABD website operates entirely through frames, so it is not possible to give precise web page addresses. The statement is reached by clicking on 'about us', viewed 22 March 2005.

Association of Australia (NMAA) is that 'for too long now motorists have been kicked around by anyone who wants to kick them' (http://www.aussiemotorists.com/faq/assoc.html).[13]

As is the case with many populist organisations, especially those dealing routinely with questions articulated as 'environmental issues', corporate backers are frequently behind the populist organisations. This does not appear to be the case with the ABD, but was certainly the case with the CVC, whose money came entirely from the car industry – individuals could join, but membership was free and members' roles were largely limited to signing and sending off letters to their politicians serving to legitimise it as a 'popular' organisation (Bradsher 2002: 66). This follows the general pattern with many populist 'green backlash' movements, for whom the term 'astroturf' (as in fake grassroots) has been coined (Rowell 1996).

But populism is not easily contained in such formal organisations. A backlash can also be seen widely in the popular media (from journalists like Jeremy Clarkson or Richard Littlejohn to 'shock jocks' like Howard Stern) where environmentalists or safety campaigners are routinely belittled and lampooned, alternatives to cars criticised (the problems on the trains, cyclists as 'lycra louts', for example) and the 'simple pleasures' of 'ordinary' people in driving their cars celebrated. It can also be seen in more subtle discourses like 'Mondeo Man' or the appropriation of protesters as in the celebration of 'Swampy' (on which more in chapter 6). Populist accounts are also prevalent in the way that anti-car backlash sentiments have been articulated by politicians, as in the UK Conservative Party's adoption of the term 'war on motorists' (see Younge and Glancey 1999; Wainwright 2004[14]).

---

[13] For other examples of similar organisations around the world, especially those involved in campaigning against speed cameras (the issue which has triggered the existence of many of them), see the links page from the ABD.

[14] This can be seen in various places at the Conservative Party's website at http://www.conservatives.com. Until 21 March 2005, it was one of the five themes highlighted on the main page under a banner of 'what we will do' – 'end the war on motorists'. This slogan was removed on 22 March 2005. But a search of their site on 'war on motorists' shows that it still appears (a total of forty times at the time of writing) in press releases and speeches going back to 2000. What was striking in terms of a populist discourse is that when they actually discuss transport policy the slogan disappears and the concrete policies are remarkably thin – supporting an interpretation that it was opportunistic and populist. See Kelly and Clark (n.d.). The Minister of Transport in the 1990s, Peter Bottomley, derided critics of the roads programme in similar manner, stating that 'more

Populism can also be seen, albeit in a more complex manner, in the protests against fuel taxes and fuel prices which occurred across Europe in 2000 in particular.[15] The protests started in France, spread to the United Kingdom and across most countries in western Europe. In the United Kingdom, for example, the protest largely entailed a group of farmers and later road hauliers deciding on 7 September to blockade oil refineries in protest against the high price of petrol, articulated as a question of the rate of fuel taxes. While the blockades only lasted a few hours, pickets of the refineries continued for a week, successfully preventing tankers from leaving.[16] While the farmers and hauliers had distinct (and, in fact, rather contradictory[17]) interests to protect and pursue, the protests can be seen as part of a populist backlash in the way that 'ordinary' people both implicitly supported the protests as they appeared to serve their interests as drivers – and (more importantly) they were articulated, even interpellated, into this subject position by the popular press. The recurrent media discourse during the

---

roads must be built for cars yet to be acquired by women, ethnic minorities and council tenants who do not enjoy the benefit of personal transport at present' (as quoted in Zuckerman 1991: 17–18): anti-roads protesters are constructed as elitists pulling up the ladder behind them.

[15] I say that this is 'more complex' as it is problematic to claim that the protesters, especially the farmers involved, were motivated by a resistance to 'anti-car' politics in any direct sense. Interestingly, at least some of the farmers involved in the UK protests, especially in North Wales, were connected to environmental movements and articulated their concerns in terms of free trade and European integration as much as fuel prices, and as such had a more complex analysis of their problematic situation than the road hauliers, the main other group involved in blockades and pickets of oil refineries. For details on the relationship between the fuel protests in the United Kingdom and environmentalism, see Doherty *et al.* (2002); for a more general analysis of the protests, on which the discussion here draws, see Robinson (2002) or Doherty, Paterson, Plows and Wall, hereafter DPPW (2003).

[16] One of the protests' oddities was that, apart from the first few hours, there were only pickets, no blockades. While there were allegations of intimidation of drivers by the pickets it was also reasonably clear that the oil companies were not overly concerned about the protest, since it allowed pressure to be brought to bear on the government to reduce fuel taxes. See DPPW (2003).

[17] Both wanted fuel prices to go down. But for the hauliers the central question was differences in fuel taxes across Europe, giving hauliers from some countries a competitive advantage over UK-based companies; for the farmers, the fuel price question was but part of a bigger problem concerning the way that European integration harmed the interests of hill sheep farmers, in particular. One favoured European harmonisation, the other delinking from the European economy.

protests was of 'the stoic struggle of ordinary folk in petrol queues, who, while frustrated, supported the protesters and were hostile to the government's fuel tax policy' (DPPW 2003: 16). The protesters themselves were largely constructed in the popular press through discourses of class and nation, as 'ordinary' 'respectable' English/British people, in stark contrast to the way that environmental protesters or trade unionists are normally portrayed.[18] The protests thus became read in terms of the standard narratives of populism.

Backlash discourse: I – naturalising the rise of the car

As is common, a backlash often operates ideologically in scattergun fashion. As it attempts to undermine its opponents it uses what strategies and tactics it feels most useful in particular circumstances and against particular opponents. One common tactic is to denigrate its critics through accusations (variously) of being communists, anti-progress, anti-freedom, anti-American, anti-poor and so on.

Behind these tactical efforts to undermine the legitimacy of their political opponents there is in backlash discourse an effort to restate automobility's basic ideological legitimation, which is rather more coherent (although as I hope to show ultimately not really so) and needs to be taken seriously. For it is this core which both connects the anti-car backlash discourse to broader political discourses and makes clear that it has at its core the politics of the (US) neoconservative right.

At the heart of the arguments is a worldview where 'the individual' is placed at the centre of things, both empirically/analytically and normatively. The car is justified by reference to an ethic which makes very strong claims about both the connection of cars to human autonomy and the rights of individuals to non-interference by others. But the individualism is not only a normative one; the emergence of a

---

[18] See DPPW (2003: 16–18), for details of the populist discourse in the press concerning the protesters. One of the quirks/problems of discussing nationalist discourses in the United Kingdom is precisely that in *England*, English and British nationalisms are routinely (and imperialistically) conflated. I did not analyse the Scottish or Welsh press while doing the work for the DPPW (2003) article, but would suspect that nationalist discourses would have worked rather differently. Note that many of these images are strikingly similar to the way that anti-car protesters were normalised shortly before the fuel protests (on which, see more in chapter 6).

car-dominated society is simultaneously 'naturalised' by explaining it in terms of the outcome of a range of individual decisions (to buy cars, not use the tram or the bus, etc.). But the interaction between the empirical and normative dimensions is complex; the series of individual decisions which over time have produced a car-dominated society are simultaneously acts which express the human drive for autonomy and thus are not simply social facts but normatively desirable actions. Together, these individualist assumptions provide a powerful basis for arguing that anti-car politics are both doomed to fail (because they work against the interests of the majority of people) and immoral (as they act to limit human autonomy).

I start with a discussion of James Dunn's *Driving Forces: The Automobile, its Enemies, and the Politics of Mobility* (1998),[19] which develops the empirical side of this argument. Albeit couched in relatively academic language, the narrative epitomises the backlash account of anti-car politics.[20] Dunn attempts to create the image that:

A growing number of very vocal critics and analysts see the automobile not as a solution but as a problem, and auto policy not as a success but as a failure ... These 'enemies' of the automobile choose not [to] see it as the most successful mode of transportation and the most popular means of personal mobility ever created. Instead they view it as a voracious consumer of irreplaceable energy resources, a major source of greenhouse gases, a killer of tens of thousands of accident victims, and a destroyer of calm and cohesive communities. (Dunn 1998: 3)

Dunn conflates the various sorts of anti-car positions outlined in chapter 2, and switches between them as a tactic to find the target most suitable for particular claims, creating the image of a homogeneous, well-organised set of writers and movements that are at once both more

---

[19] For another essay with very similar arguments to Dunn's, see Wilson (1997). Dunn's 1998 book is a significantly cruder version of the argument contained, in more measured tones, in his *Miles To Go: European and American Transportation Policies* (1981).

[20] Dunn's book is approvingly cited by various corporate front groups or neoconservative research institutions, including the Heartland Institute (www. heartland.org), the Cascade Policy Institute (www.cascadepolicy.org) (an Oregon corporate front group), the Center for the New West in Denver, for whom he has spoken, and the Mackinac Center for Public Policy. Interestingly, however, the book was published by the Brookings Institution, normally considered a centrist think tank. A summary of his argument was published in the *Brookings Review* (Dunn 1999).

threatening and sinister and conspiratorial, while meaning that he does not have to take their specific claims seriously.[21] At the same time, he denigrates the claims underpinning critiques of the car, often without evidence and using arguments which have very little evidence to support them.[22] In general, he attempts to suggest that all anti-car activists have been totalising in their critique and are elitist in orientation. Writing about activists in the 1960s and 1970s, he suggests that:

These early adversaries did not want to solve specific problems caused by the automobile, they defined the automobile as a problem in and of itself. They were not interested in the details of highway congestion, traffic accidents, air pollution, or urban sprawl as such. It was the whole gestalt of the auto as the central sociocultural icon of our society that they wanted to eliminate. (1998: 6–7)

The car as a product of individual agency

At the heart of Dunn's argument is the belief that the rise of the car can be understood only as the product of a myriad of individual actions – to buy cars and drive them. This claim has the effect of naturalising the car's growth as an inevitable outcome of human desires and impulses,

---

[21] In the part of his book establishing these claims about an 'anti-auto vanguard', Dunn focuses on Jane Jacobs, Lewis Mumford, James Flink, Bill McKibben, Howard Kunstler and Jane Holtz Kay, and then discusses policy-oriented NGOs and government agencies such as the World Resources Institute (WRI) and the Surface Transportation Policy Project.

[22] The clearest example is when Dunn refers to climate change, which he does in a passage interpreting the vanguard's agenda as a 'solution in search of a policy'. He refers to 'the assumed causal connection between automobility and the potential disasters of global warming' (1998: 14). His references to global warming could read straight out of the GCC and is a significant misreading of the mainstream position on global warming among climate scientists. It would be easy to contrast this with his account of how the vanguard as an advocacy coalition 'resist[s] information suggesting that their basic beliefs may be invalid or unattainable' (Dunn 1998: 15, quoting Sabatier and Jenkins-Smith 1993: 19). Elsewhere, he states that 'the vanguard overstates the seriousness of the *problems* being caused by the automobile' (1998: 17). But he gives precious little evidence to support this claim, beyond a questioning of the conspiracy theory concerning the decline of transit (reasonably persuasive in my view, but by no means fatal) (see below for details) and a querying of the military costs of maintaining secure oil supplies (less convincing, as he merely asserts the point). Concerning global warming at least, it is pretty clear to any well-informed observer that he understates the seriousness of the problem.

implying that the car is unproblematically about freedom, progress and democracy.

A useful place to start to show this is the way that Dunn sets up the critics' arguments concerning the debate about the 'GM transit conspiracy' (1998: 7–11). This concerns the allegations that during the 1920s and 1930s GM, along with the Firestone Tire Company and Standard Oil of California, through their jointly owned company National City Lines, systematically bought up tramlines across American cities, often with the acquiescence or support of city governments, initially replacing them with bus services but with the ultimate intention of undermining public transport and engineering a rise in car use and car dependence. The companies were convicted of conspiracy in 1949 under anti-trust legislation (Hamer 1987: 22) and then investigated again in the 1970s by the US Senate (Davies 1975; Dunn 1998: 7–10). By 1949 they had replaced '100 electric transit systems with GM buses in forty-five cities' (Hamer 1987; Wajcman 1991: 128; UNCTC 1992: 55–6; Freund and Martin 1993: 135; Wolf 1996: 84). By the late 1950s, over 90 per cent of the US' tram network had been dismantled.[23]

Dunn is right that an account of this conspiracy is ubiquitous in North American anti-car discourse, even appearing in popular culture such as the film *Who Shot Roger Rabbit?* (Dunn 1998: 10).[24] But what occurs in this debate in Dunn's narrative is that both accounts are

---

[23] Wajcman (1991: 128), Freund and Martin (1993: 135–6) and McShane (1994: 115), all allude, however, to how this collusion was also made possible both by the monopolies which the tram companies inevitably formed and which were resented by their users, and by corruption on the part of the latter. More generally, Wolf (1996: 81–4) suggests that in the United States competition between road and rail early in the twentieth century reflected competition between the two leading groups of industrialists Vanderbilt/Morgan and Rockefeller. A number of factors, including the recession of the 1920s, favoured the latter group, and thus the car industry (Rockefeller having large stakes in both Ford and Standard Oil, with Morgan involved not only in railroads but also particularly in banking, which was obviously hit hard by the recessions). For an account which suggests that the collusion was unimportant, see Gordon (1991: 20) who cites Dunn (1981). St Clair (1988) argues, taking a stand between these positions, that the role of GM and others was crucial but cannot properly be called a 'conspiracy'. However, he is at pains to show that the motorisation of US cities was not the 'natural' result of people's innate desire for cars.

[24] There is a substantial literature on this, much of which is cited by Dunn. (For a selection, see Foster 1981; Bottles 1987, 1992; Slater 1997; Goddard 1994.) What is hopefully clear is that while anti-car activists and writers

assumed to have an agency-centred discourse. In explanations of tran-sit's demise by both the 'conspiracy theorists' and by Dunn himself, agency dominates. For the car's critics, it is that the agency of powerful companies, enabled by many city governments, made possible the demise of transit. For Dunn, it is the agency of millions of individuals choosing cars over transit that caused it to decline. In neither is an account evident of the structuring of the choices faced by companies, government institutions, or individuals.

But the anti-car position is much more clearly consistent with a more complex way of thinking about structure and agency. Clearly conspir-acy theory can be tactically helpful to oppositional groups, enabling the finding of a 'smoking gun' which 'proves' the culpability of parti-cular groups or individuals. Conspiracy theories are perhaps particu-larly evident in highly individualist cultures such as the United States where a high degree of presumptions of causality on individual agency is presumed, especially when combined with a form of individualism which is hostile to government. This has helped to produce the range of conspiracies in US culture – around, for example, Roswell, the assassi-nation of J. F. Kennedy, the Waco incident and the Oklahoma bomb-ings, and among American 'Patriots' more generally about conspiracies such as the 'New World Order'.[25] But this individualist presumption is also one of the reasons why Dunn finds it difficult to understand an anti-car position which refuses such a simple explanation for the rise of the car and the decline of alternatives, but also refuses the opposite simplistic individualist explanation (offered by Dunn), that it was simply the outcome of millions of individual choices.

In Dunn's narrative, individual choice is naturalised, and thus outside the scope of appropriate analysis. Some of this is achieved through reference to economics. Commenting on Bradford Snell's conspiracy theory, Dunn writes that 'Cliff Slater studied the economics of streetcars versus buses. He concluded that "GM did not cause the destruction of

---

obviously pounce on this 'conspiracy' the force of the anti-car position by no means depends on acceptance of it. I am perfectly happy to accept that the conspiracy theory is at the very least highly simplistic. But this does not under-mine an anti-car position in part because that is primarily based on a range of normative assessments of the impacts of the car on society and also because the explanation for the emergence of car-dominated societies need not (perhaps indeed needs to not) rest on such simplistic explanations in terms of individual agency.

[25] On the latter, see Rupert (2000: chapter 5); Ronson (2002).

streetcar systems . . . GM simply took advantage of an economic trend . . . that was going to continue with or without GM's help"' (Slater 1997: 60, quoted in Dunn 1998: 10). The hegemonic discourse of economics is here used to obscure questions about how any 'economically rational choice' is always structured – in these instances, by land use policies, tax structures and so on. These help to produce what in any particular case is 'economically rational', while economics as a discipline is founded on the deliberate neglect of this structuring of choice (in technical language, preferences, in economics, are 'exogenously given').[26]

For Dunn, the only analytical choice is one of an elite conspiracy or a pluralist outcome of struggles between different transport modes: 'What the critics decry as a deformation of democracy is, from a less partisan and more analytical point of view, nothing more than politics as usual in our wide-open, rough-and-tumble republic' (1998: 10). An account of 'normal' politics as structurally favouring particular interests is precluded in his narrative.

Elsewhere, Dunn makes individual agency similarly paramount, but this time in both an analytical and a normative sense (despite his pretensions to 'scientific neutrality'). He writes:

After all, transit still enables people to move from point A to point B. If one responds that people would rather go from point A to points C, D, E, and Z on their own schedule while listening to a new CD on their car stereo, the vanguard tends to respond with condescending comments about advertising hype, false consciousness, the costs of sprawl, global warming, and shifting paradigms. (1998: 18)

---

[26] That economics is hegemonic in these debates is shown by the fact that, when he gets to the detail of the 'vanguard's' strategy policy proposals in the 1990s, they are all couched in terms of costs and benefits. The problems of the car are all reduced to costs in terms of subsidies or external costs (Dunn 1998: 15). Dunn misses the point at times – for example, where he argues that 'counting $85bn in free parking as a subsidy is odd accounting, to say the least' (1998: 16). He presumes that everything we call a subsidy must be something coming from the state, rather than referring to any form of external cost not accounted for in the price of an activity (in this case, parking). The fact that free parking costs do not come from government does not mean that free parking is not a subsidy to car driving. Others, however, starting from similar perspectives, seem to get this point – see for example, Cobb (1999: 64–5). One could go further. Neoclassical models were used, as early as the 1970s (so long before anything such as climate change costs would have been included), to calculate the costs and benefits of cars and to conclude that 'the car imposes such diseconomies on the community as a whole that it should be abolished altogether' (Mishan 1977; Ward 1991: 11).

There is no structure or cultural discourse shaping individual choice, there is only agency – that of individuals and that of elites. Dunn continues: 'The vanguard is deeply averse to acknowledging the material and psychological value of the auto to millions of individuals' (1998: 18). Perhaps, but Dunn is deeply averse to asking critical questions about the interplay of social structures with individual agency in producing these material and psychological values: it is simply too easy and too simplistic to construct the debate as a dichotomy between individual choice and false consciousness.

This lack of questioning of individual agency serves ultimately to naturalise the way in which the car has become the dominant mode of transport. For as everything is only the outcome of millions of individual decisions, and people 'naturally' make 'superior' over 'inferior' choices, the domination of the car can be presented as inevitable. Referring to attempts to shift away from the car and to other transport modes and to limit sprawl, Dunn says:

> They seek to bring about a massive modal shift from one dominant pattern of transportation and land use to another. In the past such modal shifts have always involved replacing an older transportation technology with a newer one that offered greater output in terms of mobility. For example railroads moved passengers and freight farther and faster than did canals and soon relegated barge traffic to a much less profitable market niche. But the newer mode also required greater inputs in terms of land, labor, and capital. Achieving the vanguard's goal would be the first modal shift in transportation history to reverse the process by restricting physical mobility and restraining land development. (1998: 17)

There is a clear determinism here in the way that progress and mobility are discursively linked, a point which will be revisited in chapter 5. At times, Dunn engages in interpretive moves that serve to reproduce this naturalist reading of the car's dominance. He suggests that Americans (uniformly) understand their cars as 'empowerment': 'That this sense of empowerment really exists [is] revealed by the fact that the owners of 160 million American autos pay thousands of dollars every year to empower themselves and ensure they have these choices [of types of journey, flexibility, etc.]' (Dunn 1998: 2). But this statement of fact could easily be interpreted to mean that many of these same 160 million Americans do not feel they have the choice but to own a car (cf., for example, Rosenbloom 1992).

The critics as vanguard

There are (at least) two important consequences of this individualist framing of the rise of the car. The first is that anti-car politics become interpreted as representing the interest of elites. Dunn makes a fairly standard move in suggesting that those opposing car-led development are involved in 'elitist social engineering schemes' (1998: 4). His intent is to portray an image of a well-organised minority attempting to impose its vision of urban development on a reluctant American public unanimously in favour of the dominance of the car and lacking ambivalence about the way cars have shaped both American cities and life. He argues that this group should be referred to as a 'vanguard' – 'an elite group of anti-auto activists whose progressive ideas and individual agendas complement and reinforce one another' (1998: 15). He refers to a member of this group (as he sees it), Elmer W. Johnson, saying that anti-car reformers 'must build a small, but powerfully persuasive, community of concerned citizens ... to develop a visionary and hopeful program that spells out the seriousness of the nation's social ills and ... tough but equitable solutions ... to address these ills' (Johnson 1993: 45, quoted in Dunn 1998: 15).

The charge of elitism is made more strongly by Sam Kazman of the CEI (Kazman 2001). Kazman regards the critics of the car as inheritors of an elite discourse which he traces back to the Duke of Wellington in the early nineteenth century complaining that the railways 'would just encourage common people to move about needlessly' (Kazman 2001), and follows it through the commonly cited claim (see chapter 2 above) by British Prime Minister Herbert Asquith (Kazman has him as an unnamed 'British MP') in the early 1900s that cars were 'a luxury that is apt to degenerate into a nuisance', to Al Gore claiming, in *Earth in the Balance* (1992) that 'the internal combustion engine is a mortal threat to society, deadlier than any military enemy' (as paraphrased in Kazman 2001) and to a series of adverts advocating car pooling suggesting that we are 'addicted' to our cars, or a Greenpeace advert announcing 'the end of the automobile age'. Kazman makes the claim that contemporary anti-car advocates are not motivated by particular concerns with the consequences of automobility (Kazman, in fact, never discusses these) but rather by a 'disdain that the Duke of Wellington expressed over a century and a half ago: the common people are moving about needlessly, if not via rail then via [a] sport utility vehicle' (Kazman 2001).

But the elitist argument is largely a result of individualist premises. It is worth recalling from chapter 2 that some of the anti-car critics of the 1970s (e.g. Jerome 1972) picked up on the same theme – that some forms of anti-car politics might have the effect of discriminating against the poor. But that was in the context of recognising that the car-dominated society had already created a set of inequalities through the spatial organisation of cities, etc. In Dunn's or Kazman's discourse, that spatial shift occurred through the 'natural' actions of millions of individuals not through complicated political processes involving class and racial divisions, land development policies and strategies by developers, and so on.

The impossibility of change: uncontested culture

The second consequence of the individualism in Dunn's discourse is that the overall culture within which individual actions can be placed becomes regarded as unchanging – or, at least, unchangeable by conscious political practice. In addition to attempting to denigrate and delegitimise the car's critics, he also uses the 'elitist' charge to suggest that anti-car policies are doomed to fail. '"Don't those short-sighted motorists see that they are driving the planet toward its doom?" they exclaim. The motorists fire back: "Increase gas taxes by a dollar a gallon to discourage driving – over my Congressman's (politically) dead body?"', he writes (1998: 3–4).

In his account of the anti-car writers of the 1970s Dunn reinforces the sense that an automobile-dominated development is (and was) almost inevitable by emphasising their optimism. He quotes James Flink: 'Achieving it [the alternative future, not oriented around the car] requires only our will, intelligence, and collective effort' (Flink 1975: 233) and Emma Rothschild arguing that 'auto power is comprehensible, contingent, reversible' (1973: 247) (both as quoted in Dunn 1998: 7). Later on, discussing anti-car critiques in the 1990s, Dunn makes a similar emphasis. Jane Holtz Kay, for example, believes that the 'old consciousness is waning and with it confidence in our car-bound destiny' (Holtz Kay 1997: 2, quoted in Dunn 1998: 13). Part of this is because, as Dunn correctly asserts, critics in the 1970s sometimes confused the problems of Detroit with the problems of the car more broadly. 'Clearly, their hopes for an immediate revolution in transportation and community planning were not realized. Developments in the

1970s and 1980s showed that Detroit can take quite a beating in both the market and in Congress without the automobile losing any ground to other modes of transportation. Americans will as readily drive a Toyota as a Taurus' (1998: 8–9).

Elsewhere, Dunn asserts repeatedly that there simply is no possibility of having anything other than a car-dominated transport system in the United States: 'The critics are historically anachronistic and politically unrealistic in thinking that the struggle between the [transport] modes *could have had a different ending*' (1998: 10, my emphasis). His standard argument is that there would be no popular support for such measures: '[People] will not flock to a lifestyle that includes strong metropolitan land-use controls, high-rise living, and greatly increased dependence on public transit' (1998: 9).[27] Later again, Dunn states that 'it is virtually certain that the laws and taxes necessary to discourage driving would not be accepted by voters' (1998: 19). What is interesting here is that throughout the book Dunn provides no direct evidence for this sort of claim; indeed, he seems to have to work hard to compensate for its absence. In a passage on how the 'vanguard' operates, he 'concedes' that 'sometimes its views can be *made to appear* in the majority' (1998: 17, my emphasis). Perhaps he feels no need to provide evidence to support his contention as the views of the American public are so self-evident, uncontested and lacking in ambivalence.

The combination of the accusation of elitism with the fact that Dunn provides no evidence for his claim that the majority of the American public would strenuously oppose moves towards more dense communities, more use of transit and so on, means that ultimately his book can be read as (part of) a hegemonic project. It is an attempt to represent particular interests as universal ones; it is simultaneously an attempt to present culture as uncontested, an attempt at closure. But the very necessity of this effort on Dunn's part shows perhaps the irreducible contestability of (car) culture; that it needs to be continually reproduced through discursive moves in a variety of contexts (academic books, advertising, political lobbying; see more in chapters 5 and 6).

---

[27] In fact, survey evidence is significantly less clear on this than Dunn might hope for. See, for example, Patterson (1995); although the paper is on attitudes to urban spatial form in Canadian cities, the context and culture is sufficiently similar to be useful. It is clear there that attitudes to low-density living are significantly more ambivalent than Dunn assumes.

This is perhaps rather odd since 'the critic's own agenda' is read as a cultural challenge to 'the values of American political culture' (1998: 11). Later, Dunn quotes a critic who shares this assumption. Elmer W. Johnson (formerly of GM, now a member of the 'anti-car vanguard') says that 'America's individualist and consumerist culture' is the main obstacle to ending the dominance of the car (Johnson 1993: 44–5, quoted in Dunn 1998: 14). But what Dunn regards as a critique of American culture can just as easily be read as a critical contestation *within* American culture, a set of debates going back to the War of Independence, an essentially normative debate about the form American society ought to take, read back by Dunn as a description that the Washingtonian model has become what American political culture *is*. American political culture is misleadingly taken by Dunn to be homogeneous, uncontested, settled. But this is always a discursive move which attempts to call into being what (in this case American) culture is to bring about that which it merely claims to describe. That such an understanding of the political/cultural dynamics at work here in the minds of anti-car writers is evident even in the quotes Dunn gives. He cites Bill McKibben, for example, saying 'The only way out of the dilemma is for Americans to "rethink what we mean by 'development'"' (McKibben 1995, quoted in Dunn 1998: 12). This is a contestation of a culture, not a rejection of it in favour of a completely different one. Similarly, when he quotes Kunstler writing that the car culture 'reflects much confusion over the ideas of freedom and democracy' and its definition of freedom is 'whatever makes you happy. This is the freedom of a fourteen-year-old child' (Kunstler 1996: 60–1, quoted in Dunn 1998: 13) what is being contested is not the importance of freedom for American culture, but its meaning and its content.

Backlash discourse: II – autonomy and automobility

The ownership of a motor car belongs to human rights. (Ingmar Carlsson, Swedish Prime Minister, quoted in Zuckerman 1991: 17)

Dunn's account of the rise of the car serves to explain the inevitability of a car-dominated society; in effect, why the car's critics and anti-car policies are doomed to fail. It does so largely through arguing that the situation has arisen because of the myriad actions of individuals who have in effect 'chosen' to drive and thus to live in a society dominated by cars. The other side of backlash discourse, however, is the more explicitly normative argument that not only can automobility not be stopped, it *ought* not to be, either. This is so since cars represent an, if not *the*, expression of human autonomy, and thus to criticise cars is in effect to be 'an enemy of freedom'. The best expression of this argument is in Lomasky's *Autonomy and Automobility* (1997).[28]

Lomasky's essential concern is to make an extremely strong claim about the link between human autonomy or freedom, on the one hand, and car driving, on the other. The overall effect is to try to argue: (a) that to act to limit car driving is to limit the realm of human freedom; (b) that freedom is the principal human instinct or drive and the principal set of rights to which individuals are entitled; and thus that (c) no justification can be made for attempts to limit car use. He sets his ambition admirably high, perhaps. As suggested in his title, the conceptual foundations of his argument are twofold, and I will deal with them separately.

Concerning automobility, Lomasky never defines in a clear manner what he means by this. He writes variously, 'I shall concentrate on automobility's intrinsic capacity to move a person from place to place. As such automobility complements autonomy' (1997: 7); 'automobility has value because it extends the scope and magnitude of self-direction' (1997: 8); and 'the automobile, definitionally, promotes automobility. The complementarity of autonomy and automobility is only slightly less evident. In the latter part of the twentieth century, being a self-mover entails, to a significant extent, being a motorist' 1997: 15). In effect, Lomasky works with a definition which looks like this: automobility is first and foremost an attribute of individual humans; it is the act of their moving autonomously. It is also therefore phenomenological – it refers to their experience of this movement as expressions of their autonomy. Finally, it is for him at the same time ahistorical and intrinsically connected to the car. That is to say, while humans intrinsically connect their autonomy to the capacity to move

---

[28] Lomasky's piece was commissioned by the CEI but Lomasky is a Philosophy Professor at Bowling Green State University. Waldemar Hanasz, the author of one of the other CEI reports on automobility, was a graduate student in philosophy at Bowling Green and one assumes a graduate student of Lomasky's. It is not necessary to assume that either is in any simple way a 'hired gun' for the CEI, but nevertheless using university professors to write reports of this nature is a highly effective means of legitimising an essentially ideological discourse.

about (a line in western thought he traces back to Aristotle), it is the car which is the apotheosis of human achievements in realising this impulse as a daily reality. As a consequence, the strength of this connection permits in effect a conflation of the artefact of the automobile with the general concept of automobility, since no other artefact similarly enhances human autonomy in relation to mobility. So while the most immediate use of 'automobility' is simply as a noun-form of the act of driving a car, Lomasky also claims for it a set of deeper philosophical connections.

Concerning autonomy, Lomasky first makes it not only something intrinsic to humans (something shared by many traditions of thought in political philosophy) but a value that always trumps other values. Critics of the car must 'surmount a stronger burden of proof than they have heretofore acknowledged. For not only must they show that instrumental costs of marginal automobile usage outweigh the corresponding benefits, but they must also establish that these costs outweigh the inherent good of the exercise of free mobility' (1997: 8).[29] Human autonomy is secondly enhanced by technology – the use of particular technologies by humans can extend the realm of their possible freedom. Along with the automobile, Lomasky regards the printing press and imminently the microchip as the pre-eminent 'autonomy-enhancing contrivances of technology' (1997: 14). Third, autonomy is opposed to planning in Lomasky's discourse: 'People who drive automobiles upset the patterns spun from the policy intellectual's brain. The precise urban design that he has concocted loses out to suburban sprawl.' He then continues with a list of 'what ifs', if planners succeeded in promoting smart growth, public transport, etc. 'Perhaps ... but why go on? These lovely visions give way before the free choices of men and women who resist all blandishments to leave their cars in the

---

[29] It is also instructive in this quote that the site at which ethical/political decisions are to be judged is also only that of the individual. Obscured in the economics language of 'marginal automobile usage' is the notion that what is to be judged is each individual car journey. 'Marginal automobile usage' refers simply to each additional car journey, over a base of already existing (and taken-for-granted) car journeys. Of course, the marginal costs of individual car use are negligible; the costs arise precisely from their absolute level of use and Lomasky in effect has no framework within which collective decisions about absolute levels of use can be negotiated – consistent with libertarianism generally, he in effect assumes that such collective decisions are in any case illegitimate, infringing as they do individual 'rights'.

garage. They wish to drive, and by doing so they powerfully express their autonomy, but their exercises of choice also have the effect of rendering the planners' conceptions moot' (1997: 26).

Finally, and most fundamentally perhaps, autonomy is in Lomasky's view fundamentally connected to movement. He traces this back to Aristotle: 'For Aristotle, being a self-mover was the crucial feature distinguishing animals from plants and, thus, higher forms of life from lower' (1997: 8). He spends considerable energy differentiating plants from animals along this dimension, and then between humans and other animals in suggesting that while animals 'merely react to stimuli in [their] environment', 'we deliberate among available alternatives of not only as pleasing or displeasing but also in terms such as "dishonourable", "what justice demands", ... and so on' (1997: 9). In other words, humans make conscious choices which then direct their movement.

There are several things that are problematic about Lomasky's use of this hierarchical Aristotelian framework, not least that modern biology would regard it as more or less useless in describing differences between different types of organisms. That biologists do not in any simple sense distinguish between plants and animals, nor limit the biological realm to these two categories, nor place humans in some separate category, nor regard processes of evolution as plausibly about the movement from 'lower' to 'higher' forms of life, is neither an obscure point at the frontiers of biological science,[30] nor is it trivial. Even beyond biology, contemporary science would not make a distinction between the 'alive' and the 'not alive' in terms of movement – witness plate tectonics, which has shown how the earth's crust is made up of a series of plates of constantly moving rock, and the form of the earth's surface (its mountains, oceans, etc.) has produced by the collisions of these moving plates. Lomasky would probably claim that there is a distinction of a moral kind being made which is separate from any empirical claims; but ultimately his hierarchy of 'plants–animals–humans' rests on the plausibility of the empirical/ontological claims about what different organisms are like, and his account of this is simply incorrect. But what is crucial for Lomasky's argument is that the hierarchy is founded fundamentally on the nature of the universe as dynamic, whose funda-mental constant is change and motion. Now while this is empirically

---

[30] A glance at any decent popular science book of the last fifteen–twenty years would show this (see Bryson 2003).

reasonable (and unlike his biological categories, reasonably consistent with contemporary science) it does not follow that we need to turn this into a normative claim, as Lomasky does (1997: 10). For Lomasky and Aristotle, movement is not only an ontological claim about the universe; it is a moral category, since it represents attempts at 'self-realisation'. 'The concept of motion has a wider scope than travelling from place to place ... going from here to there constitutes movement, but so also do an organism's growth, someone's coming to know something, the development of a faculty, and so on. In an Aristotelian universe, motion is ubiquitous because everything tends to progress toward the highest possible self-realization' (Lomasky 1997: 10). As an ultimate consequence, 'intelligent automobility is crucial to the elevated status of human beings vis-à-vis other beings' (1997: 10). It is then a fairly short step to making autonomy a principal political virtue, to define it in terms of the ability to move in a self-directed manner and to define this ability to move autonomously in opposition to varied abilities of society to define individuals' ends for them.

Lomasky concludes this part of the argument with a quote from John Stuart Mill on censorship and the statement that 'autonomous people "Just Say No" to the yoke' (Lomasky 1997: 15). The 'Just Say No' allusion is (unintentionally, I'm sure) highly ironic. Lomasky's argument concerning how autonomy is in opposition to social control (he wants to end up with 'planning', or 'the state' as the opposition to autonomy, but doesn't quite manage to get there) is in fact founded on an example from Mill about censorship, not only in terms of direct state repression of individual's autonomy but in terms of how this produces a conformist culture which quashes individual autonomy. The irony is that 'Just Say No' was coined most prominently in the 1980s in Nancy Reagan's campaign against drug use, in particular cocaine use – i.e. in a campaign which was aimed precisely at the repression of individual behaviour and the cultivation of conformist attitudes. The more substantive point, perhaps, is that Mill's argument is about censorship – and it is not clear that the political arguments here translate well into arguments about mobility, except perhaps in the banal and ultimately tautologous fact that since anything we do is movement (in the Aristotelian sense) therefore speech and driving cars are the same sort of thing since they are both movement.

Within his own terms, Lomasky fails to demonstrate the links necessary to show either that the political value of freedom of movement is so fundamental to human autonomy that no restriction on movement is permissible, or that such automobility can be pursued only through the technology of the car. For the first point it is perhaps rather the case that what needs to be explained is not so much whether the normative value of autonomy means that active restrictions on (particular means of) movement are legitimate, but more whether such a value necessitates enormous investment by public authorities to make the realisation of such autonomy possible. For the ability to 'move autonomously' in cars is (as emphasised above) made possible only by huge investments in road construction, maintenance and so on. By emphasising that proposals to 'limit' automobility constitute a threat to freedom Lomasky works within a standard libertarian account of freedom in 'negative' terms – the absence of laws and regulations, restricting people – whereas the realisation of the normative value of automobility as freedom makes sense only within a 'positive' account of freedom – the state being regarded as an institution which enables people to realise particular freedoms. The conscious collective choice about *which* freedoms are to be favoured by state activity is thus unavoidable. This 'positive freedom' account is also the version consistent with the Aristotelian arguments upon which Lomasky claims to build his case, but this vacillation between negative and positive accounts of freedom is perhaps at the root of his problems. If he wants to make a negative freedom argument he cannot explain the absolute right to a car, since the lack of a car is not literally an infringement of our freedom of movement. Only in terms of positive freedom can the car 'enhance' one's freedom, but this then undermines the overriding priority Lomasky gives to movement, since under a positive conception of freedom what is necessary is to promote the conditions under which people can flourish. There are, however, many ways to do this and Aristotle cannot be invoked to promote one particular means over others.[31]

For the second point, Lomasky's account of how the car acts as an extension of human freedom can easily be applied to other modes of movement. 'To be autonomous is, minimally, to be a valuer with ends taken to be good as such and to have the capacity to direct oneself to the realization or furtherance of these ends through actions expressly

[31] I am grateful to Paul Saurette for this point about positive and negative freedom, as well as comments more generally on my critique of Lomasky.

chosen for that purpose. Motorists fit this description' (Lomasky 1997: 7). But so do bus or train users, cyclists, or pedestrians. In other words, it is not the primary value of autonomous mobility which explains the hegemony of the car but some specific patterns of development which favour particular expressions of autonomy/mobility; to criticise the car is not to oppose oneself to autonomy. More strongly, one might argue that Lomasky's definition of 'autonomous mobility' in fact excludes car use. Since 'unlike plants, animals perceive and they move themselves' (Lomasky 1997: 8–9), and the human application of intelligence merely adds a level of conscious decision to this action, car use is not autonomous mobility since people do not 'move themselves'. This suggests a contradiction at the level of the 'thing' which is autonomously moving, to be followed up below and in chapter 5.

But beyond this, the conception of the relation between 'planning' and the automobility entailed in car use is flawed. Throughout, as already noted, Lomasky (with Dunn, or the various ideologists using their work in their political advocacy) opposes individual autonomy, with car driving as its extension, to planning. But this is a fundamental mistake, which is clearest in his brief history and explanation of suburbanisation. The patterns of development which have made car driving in many instances practically the only means of navigating urban areas, and in most places significantly more convenient than other modes of transport, are interpreted by Lomasky (as by Dunn) as the outcome of a myriad of choices by individuals. 'People who, individually and collectively, could have devised for themselves residential and occupational patterns not incorporating lengthy commutes chose to do otherwise' (1997: 15). Later, he counters critics of suburban sprawl with the proposition that 'they are genuine objects of choice for those who live there' (1997: 16).[32] But to present this process in this manner is to ignore the fact that those choices were throughout the entire period heavily structured, and structured by planners who wanted to promote car use and low-density development. The pattern of suburban development was in effect created less by these individual choices

---

[32] One contradiction within the arguments here (and in those of Dunn) is that while both are happy to base their understanding of the economy on neoclassical principles, both manage to miss the obvious conclusion from this perspective: that people in fact *do* prefer dense cities to sprawling suburbs; otherwise one cannot explain within a neoclassical framework why house prices are consistently higher in dense city centres than in low-density suburbs.

than by modernist philosophies of urban planning, relations between city planners and land developers, jurisdictional competition between different metropolitan areas attempting to attract people to their area and thus increase the tax base, the aggressive development of road building and road surface improvement from the 1910s onwards (as opposed to reforming and modernising public transport systems) and so on. The condition of possibility of 'autonomous mobility' through the car is in fact extensive state planning, so to oppose 'freedom' to 'planning' as Lomasky suggests is fundamentally flawed.

Finally, and following from the previous point, Lomasky's concept of automobility is flawed. As processes of planning should be regarded as integral to automobility (understood narrowly as the driving of cars), this suggests that automobility should be regarded less as a feature of individuals, conceptualised as 'antecedently individuated' – i.e. ontologically existing prior to their membership in society – and more as a system or regime within which concrete individuals are situated. Automobility is thus not only the fact of an individual moving around by car but all of the things which go to make it possible, and to make that act appear as a moment of 'autonomous mobility', as developed in chapter 1. In Rajan's phrase, automobility should be regarded as 'automobile use and everything that makes it possible – roads, highways, parking structures, and traffic rules' (1996: 7). The point for present purposes is that the 'autonomous mobility' of car driving is something which has to be socially produced, rather than being something which can legitimately be regarded solely as a facet of individuals, as suggested by Lomasky. The 'intrinsic' autonomy of driving is brought into being by a range of interventions which have made it possible (from road surface improvements to insurance schemes) and which render it an expression of autonomy. Thus the way that the car has come to figure symbolically as the pinnacle of human 'urges' to 'autonomous mobility' is fundamentally historically contingent.

Automobility is, from this point of view, and in direct contrast to Lomasky or Dunn's representations, fundamentally contradictory. I will pick up on three elements of this contradiction here, and more are apparent later in the book. Within their own restriction of automobility to the act of driving, there is as widely noted a basic contradiction in terms of what is doing the autonomous movement. Is it the car or the driver which is moving, and is it the car or the driver which is autonomous? This tension is at the heart of the noun 'automobile'. As

Urry points out, the 'auto' in 'automobile' can be seen to operate in two senses: 'On the one hand, "auto" refers reflexively to the humanist self, such as the meaning of "auto" in autobiography or autoerotic. On the other hand, "auto" refers to objects or machines that possess a capacity for movement, as expressed by automatic, automaton and especially automobile' (Urry 2006).[33] In Lomasky's discourse, he never quite succeeds in making the move from Aristotle to the car that he wants to, in part because (his account of) Aristotle works with a much closer immediate connection between the thing which decides and the thing which moves than exists in the relationship between a car and a driver. Of course, in a car the person in fact hardly moves at all.

The second contradiction is at the level of the 'system' of automobility (Urry 2004; Böhm *et al.* 2006). The simplest contradiction here is that the universalisation of automobility has diminished the actual possibility of, and perhaps the significance of, movement itself. Congestion has become a daily feature of life in many places, to the extent that in many cities around the world those moving in cars move around less flexibly and less fast than those using other modes of transport. The more complex ones are to do with the way that the 'external' effects of mass car use generate forms of political and social response which then serve to intrude progressively on the 'freedom' associated with driving (Rajan 1996).

The third contradiction, however, concerns the way that Lomasky concludes his argument. He begins his conclusion with the statement

---

[33] The picture gets murkier when we consider the meanings in French, the language in which the term '*automobile*' was first articulated, in 1861 (Robert 1985, on '*automobile*' as a Gallicism in English, used first in the United States, see *The Oxford English Dictionary (OED)* online, http://www.oed.com). In French '*automobile*' was originally and first an adjective – '*qui se meut de soi-même*' ('that which moves itself', although the double reflexive in the French emphasises the *self*-moving aspect more than the English can convey – in effect 'that which itself moves itself'). '*Une véhicule automobile*' and '*un camion automobile*' are given as its primary examples. Only later (1890) does '*automobile*' become a noun – '*une automobile*', with its contraction '*une auto*'. It is clear in this etymology that the ambiguity we now play with in English through the term 'automobility' – which is autonomous, the person or the driver? (on which, see more in chapter 5), – is not there in the original usage that is clear that it is the vehicle or the truck (*camion*) that is self-moving. When words developed for those using cars, or the activity of driving – such as *automobiliste* (1897), *automobilisme* (1895), or *automobiling* (1898) (Imbs 1974; *OED* online), it is clear that this refers to the use by people of an automobile.

that 'I have argued that the automobile does not merit the opprobrium its critics have showered on it' (1997: 24). This misrepresents his own argument, however. What Lomasky argues is rather that even if the car 'merits the opprobrium', then the 'autonomy-enhancing' aspect of cars means that this opprobrium is for him ethically irrelevant. But if autonomy does not trump other values in the way that Lomasky assumes/asserts, or the relationship between autonomy and car use is less simple than he argues (both in that the 'autonomy' of a car driver has had to be produced by planning, etc. and that there are other transport modes which similarly express a desire for autonomous movement) then the appropriate conclusion is not triumphalism but *ambivalence*. Cars are simultaneously experienced as autonomy-enhancing and at times autonomy-limiting. And even while they are experienced as autonomy-enhancing they create a range of consequences which harm other aspects of individuals' lives. As one of the car's critics puts it: 'like many of us, I too am torn between the pleasure of using a car and the knowledge of what its use implies' (Zuckerman 1991: xvii). As I shall show in chapter 5, this reading of Lomasky's most logical conclusion fits well both with empirical work done on people's actual attitude to cars (e.g. Macnaghten and Urry 1998; Lex Service 1999), which is deeply ambivalent rather than unambiguously positive, or associated aspects like road building (Berman 1982) and with general arguments about the 'experience of modernity' (Berman 1982; Bauman 1991).

Conclusions

I have tried to show in this chapter that there is a set of forces resisting arguments and political projects to limit car use or reshape societies away from being dominated by cars. But the chapter has also endeavoured to argue that these arguments have at their heart a set of philosophical beliefs which cannot seriously be sustained. Specifically, they rest on a simplistic account of cars as technologies which 'extend' the range of human autonomy, on the opposition of such autonomy to 'planning' and on a hyper-individualism which assumes that individuals logically and ethically precede their membership in society. These basic flaws mean that pro-car ideologists end up with arguments for continued unrestrained expansion of a car-dominated society which have a flawed set of ethical underpinnings, but also (and perhaps more importantly) that they produce and depend on a history of the rise of the car in these individualist terms which simply bears very little relation to the historical record.

As the authors' ideological underpinning of the backlash against anti-car sentiments fails to either explain the rise of the car adequately, nor to justify morally why no restrictions on car use are legitimate, the arguments presented in chapter 2 come back into the frame. One of the interesting things about the backlash writers is that they rarely address the concrete claims made by the car's critics, and thus have no basis for refuting the basic challenge to a car-dominated society. Their arguments for cars as extension of human freedom fall back onto lumpen 'I want my SUV' pleas and knee-jerk reactions such as destruction of speed cameras, recalling Kunstler's 'freedom of a fourteen-year-old child'.

If automobility is at least potentially unsustainable and thus in need of some sort of transformation, then we need to take seriously the question of why cars have become so dominant in societies across the globe. Chapters 4 and 5 address this question in more detail, and demonstrate that the hyper-individualism which underpins the arguments discussed in this chapter is completely unpersuasive.

4 | *Automobile political economy*

As seen in chapter 3, the pro-car arguments of Dunn and Lomasky, as well as those seen in more general political discourse, rely on an assumption that cars have become dominant principally through the separate and combined choices of millions of individuals to purchase and use cars, move to the suburbs and so on. Such choices reflect a strong desire for freedom which Dunn and Lomasky both argue is extended by car use. But this raises the question: is this implicit history of the car's rise persuasive? This chapter and chapter 5 show that it is not. This chapter shows that the rise of the car is better explained in terms of an intertwining of the particular developments of capitalism in the twentieth century while chapter 5 focuses on the production of particular types of individuals attuned to constant mobility.

Introduction

This chapter proceeds from the proposition that to explain the rise of the car it is useful to think in terms of *political economy*. Specifically, it is the relationships between automobility and economic growth (or capital accumulation[1]), those between economic growth and the state and the appropriate ways to theorise such relationships, which enable a

---

[1] Economic growth and capital accumulation are not strictly the same thing, although they are clearly related. Strictly, from the perspective developed below, capitalism entails the relentless pursuit of accumulation by capitalists – that is, the turning of investments in commodities into profits and into further investments (and consumption by capital), while economic growth refers more conventionally to the aggregate increase in the money throughput in the economy (gross domestic product, GDP). While in some contexts it is important to distinguish more carefully between the two for present purposes this is not important, and I use the terms interchangeably. For an elaboration of the importance of the distinction in relation to climate change policy, see Matthews and Paterson (2005).

more adequate account of why cars have become so dominant. Across a wide range of political/economic discourses cars have been seen to play a fundamental role in the promotion of economic growth in the twentieth century, and thus in the reproduction of capitalism as a system. Proponents and social critics argue that both in terms of its direct stimulating effects on the economy and the broader political/economic shifts effected because of the motor industry's role in reorganising industrial production ('Fordism'), the car has been central to promoting growth. This role has therefore been crucial in legitimising the car's expansion, enabling the car to become perhaps *the* symbol of progress for most of the twentieth century.

I traverse three broad sorts of approaches to this question. I start with those which rather take for granted the relationship between cars and growth, that tend to 'naturalise' it. They discuss it in a way which leads them to the conclusion that, in Overy's words, the rise of the car 'needs little explanation' (1990: 57). These approaches (principally those of neoclassical economics as reflected in history and business studies, modernisation theory in development studies and 'realist' IPE) can be seen as connected to those of Lomasky and Dunn discussed in chapter 3, although without necessarily having the same explicit political project. I then move to accounts which take more seriously both the political and the historically contingent character of the connections between cars and growth. This approach serves better to explain the growth of the car as a feature of a particular pattern of capitalist development. But while it gives us the resources to do this, these accounts, coming out of various versions of Marxist political economy, tend (reasonably enough) to pose questions about the character of a historically specific form of capitalism and can be pushed further in order to explain specifically why it is that this form favoured cars over other transport modes. In my third section I thus try to do this by making the connection between this sort of political economy and state theory to show that as a consequence of the car's importance to capitalist development for most of the twentieth century (and into the twenty-first), states have systematically promoted cars over their competitor modes.

Liberal/economic discourses

It is a commonplace to observe the sheer size of the car industry. In the middle of the twentieth century business management analyst Peter

Drucker wrote that: 'the automobile industry stands for modern industry all over the globe. It is to the twentieth century what the Lancashire cotton mills were to the early nineteenth century: the industry of industries' (Drucker 1946; Dicken 1998: 316). Car manufacturers have for much of the twentieth century been high in the list of largest corporations in the world, with General Motors (GM), Ford and Toyota near the top of the list.[2] In industrialised countries, the car industry accounts for around 13 per cent of GDP (Maxton and Wormald 1995: 3). While for the most part this is evidence of the economic and political importance of these firms and the people they employ, at times stronger claims are made in terms of the way that cars create growth (not least by the industry's lobby organisations – see AAM 2001 or Institute of Labor and Industrial Relations *et al.* 2001). In other words, the connection to growth is not just perhaps that the production of cars has made some firms very large because of the demand for cars and the concentration of market share in a small number of firms.[3]

It is also, however, a commonplace to observe relationships between transport and economic growth, and even more specifically cars and growth. In statistical analyses, for example, a relationship between various aspects of transport consumption and GNP *per capita* is commonly noted. OECD reports observe this sort of relationship (e.g. OECD 2003), as do numerous studies by national government bodies. An influential report by the UK government's Standing Advisory Committee on Trunk Road Assessment (SACTRA) in 1999 details the close fit between GDP growth and transport use in general, but specifically the growth in car use (SACTRA 1999: 23–4).[4] Dimitriou (1990: 56) reproduces a World Bank study (1986) showing a close fit between *per capita* incomes and levels of car ownership across the world. Rae (1971: 101) and the AAM (2001: 11) give similar relationships between vehicle miles travelled and GNP in the United States. This is sometimes interpreted in terms of increased car consumption

---

[2] Many of the others are, of course, oil companies, closely related to the car industry.

[3] Dicken reported in 1998 that 71 per cent of sales world-wide were concentrated in ten firms, and there have been mergers since then which increase this concentration. See Dicken (1998: 316, 335).

[4] OECD (2003), for example, uses the SACTRA analysis and generalises its implications across the OECD countries. For other expressions of this assumed relationship, see Chatterjee *et al.* (2003: 15–18).

following economic growth – as people get richer, they are more likely to buy a car (e.g. *Economist* 22 June 1996, Survey: 4) and as a consequence car sales fluctuate with business cycles (e.g. Brown *et al.* 1979: 18). But it is often argued or asserted that the causal relationship also works the other way round: that the production and consumption of cars has helped to accelerate growth. 'Automobility was the driving force behind Coolidge prosperity, and the boom of the 1920s was shattered with the saturation of the market for new cars after 1925', writes James Flink (1975: 167). The (1999) SACTRA report presents a model of the way that traffic growth affects economic growth which has become widely used in other governmental and intergovernmental studies (for example, in OECD 2003: 13–14). In this model, provision of transport infrastructure produces a number of effects, including improved labour supply, expansion of markets and increased traffic volume, which then create positive externalities across the economy, improvements to productivity, growth of fixed capital *per capita* and technical innovation, which combine to produce growth in GDP *per capita*.

The debates concerning transport and developing countries also reflect this argument. Car ownership is expanding much faster in developing than in industrialised countries, partly reflecting saturation in the latter group (Lowe 1990: 7–8; Dimitriou 1990)[5] and partly the assumption that increased vehicle ownership is related to increased incomes (World Bank 1986; Dimitriou 1990: 17, 53), but also reflecting cultural assumptions concerning connections between transport and development. Modernisation theory, the dominant approach to development practice in the post-colonial period, has routinely assumed a linear relationship between transport growth and development. Although there has been a shift from assuming that transport growth leads directly to economic development (understood to mean GNP *per capita* growth) towards assuming only that transport creates permissive conditions for growth (Tolley and Turton 1995: 76; Hoyle and Smith 1998), a strong connection is still assumed both in academic studies of transport in economics, geography and sociology and by transport planners (Simon 1996). The pervasive assumption in both

[5] Dimitriou also suggests (1990: 52–3) that the increase in car ownership in developing countries was stimulated by aggressive marketing techniques by car manufacturers in the early 1980s because of reduced demand in industrialised countries as a result of the recession and general saturation of markets.

such circles is that as countries move up the development ladder cars become the favoured transport mode because of its flexibility and associations with personal freedom.[6] *The Economist* illustrates this assumption in its most crude form, writing that 'whenever income per head in a country reaches around $6,000 a year, car sales rise steeply' (*Economist*, 22 June 1996, Survey: 4). The way that the relationship between cars and growth is often characterised can be divided into three elements, which collectively have enabled an acceleration of production and consumption: technical innovation, the flexibilisation of mobility and the extensiveness of forward and backward economic linkages.[7]

Technical innovation

It is principally technical change in the production process (not the cars themselves) that has been regarded as important (e.g. Maxton and Wormald 1995: 11; Ross 1995: 19). The development of the assembly line, the intensified division of labour, the mechanisation of increasing numbers of tasks and then later flexibilised production, just-in-time (JIT) delivery, robotisation and so on all led to productivity gains which meant that prices could be radically reduced and thus more widespread consumption enabled (e.g. Dicken 1998: 325). 'Twice in this century it [the car industry] has changed our most fundamental ideas of how we make things' (Womack *et al.* 1990: 11). Ford's introduction of the assembly line, for example, fully developed by 1913, reduced the price of a Model T Ford from $825 in 1908 to

---

[6] The studies just cited all note how car ownership in developing countries is concentrated in the relatively high-income Newly-Industrialising Countries (NICs), and make the connection to a relatively high income in such terms. Countries also promote the car over its alternatives in order to promote an emerging indigenous car industry – as, for example, in China's attempts to restrict bicycle use in Beijing to enable faster movement by car, as noted in chapter 1 (Chu 1998).

[7] I exclude discussion here of the direct public provision of transport infrastructure which figures highly in SACTRA (1999) or OECD (2003). Transport infrastructure provision is considered both a direct contribution to economic growth (spending by the state directly increases GDP) and a permissive condition for growth through the way it makes transport of goods, services and consumption of transport itself possible. In the latter sense (perhaps also the former, but the link is less clear) infrastructure provision may be thought of as a special instance of the extensive forward and backward linkages of transport, in particular cars, on which see below.

$290 in 1926 (Maxton and Wormald 1995: 68–9). The car industry also stimulated technological innovation in related industries such as steel and petroleum (Flink 1975: 140–1).

Flexible mobility

Cars produced a form of mobility which enabled people to move around in a significantly more flexible manner than had been previously possible. '[T]he freedom of personal movement conferred by the automobile and the surfaced road has been a major contributor to economic growth' (Rae 1971: 107) principally because of the way this increased flexibility created the possibility for trips and thus business opportunities both for those who have wider travel options and for those who might sell goods and services to the automobile. 'Historically, railways provided the pioneer transport arteries in many world areas, but over time roads have proved more flexible and more competitive as well as providing more convenient door-to-door transport' (Hoyle and Smith 1998: 15). This significantly reduced costs of goods and services (Hoyle and Smith 1998: 33–4) and, as Flink (1975) notes, a wide range of people – doctors, insurance agents, clergymen, farmers, school supervisors and so on – experienced increases in incomes and/or efficiency as a consequence of car ownership (Flink 1975: 160).

Forward/backward linkages

The development of the car industry has had particularly extensive forward and backward economic linkages. Investment in a car simultaneously presupposes a range of backward linkages – in steel, aluminium, oil, rubber, plastics, lacquers, glass, construction, lead, platinum (to name just some of the more important) – and entails or creates an even wider range of forward linkages – filling stations, tourist cabins, trailer parks (Dunn 1998: 26–7), insurance, health care, advertising, maintenance (of both cars and roads), spare parts, legal fees, in-car gadgets and so on. A banal example is instructive. Flink (1975) quotes a New York City health commissioner writing in the magazine *Motor* in 1922: 'do you realize, that without the motorcar golf could never have become the popular game that it is today' (1975: 166). The investment in cars or associated activities helped to stimulate activity across great swathes of the economy, even without considering the dynamic effects: if one includes the process of suburbanisation as an 'effect' of the development of automobility, then increased highway construction (which was the second largest US government expenditure in the 1920s) and the suburban real estate boom (with associated investment in sewers, telephones, electricity provision, schools, shopping malls, etc.) all become part of the knock-on economic consequences of the emergence of the car (Flink 1975: 140–1; see Rae 1971: 101–7).

For much of the twentieth century, then, the motor and associated industries (oil, steel and construction, in particular) had growth rates noticeably above those for the economy as a whole. A fairly common assessment would be along the lines given by Overy:

> The motor and aviation industries have both contributed to sustaining high levels of economic growth and technical change at a vital period in economic development, when the technical and market possibilities of the first industrial revolution were reaching a climactic point. (Overy 1990: 71)

To observe these relationships is important; however, what most writers tend to do is to 'naturalise' the car's relation to growth – to render it an objective fact outside political agency. Cars just appear to have grown in a more or less autonomous, haphazard manner, principally because of the actions of either business geniuses such as Ford or Sloan (of GM), or millions of (American) consumers 'choosing' cars over their alternatives. This naturalistic tendency is particularly pronounced among economists or business historians. Overy (1990), for example, argues that 'the reception and rapid evolution of the motor vehicle ... needs little explanation' (1990: 57). The way writers often discuss the (usually American) 'love affair' with the car reinforces such naturalistic notions (e.g. Davies 1975: 7; Flink 1975: chapter 1).

Hoyle and Knowles (1998) reflect this tendency well. They conflate the historically specific patterns of, and tendency towards, enhanced mobility in the nineteenth and especially twentieth centuries with an ahistorical account of 'human needs':

> The study of transport rests essentially on two cardinal principles. The first is that *mobility is a fundamental human activity and need*. 'When the history of the late 20th century is written, there seems little doubt that mobility ... will be one of its touchstones'. (Hoyle and Knowles 1998: 3–4, quoting from Johnston *et al.* 1995: 13)

So, as with Lomasky, mobility is simultaneously a feature specific to
the way we might characterise a particular age and a timeless aspect of
human needs. As a consequence, the shift from one transport mode to
another over time is presented effectively in teleological terms, as a
succession of modes to a 'final stage' where the automobile 'which
offered a greatly improved alternative to either bus, streetcar or rail' is
the pinnacle of achievement in urban mobility, in much the same way
as conceptualised by Dunn or Lomasky (Hoyle and Smith 1998: 25).[8]

This tendency explains the rise of the car in terms of the natural
advantages it has over other forms of transport and the way it taps into
powerful forces in human psychology. Maxton and Wormald (1995)
indulge in some bizarre psychologising:

The truth is that our attachment to cars is profoundly rooted – not only in the
practical necessities of life but also in our emotions. Research shows that
there is a deep psychic connection between freedom and movement. Babies
achieve locomotion. Adults re-experience it through the motor car. Waiting
for a bus or a train unleashes hidden, unconscious fears of abandonment in
many. (Maxton and Wormald 1995: 33)

Economic nationalist IPE

When cars appear in discussions of IPE the legacy of this understanding
of the relationship between the car and growth is strong. Discussions of
the car industry within IPE tend to focus on two themes. First, there is a
concern to explain the changing spatial organisation of the car industry, reflecting broader concerns with shifts from 'national' to 'international' and more recently from 'international' to 'global' economies.
The car industry is often taken as a paradigm case of a globalised
industry (Dicken 1998; Held *et al.* 1999: 262–3). Dicken emphasises
how the car industry was organisationally one of the most globalised of
all manufacturing industries and had transnationalised early. Ford and
GM had set up plants abroad during the 1920s and by 1994, for
example, 57 per cent of Ford's production was taking place outside
the United States. Over 40 per cent of the production of the largest car
manufacturers is outside their 'home' country (Dicken 1998: 316–18,

---

[8] That this citation is from an undergraduate textbook should not be taken as a
weakness in the argument here; it is a key site where 'received wisdom' is passed
down to a new generation of transport planners.

335–6); although a substantial majority of final car assembly is still carried out in 'triad' countries in North America, Japan and western Europe, 20 per cent is now outside that area and component manufacture is even more widely spread (Dicken 1998: 319).[9] Car companies have been highly innovative in relation to emerging forms of interfirm alliances as a response to the increased competitiveness pressures associated with globalisation (Dicken 1998: 337–8). These 'various types of joint venture' include 'equity, vehicle swapping, manufacturing and assembly, parts swapping, engineering and design, and distribution' (Munkis *et al.* 1993: 628).

Secondly there is a concern to explain this spatial distribution of production facilities in terms of government policies. A successful car industry was in the twentieth century widely taken to be a necessary condition for a successful economic development strategy (Dicken 1998: 316). Many states established various forms of protection to ensure the dominance of the domestic car market by domestic firms and several created nationalised car companies as 'flagship' industries. The changes in production techniques and labour relations collectively known as 'Fordism' laid the foundation for the projection of US global power in the mid-twentieth century (Rupert 1995). Within a globalising economy, the imperative for governments to compete to attract investment is taken as a background of this concern.

There is often a clear connection in this literature to normative policy-making concerns with how 'we' (nationally understood) promote 'our' car industry, as well as a concern to evaluate (and often emphasise) the role of the state under conditions of globalisation. Reich (1989), for example, shows that the success of 'national' car industries is dependent primarily on the degree of access to the domestic market which overseas producers have, and the varied types of support given to domestic firms by the state (Reich 1989, 1993; Plumstead *et al.* 1993; Kawahara 1997; Dicken 1998: 330–2). Gradually, as the economy has globalised, most countries have disbanded nationally owned or otherwise systematically favoured car companies in favour of opening up markets and simultaneously providing inventive packages to attract investment from transnational firms. Such incentives include various

---

[9] Indeed, at times, a process of 'continental' integration is analysed as opposed to globalised integration (e.g. Molot 1993a) – but the logic is ultimately the same, only the scale differs.

forms of tax breaks as well as state investment in infrastructure for the factory concerned (Dicken 1998: 271–2). In extreme cases, the value of the subsidy provided by states to get investment far outweighs its direct employment benefits (illustrating the importance of forward/backward linkages, as suggested above). In one case, Dicken (1998) reports that Alabama offered the equivalent of $167,000 per job created to attract a Mercedes–Benz plant in 1993 (1998: 272). Transnational firms have also worked to re-present themselves as 'insider' firms to overcome the legacy of nationalism in the car industry, the paradigm being Japanese firms in North America (Eden and Molot 1993). One final concern often raised in these debates is that of the position of developing countries – whether or not it is possible for developing countries to emulate industrialised countries in developing a car industry, or how they might develop other policy tools to promote such an industry (Gwynne 1991; Maxton and Wormald 1995: 132–41).

This form of political/economic discourse is the dominant one in political representations of the car industry, with anxiety about employment, investment and economic performance all being prevalent. These routinely intertwine debate about the success of individual firms, the system-wide problems of the industry (notably persistent overproduction) and those of national economies (e.g. Kalawsky 2001). Witness the debates in the United Kingdom over the perennial crises of Rover, being sold to BMW in 1994, downsized by BMW, sold by BMW, with Ford picking up profitable Land Rover, the rest reverting to a UK-based group of investors in 2000 and then going into receivership in April 2005. In all of these episodes a series of concerns framed in nationalist terms about productivity and competitiveness, employment, management versus unions (both as a narrative within the events and as competing explanations for Rover's woes) is prevalent. When Rover was sold to BMW the moral panic was that there was no longer a 'British car industry' left, a general concern over the competitiveness of the 'British' economy and so on.[10] Similar crises and concerns can be seen in recurring crises of car firms around the world – Chrysler, from at least the 1979 bailout onwards, Fiat, Volkswagen, Volvo, Saab,

---

[10] At times, this is overlaid with localist concerns – in Rover's case, in the West Midlands in particular. But whatever the spatial scale, the logic is the same – of increased competition between places in a global economy and a concern to protect jobs and investment in a particular place.

Renault – even GM worrying about when Toyota will overtake it as the world's largest car maker.

While it is not surprising that this sort of discourse is prevalent in a broader political arena it is perhaps more surprising how dominant it is in academic discourse about the car industry in IPE. Maureen Molot's edited volume *Driving Continentally* (Molot 1993a) stands as a paradigm case, as does much of her more recent edited AUTO21 volume (2003). Both stem from large conferences involving academics, car industry people and government officials. Molot begins her introduction to *Driving Continentally* with the assertion of the 'enormous importance [of the car industry] to the economies of Canada, the United States, and Mexico (Molot 1993b: 1). The overall concern is with the fate of the industry based in North America in the face of continental integration (both political and corporate), intensified competition (especially from Japanese firms) and emerging pressures such as environmental regulation. This literature in general assumes the centrality of the car industry to national economic success; it then focuses on government policies (and shifts in them) to channel investment into the car industry, to protect national industries, etc. There are some obvious limits to the nationalist agenda. From my perspective here the central one is that it does not really explain the relationship between cars and economic growth: rather, it assumes such a relationship exists and looks at one of the consequences. As Molot states, within this mode of analysis, such a question would appear redundant: 'that the economic viability of the auto industry has a direct impact on the overall health of each of the North American economies is to state the obvious' (1993b: 4).

The focus on national strategies in an international/global economy has generated much attention on the relationship between such national strategies and economic integration on a world, regional, or bilateral basis. The potential conflicts between regional or bilateral schemes and multilateral ones, as in analyses of the Auto Pact between Canada and the United States (Donaghy 1998; Anastakis 2000), or of the North American Free Trade Agreement (NAFTA) (Weintraub and Sands 1998) have been considered. These often generate specific contexts for such interstate competition for locational advantage and, as knock on consequences, generate rules (mostly involving harmonisation of standards) designed to level competitive playing fields (most work here is on NAFTA and the European Union (EU), see various chapters in Molot 1993, especially Holmes 1993; see also Weintraub and Sands 1998; Freyssenet *et al.* 2003). The environmental features of such integration schemes are prominent and are often stress environment/economy conflicts. The MMT case is a paradigm example and the debate in the EU over catalytic converters in the late 1980s and early 1990s was similarly important (Arp 1993; Kirton 1998). In the former, the US company Ethyl Corporation successfully sued the Canadian government in 1998 under the provisions of chapter 11 of NAFTA for the latter's ban on the former's gasoline additive on grounds of health and environmental impacts, gaining compensatory payments and an overturn of the ban (Kirton 1998). In the latter, there was a fierce debate in the EU between advocates of catalytic converters and those of lean burn engines in the late 1980s and early 1990s, which turned as much on whose car industry had a strategic advantage in one or the other (the United Kingdom versus Germany, principally) as on the environmental benefits of each (Arp 1993).

Regimes of accumulation

While these arguments concerning the importance of cars to growth are a useful starting point, they remain partial. It seems to me more fruitful to start with Marxian political economy, particularly combinations of regulation theory and neo-Gramscian IPE as well as a little dose of Schumpeter to illustrate and explain the centrality of cars to growth. It is not just a matter of certain features of cars (as, say, in Overy's account – e.g. the forward/backward linkages point) but the presence of a whole 'regime of accumulation' in which cars (both their production *and* consumption) have figured centrally.

Some of the historians of cars, or commentators on the car industry's problems in the 1970s, get part of the way here. Flink (1975), for example, has a subtle appreciation that the development of the car in the 1920s and 1930s in America relied simultaneously on the expansion of productive capacity through massive capital investment (both private, in manufacturing capacity for cars as well as steel, oil, rubber, etc. and public, in roads and improved surfaces) and consumptive capacity through credit creation and so on. Flink also recognises that the specific patterns shift over time – for example, showing that the massive capital investment in the 1920s generated growth in that decade but that in the 1930s this could not be sustained and growth instead shifted towards planned obsolescence (Flink 1975: 174). Rothschild similarly emphasises that the development of the car depended not so much on people's 'innate' desire for cars as on 'the sustenance of social and institutional partiality. Such support provided roads, a favourable tax structure, a dispersal of cities and jobs. It encouraged the decay of alternative modes of transportation, and suspended rational calculations of the costs of auto development and auto waste' (Rothschild 1973: 245). Protesters against the car also often understand the political economy here, as noted in chapter 2. John Tyme (1978) provides a good example of how the growth of cars stems from a 'technological imperative' which guides the age – consisting of the technology itself, the industrial/financial complex which promotes and profits from it; a lobby organisation which promotes the interests of the industrial bloc to governments; an 'interest section' in the relevant government department, predisposed towards the lobby; a body of expertise dependent on the industry for their careers; and a 'brainwashing organisation, loosely staffed by hack economists' whose job it is to 'establish "economic truths"' in the interests of the imperative (Tyme 1978: 93).

But a political economy which has its origins in Marxism allows us to emphasise the way in which capital accumulation requires the success of particular industries (which may change over time) and the way in which the state is structurally impelled to intervene to promote the pursuit of continued accumulation and thus to promote key industries. I show how the specific material practices involved in the car are organised as part of the ongoing reproduction of capitalist societies and are increasingly organised transnationally rather than simply within national borders. But, at the same time, the car industry is not simply something which has been organised through capitalist enterprises; it is an industry which has been seen ubiquitously as a key industry in ensuring continued accumulation.

It is necessary at this point to go 'back to basics' to clear the ground for what follows. Central to all accounts of capitalism from Marx onwards is that, as a social form, capitalist society is defined principally by a combination of the specific commodification of human labour – the emergence of the wage form as the principal means by which most people meet their subsistence needs – and the way that capitalists face each other in competition in the marketplace. These fundamental features create a number of conflicting consequences. First, they generate endemic class conflict as wage labourers and capitalists with antagonistic interests face each other. Second, the interests of individual capitalists and those of capitalists collectively are in conflict with each other. Individual capitalists tend to want to keep workers' pay to the minimum necessary to enable the reproduction of their labour power while collectively capitalists (at least once the productive capacity of society has got beyond the point where all production can be consumed by a minority of the rich) increasingly need wages to rise to facilitate consumption of industry's products. A tendency for underconsumption/overproduction is thus built into the structure of capitalist society. This tendency is used to explain the boom/slump cycles endemic to the history of capitalist society; at various points in a business cycle it produces a crisis of overproduction, an inability to realise profits and a recession which shakes out productive capacity and 'surplus labour' until profits can again be realised. A third feature of this dynamic is that capital attempts to substitute labour for machinery in order to realise increased profits by reducing wage bills. This is one of the principal reasons why capitalist society is so enormously dynamic as a system, but it also exacerbates underconsumptionist tendencies through unemployment and depressed wage levels as workers compete not only with each other but also with machinery. Finally, the modern state has emerged as a political institution which attempts simultaneously to secure the rule of capital (through the principal institutions of private property and contract, as well as through specific laws to discipline labour and occasional violence and repression), to manage class conflict and to secure the conditions under which accumulation might continue reasonably smoothly – specifically through intervention to mitigate the problems caused by capitalism's underconsumptionist tendencies.[11]

It is at this point that the branch of Marxism known as 'regulation theory' enters the picture.[12] At least for present purposes, regulation

---

[11] As well as skirting many controversies, this brief account of Marxist political economy draws on a huge literature. For two accounts similar to that shown here, see Held (1987: chapter 4) or Harvey (1990: 121–41).

[12] The account here draws principally on Aglietta (1979, 1998), Boyer (2004) and useful reviews by Jessop (1990), Amin (1994b) and Dunford (2000). Other key works in regulation theory are Boyer (1986) and Lipietz (1987).

theory focuses on the means by which capital attempts over long periods of time to mitigate underconsumption. The more general premise of regulation theory is that neoclassical economics fails to understand that social institutions are necessary conditions of the continued reproduction of capitalist society. 'Regulationist research insists on the fact that the market relation, and therefore its expression in markets, results from *a social construction* and not from the information coming from the spontaneous confrontation of economic actors' (Boyer 2004: 17, my translation). 'The essential idea of *A Theory of Capitalist Regulation* is that the dynamism of capital represents an enormous productive potential but that it is also a blind force. It does not contain a self-limiting mechanism of its own, nor is it guided in a direction that would enable [it] to fulfil the capitalists' dream of perpetual accumulation' (Aglietta 1998: 49). But at the same time, regulationists resist the idea, which they suggest most Marxists hold to, that capitalism's basic principles (wage labour, commodity production) determine a singular path of development; social institutions thus create historically and spatially specific patterns of growth (e.g. Boyer 2004: 17).

These specific patterns are termed 'regimes of accumulation' in regulation theory. They refer to the historically specific way in which surplus value is extracted and realised and a long-term model articulated which creates a general consistency between conditions of production and 'the conditions under which production is put to social use (household consumption, investment, government spending, foreign trade)' (Lipietz 1992: 2; for a similar definition see Amin 1994a: 8). But these regimes do not arise spontaneously, nor do their inevitable contradictions resolve themselves. Specific regimes of accumulation also entail particular modes of regulation which are referred to as the socio-political institutions and ideologies through which capital attempts smoothly to reproduce a specific regime of accumulation, the 'mechanisms which adjust the contradictory behaviour of individuals to the collective principles of the regime of accumulation' (Lipietz 1992: 2; Aglietta 1998: 44). These elements are not simply to do with state intervention or regulation, narrowly understood; they entail 'a wide range of areas, including the law, state policy, political practices, industrial codes, governance philosophies, rules of negotiating and bargaining, cultures of consumption and social expectations' (Amin 1994a: 4).

Fordism and after

Although other regimes of accumulation, and their crises, can be identified,[13] regulation theory arose out of the economic crisis of the 1970s
and took as its principal object of study the regime of accumulation
known most commonly as Fordism, occasionally also as 'organised
capitalism' (Lash and Urry 1987). Aglietta's *A Theory of Capitalist
Regulation* (1979) was principally an investigation of how this regime
was put together and maintained in the United States throughout much
of the twentieth century. Fordism entailed an integrated (if not necessarily 'planned' in the conventional sense of the word) set of policies,
practices and projects developed from the 1910s to the 1940s, and then
fully integrated through to the 1970s, albeit with variants in different
countries (Dunford 2000: 152, quoting Boyer 1996: 26–9). At its heart
was a set of technical and labour organisational changes which enabled
massive productivity gains, often known as 'mass production'. But
such productivity gains and the mass production they enabled also
went along with a set of social compromises which enabled the development of *mass consumption*, mass production's logical corollary. The
first of these involved Taylorism (or the scientific management of
work), increased mechanisation – in particular, through the development of the use of the assembly line – and the rise of managerialism to
effect enhanced control over labour. Collectively these produced huge
and ongoing productivity gains in the industries which adopted them
from the 1910s through to the 1970s. But the second element, the mode
of regulation, was just as important. This entailed first and foremost a
shift in capital/labour relations where capital forwent a high rate of
profit in order to realise higher absolute profits by increasing wages
above the rate required for the physical reproduction of labour, and
labour accepted enhanced managerial control in return for increased
wages and acceptance (after a struggle) of unionisation. Its symbolic
starting point was Ford's 'five-dollar day', started in 1914, but two
other elements were key to the success of Fordism over time. One was

[13] Dunford (2000: 148) suggests that capitalism's history can be characterised by
four periods of crisis with distinct regimes of accumulation between them. The
four crisis periods are those following the post-Napoleonic war (both the first
crisis of industrial capitalism and the last crisis of the *ancien régime*), the
depression of the 1890s, the interwar crisis of 1918–39 and the crisis of
Fordism starting at the end of the 1960s.

the emergence of what Aglietta calls a 'norm of working class consumption' (1979: 152): that workers had to be acculturated into a
culture of consumption in order that increased wages would result in
cycles of production/consumption necessary to sustain the regime of
accumulation. It also entailed the emergence of the state as both a
significantly increased consumer of goods and services directly (notably with the public works programmes in their New Deal/Keynesian
and fascist variants in the 1930s) and as the agent with the key responsibility of managing labour conflicts, redistributing wealth to those not
in work (again to enable the spread of consumption), stabilising aggregate demand at national levels (through Keynesian demand management) and negotiating the international tensions brought about
through such nationalist economic management techniques at international levels (the Bretton Woods system after the Second World War).[14]

As we have seen above, many writers illustrate the centrality of cars
in promoting growth from the early twentieth century onwards in
relation to a number of specific features – forward/backward economic
linkages, the acceleration and flexibilisation of mobility, the reorganisation of industrial production and so on. The regulation-theoretic
account also enables us to understand these specific features as an
integrated whole. At the same time, it enables us to revisit Fordism's
central elements in the car industry as both paradigm example and
principal 'driving force'.

That the car industry was central in such reorganisation/productivity
gains is clear from its most commonly designated name – Fordism. Ross
claims that 'the car *is* the commodity form as such in the twentieth
century – "Taylorization" [the methods of rationalising work in fac-
tories central to Fordism] . . . was developed *in the process of* producing
the "car for the masses" and not the inverse' (Ross 1995: 19).
Taylorisation involved the breaking down of production tasks into
their simplest elements. Previously each worker had done multiple
tasks, so that an individual worker could be said to have built a car.
Instead, each worker would now do only one task, repetitively,

---

[14] This is inevitably a whirlwind overview of the principal elements of Fordism and
glosses over debates and details. For fuller accounts, see Aglietta (1979), Lash
and Urry (1987), or Harvey (1990: 121–200). On the interpretation of the
relationship between Keynesian management and Bretton Woods given here
(the latter is often overlooked in accounts of Fordism), see Ruggie (1983) or
Leyshon and Thrift (1997: 59–82).

throughout the day, and the car would be built by the work team as a whole. As introduced by Ford this involved the use of the assembly line where the car in production would be moved mechanically around the factory, each worker adding their part as it passed them. This method of production greatly increased worker productivity and thus reduced prices for the finished products.

But this reorganisation and mechanisation of work and worker/ manager relations needed to be managed politically. The car industry became one of the principal sites of labour disputes and disputes over unionisation (e.g. Rupert 1995).[15] The productivity gains enabled by Fordism produced deep struggles over how they should be distributed. It was struggles in the car industry above all which had produced by 1945 the key elements in the Fordist class compromise involving recognition of union rights, full employment policies, the 'family wage' principle underlying wage rates and so on. This in turn enabled the spreading of consumption across much broader segments of the population and the thirty years of unprecedently high economic growth across the western world from the mid-1940s to the mid-1970s.

But cars were not only important in terms of their role in transforming production relations; they became one of the principal consumption items around which the consumption side of the equation was structured. Fordist consumption 'is governed by two commodities; standardized housing that is the privileged site of individual consumption; and the automobile as the means of transport compatible with the separation of home and workplace' (Aglietta 1979: 159; cf. Freund and Martin 1996: 8). Through the relation of these two, the processes of urban spatial change – in particular, suburbanisation – thus becomes integral to the success of Fordism as a regime of accumulation. Consumption of cars becomes the process of commodification through which other consumption (houses and the things to put in them) is thus

---

[15] Indeed, if we look at the field of study known as industrial relations it is hardly too strong to say that it was almost exclusively founded and developed on the back of studies of the car industry, or on conceptual tools drawn from that study. The classic study is Braverman (1974). The literature on industrial relations in the car industry, practically all of which proceeds from this premise about the management of labour relations as part of the development of Taylorism, and more recently of 'flexibilisation', is enormous; for a small selection, see Tolliday and Zeitlin (1986); Law (1991); Jürgens *et al.* (1993); Deyo (1996).

enabled, and which occurs in a manner which starts off appearing as 'freedom', but increasingly becomes a necessity.

As means of managing capitalism's internal contradictions, regimes of accumulation and modes of regulation are able to stabilise growth for only a period of time. Fordism started to come under pressure from the late 1960s and as a regime of accumulation it is usually seen as exhausted by the mid-1970s. At the heart of the crisis were slowdowns in the productivity gains produced by the Fordist combination of high wages, strict labour discipline, the assembly line and Taylorism. At the same time, enhanced international competition (in part because of the Bretton Woods system, one of Fordism's regulatory elements) placed competitive pressures on firms and downward pressures on profits. By the 1970s many western economies were experiencing the contradictory phenomenon of *stagflation*: simultaneous economic stagnation (as investment and output stalled and unemployment rose) and inflation (with prices rapidly rising). The oil crisis of 1973–4 helped to prolong the problem.

The 1970s and 1980s saw a series of debates about how to characterise what was emerging as a response to the crisis of Fordism. Various prefixes (neo, post, *après*) were added to Fordism to indicate the relationship to what had gone before and the transformations in the way the political economy operated. Others preferred a terminology invoking a distinct break from Fordism – 'the second industrial divide', 'flexible accumulation', 'flexible production', 'disorganised capitalism', 'New Times' were all proposed. For some the crisis was contained within the organisation of production and had to do principally with technology and labour relations (with differing emphases on each element); for others it was a crisis simply of Keynesian economics and economic management; while for others again (including regulationists), it was a crisis of the regime of accumulation as a whole.[16] Within the regulationist school (e.g. Aglietta 1998) there is a sense that no fully fledged regime of accumulation has successfully emerged to replace Fordism and as a consequence overall growth rates have been significantly lower than during Fordism's heyday and the global economy has

---

[16] For a useful survey of these debates, see Amin (1994b). For key contributions where these terms were articulated, see Piore and Sabel (1984), Offe (1985), Lash and Urry (1987), Lipietz (1987), Hall and Jacques (1989) and Harvey (1990).

been significantly more prone to recurrent crises. Nevertheless the years since the 1970s have been characterised by a search for such a regime; Harvey (1990) provides a useful starting point with his emphasis on the word 'flexibility'. The 'inability of Fordism and Keynesianism to contain the inherent contradictions of capitalism' which became evident during the 1970s, 'could best be captured by one word: rigidity'. As a consequence, 'flexible accumulation ... is marked by a direct confrontation with the rigidities of Fordism. It rests on flexibility with respect to labour processes, labour markets, products, and patterns of consumption' (Harvey 1990: 142, 147).

Asking questions about the transition from Fordism to post-Fordism can also serve to illustrate more fully the centrality of cars to both regimes of accumulation. First, car firms were at the centre of the crisis of Fordism, as both its problem and its solution. One of the elements in the crisis was enhanced international competition which placed downward pressure on profits, particularly noticeable in terms of US/ Japanese competition. As we saw in chapter 2, one of the particular problems of the car industry – in fact, probably outstripping that posed by the critics of the car (on environmental, safety, or other grounds) in the day-to-day lives of US car executives – was the pressure on profitability produced by enhanced Japanese competition. At the root of this competitiveness was a distinct productivity regime in the Japanese workplace which enabled it to combine the economies of scale of the assembly line with flexibilities unavailable to US manufacturers. Japanese firms had been developing what became most commonly called 'lean production', sometimes 'Toyotism', since around 1960. Lean production entailed an attempt to continue to realise the economies of scale produced by the assembly line and Taylorism, but to strip out the rigidities and inefficiencies in mass production. In particular it involved the application of JIT principles throughout the industry. JIT refers to a way of organising an industry where everything arrives where it is needed 'just-in-time'; the principle is effected from supply of parts, to manufacture, to distribution of end products, with the result that many cars are in effect now not produced until they are ordered. JIT replaced older systems of planning which entailed, for example, manufacturers holding huge stocks of parts (with their associated costs) and were often vulnerable to running out of one part, as they did not intensively manage inventory. JIT thus significantly reduced the costs of holding inventory, reduced the risks of running out and also enabled much swifter responses to changing market conditions, at the same time limiting problems of overcapacity. It also entailed significantly reorganised work practices, from individualised jobs on the assembly line to team working, an ideology of 'co-operation in place of conflict, leadership by demonstration rather than imposition, multi-skilling and appealing to individual creativity' (Maxton and Wormald 1995: 71–2). Japanese firms could then sell cars at highly competitive prices in US markets, even taking into account protectionist measures in place.[17] But flexibility was an additional and qualitatively important difference: Japanese firms were able to respond to changes in market demand much more quickly than their American counterparts.

So while the origins of Fordism are to a very significant extent in the development of the car industry, so are the origins of its demise as well as the rise of an alternative way of organising production. The implications of the Japanese challenge to US dominance in car manufacturing and the whole regulatory apparatus of Fordism were profound. Stagflation had as one of its causes the overproduction and enhanced competitiveness problems in car markets. Although most commentators looking back identify the crisis of the Bretton Woods system, in particular, the fixed exchange rate mechanism – with either declining US hegemony (Kindleberger 1973; Keohane 1984), the rising costs of the Vietnam War, or the emergence of the Eurodollar markets and the consequent downward pressure on the dollar (Helleiner 1994; Leyshon and Thrift 1997: chapter 2) – some contemporary commentators noted that 'Nixon at the time explained the devaluation of the dollar in terms of its adverse effect on people who wanted to buy foreign cars' (Rothschild 1973: 10).

Second, and perhaps more importantly for my concerns, what is often overlooked in discussions of Fordism – although it is discussed (if on the brief side) in Aglietta (1979: chapter 3 – is that Fordism was not only a series of innovations in production, to do with production technology, industrial relations, corporate organisation, state/firm relations, and internationalisation but was also a restructuring of

---

[17] There was a widespread view early on in the United States that the Japanese advantage was purely in terms of low wage rates. But car industry executives quickly knew that this was not the case. What was (and is) the case was that US firms expected significantly higher profit rates than Japanese (and European) firms (Flink 1975: 203).

consumption and the integration of the working class into capitalist society through such consumption. Aglietta emphasises that Fordism entailed a 'norm of working class consumption' (1979: 152) and that the key sites of such a norm were in housing and transport. Cars were thus central to Fordism through the stimulation of demand and the creation of a set of ideological mechanisms and consumer credit practices which served to close the circle between production and consumption necessary to secure a regime of accumulation.

We can revisit the question about the notion of 'post-Fordism' in this light. Implied both in the name and often more generally is the fact that post-Fordism signifies an eclipse in the centrality of cars. This narrative, however, suggests a different line. Within automobility's relation to Fordism are contradictions which help interpret both the unravelling of Fordism and the continued importance of cars. One central weakness in many approaches to post-Fordism (e.g. Amin 1994a) is precisely the positing of a 'break'. But when we focus even in a traditional manner on the organisation of production it is rather more useful to think of 'lean production', etc. as a *continuation* of the basic principles of Ford's innovative ideas rather than a break with them. Kawahara's (1997) account of the development of the Japanese industry, while highly ideological in orientation, is nevertheless useful here, as he shows that lean production arose in Japanese industries out of innovations within methods of mass production as transplanted from US firms in Japan, with the Japanese firms then simply working to improve the efficiency of the methods. In this sense car industries were still central in innovating in both the organisation of production and productivity gains and also in industrial organisation and labour relations (Kawahara 1997; Dicken 1998) in a 'globalising' economy.

But one can also think about the importance of automobility as one of the contradictions of Fordism itself, and the transition to post-Fordism as produced in part because of the unravelling of this contradiction. Take Harvey's classical account of 'flexible accumulation', for example. This is broadly centred on the production side of the 'regime of accumulation' (although there are some nods in the direction of consumption), and therefore suggests that the central 'break' is between rigidity (Fordism) and flexibility (post-Fordism). But, as illustrated already, the central 'competitive advantage' of cars at the consumption end, and thus their ability to generate accumulation, was always a question of 'flexibility' – they increased the flexibility of many individuals' mobility and thus their ability to produce and consume services and create cycles of accumulation. Cars in this sense can thus be seen to play a part of an 'immanent contradiction' within Fordism, their flexible modes of transport and thus consumption (not just of themselves but of a whole range of other commodities) tending to breach the limits of a production regime based on rigidities. In other words, Fordism tended to become a limit to the realisation of the potential of automobility to produce limitless, mobile, accumulation.

Aglietta (1998: 56–7) also makes a similar argument when he suggests that one of the contradictions within Fordism was the way it encouraged individualism both through consumption and what elsewhere is called 'detraditionalisation' – in particular, through the emergence of large organisations as the principal sites of work – but that this individualism increasingly regarded such organisations as limits to its realisation. The events of 1968 are interpreted as the first major outburst of this contradiction, and the attempts in the 1970s by firms to 'make use of employees' initiatives' to enhance autonomy largely failed, with the consequence that 'productivity ran out of steam, inflationary pressures built up and the rate of profit declined' (Aglietta 1998: 57). The contradiction in automobility could be regarded as a specific instance of this tension, but I would make the stronger claim that it should be seen as its principal, and earliest, element. As in the principles of Sloanism which included the introduction of consumer credit systems, annual model changes, emphases on the importance of styling and aestheticisation, (Gartman 1994) and GM's intensified management of consumers through 'customer research' (Marchand 1998) are in this instance a corporate response to this tension.

Gartman (2004) neatly analyses this intertwining of production and consumption in the development of automobility. He suggests that there have been three principal cultural logics to the development of cars. In the first instance, cars seemed to cement and articulate class differences through ownership/non-ownership, craft-made/mass-produced and through a series of distinctions made by manufacturers, quintessentially GM (constructing a range of brands hierarchically from Cadillac 'down' to Chevrolet). But by the 1930s into the postwar period this logic was undermined by the working-class car consumption central, as we have seen, to Fordism. Workers were not

content with 'inferior' cars and the strict hierarchical logic of distinction became replaced with a mass-consumption logic, more consistent
perhaps with that of Fordist production. But this always contained a
tension between individuality and mass production which had produced by the 1960s a proliferation of styles and types of car – not
organised hierarchically but increasingly according to 'lifestyle' logics –
a 'postmodernisation' of the car market. Gartman's point is that each
of these shifting cultural logics produces alterations in the production
regime – the emergence of 'lean production', with changes in work
practices and labour relations, is driven by desires to adapt to changing
consumer tastes (themselves for Gartman driven by needs to escape
alienation in the workplace). It is thus shifts in consumer practice,
stimulated by shifts in class structure and class conflict, which then
feed back to shape the particular character of the reorganisation of
production. The problem of 'rigidity' which, in Harvey's view, is
paradigmatic of the crisis of Fordism by the late 1960s, starts in the
emergence of aestheticisation under Sloan, designed to respond to the
problems of market saturation and working-class resistance to their
status as being subjected to standardised, low-status cars. In response
to these problems in the consumer market, Sloan developed an
enhanced emphasis on the design of cars and on their aesthetic quali-
ties, but also developed the idea of the annual model change in order to
renew interest in new cars.

The relationship between post-Fordism and automobility should
thus be regarded less as an eclipse of the centrality of cars and more
of a triumph of automobility over the rigidities of the previous accumulation regime. Again, we need the concept of 'automobility' here. If
we limit our analysis to 'the car' then what we see is the persistent crises
of particular car firms, the apparent saturation of car markets and the
decline of car industries relative to 'new' 'innovative' industries such as
biotechnology, telecommunications, software, etc. and to the financial
sector. But when we think more broadly in terms of automobility its
centrality to growth is still palpable, principally through the mode of
mobility which it facilitates.

States promote the car

Given the structural role of the state in promoting accumulation it is no
surprise that once the car's potential in accelerating accumulation was

realised states began to promote the car. The car industry offered significant improvements in the capability to commodify means of mobility and at the same time accelerate the movement of goods and people in the economy. Promoting the car through hidden and not-so-hidden means has helped it to become the dominant force it is. Such promotion is perhaps best understood in terms of the state's structural role in capitalist societies, its general imperative to support the conditions for capital accumulation (e.g. Jessop 1990) and the particular understanding of the requirements for accumulation in specific historical periods. Support for the car thus helped to reproduce state power itself.

Many restrictions were initially in place which acted to hamper the use of cars (Wall 1999: 17–39). The classic case was the Red Flag Act (Locomotive Act 1865) in Britain which restricted the speed of motor vehicles to 2 mph, and insisted that three people accompany such vehicles with red flags of warning. This was repealed only in 1896 when the red flag provisions were abolished and the speed limit raised to 14 mph (Overy 1990: 61). France instituted 6 mph speed limits in some cities and in 1912 the Parisian government 'ordered gendarmes to shoot out the tires of speeding motorists' (McShane 1994: 113). In the United States, steam-engined cars had been banned earlier in the century but the ICE was not placed under such restraint. Such restrictions reflected opposition to cars on grounds of noise, smell and danger but they were dismantled in the United States more quickly than elsewhere, largely as judges ruled that cities did not have the right to impose them (Volti 1996: 664). Ironically, this initially involved dismantling restraints on the bicycle, and bicycle lobbies were in the forefront of lobbying for their restriction (Wall 1999: 22). By 1900 'activist judges had ruled against urban regulations that might impede automobility' (McShane 1994: 115). The other major restriction was imposed by the quality of roads, as both car manufacturers and municipal engineers were aware, and the former acted to promote road quality (McShane 1994: 109–10).

After car manufacturers had managed to overcome these political obstacles to the car's expansion – in most western European countries and the United States by about 1910 – the state by and large became a dedicated ally of the car companies. In some cases the car's expansion became a specific election pledge by politicians – Hoover's slogan in the 1924 election was 'a chicken in every pot; two cars in every garage' (as quoted in Wernick 1991: 71).

The promotion of the car economy by the state has had three main facets.[18] The first has been road building (both within and between urban areas). The second has been the progressive neglect and downgrading of public transport and non-motorised forms of transport. The third has been the fiscal measures which effectively subsidise car use relative to other forms of transport.

As Wolf (1996) points out, roads differ from rail in that the ownership and control of the transport infrastructure (roads) and of the means of transport (cars, lorries) can be easily separated. This separation has enabled states to promote the car, resulting in a system operating by the principle of:

Private appropriation of profit, socialisation of costs and losses. Private profits are appropriated on the vehicle manufacturers, the insurance companies and the motorway construction firms; costs are socialised by means of public financing of motorway construction, policing, hospitalisation of the injured and repairs to the environment. (Wolf 1996: 89)

The principal element of this has been road building (Luger 2000: 12). The emergence of the car demanded improvements to the quality of road surfaces and the emergence of mass-motorised societies demanded substantial increases in the quantity of roads. The provision of such investment out of general public expenditure has been something which all states have accepted as one of their basic roles. Highways became, in Wood's term, 'a natural function of the state' (Wood 1992: 107, quoted in Freund and Martin 1993: 82).

With the exception of a small number of privately financed toll roads, states have historically always paid the cost of road construction. The difference in the era of the car, however, has been that the costs of road construction (up to the standard required by the car and, in urban areas, to avoid dust) have been substantially higher than previously. The direct benefits of road construction have also increasingly been received primarily by car users whereas previously users of

---

[18] I leave out here discussions of oil geopolitics, dealt with in chapter 2, although this could be regarded as an additional dimension of the promotion of cars by the state. I also leave out discussion of the alleged collusion between states and firms in the 'GM conspiracy' to dismantle US public transport. I have discussed this debate in chapter 3, although if one is persuaded that it was a conspiracy, it is also suggestive of the length some local states would go to promote cars over public transport.

the roads of various types, employing a variety of transport modes (horse, carriage, cart, bicycle, trams and pedestrians) and for non-transport uses, such as leisure and commerce, benefited from road building and maintenance.

This development was intensified by urban freeway and parkway construction and reached its peak with the construction of motorways. What is distinctive about these constructions is that they have been designed and regulated to be used solely by motorised transport – bicycles and pedestrians are explicitly excluded. They are also specifically designed, by avoiding or going straight through city centres, to compete with/replace trains, which had previously been the primary means of interurban transport.

Motorway construction was initiated by Mussolini and then Hitler, primarily for military reasons, but other countries soon followed. Two classic accounts of the process in the United Kingdom and the United States are Hamer (1987) and Davies (1975). In both cases, the 'road lobby' (Hamer's phrase) or 'highway lobby' (Davies' term) increasingly knocked on open doors in persuading governments to spend large amounts of public money. The coalition of car, oil and construction companies, allied with highway and municipal engineers, is regarded as the single most powerful political lobby. In the United Kingdom its initial plan in the early 1930s for a 1,000-mile motorway network was taken up by the Labour government in 1946 and completed ahead of schedule by 1972. The plans were then rapidly expanded to 3,500 miles, the government again adopting very closely the plans of the British Roads Federation (BRF, the organisation providing the forum for the roads lobby) (Hamer 1987). In the United States, the Highway Aid Act 1956 created a system whereby the bulk of car-related taxes went into a Highway Trust Fund which could be used only for highway construction; the state put money into the fund from other sources to fulfil the lobby's ambitions (Davies 1975; Gordon 1991: 12–13).

The political/economic importance of automobility means that such road construction projects increasingly extend beyond the spatial scale of the state. The EU has since the mid-1980s expended considerable energy in developing such networks at a European scale while the Trans American Highway is also conceived as facilitating continental-scale trade and investment. The TransEuropean Transport Networks, of which motorway construction is the most important element, in part reflect the power of European business (Bowers 1993; Doherty and Hoedeman 1994; Richardson 1997) but also an under-standing of the importance of transport to economic growth and integration. In the words of Transport Commissioner Neil Kinnock, 'just as the development of efficient national transport networks was vital in the last [nineteenth] century in what became *national* 'single markets', so in the next century the same will have to occur *internationally*. The challenge is not so much new in nature as new in scale' (Kinnock 1996, quoted in Barry 1999: 79).

The second aspect of the state's promotion of the car has been neglect of alternative means of transport. State spending on transport since 1945 has systematically favoured roads. Rail has declined throughout this period, with many countries dismantling large proportions of their network (Wolf 1996: 75–81, 117–23). A recurrent complaint is that there is no 'level playing field' between road and rail (and as Wolf (1996) shows, canals) – for example, rail investments in the United Kingdom have to show a profit while the costs of road construction are written off by the state.

The third aspect has been hidden subsidies to the car relative to its competitors. Despite high petrol taxation in many countries the net effect of relevant fiscal policies is usually regarded as favourable to the car. The differential treatment of infrastructure investment between road and rail is clearly an important component of this but other aspects are also significant – for example, tax relief on provision of company cars. Athanasiou (1996: 264) estimates that the value of total subsidies to the car in the United States is approximately $400 billion, while Cobb (1999) puts the figure more conservatively (but still large) at $184 billion.

In addition to the structural role which states have in promoting accumulation, the favouring of the car has been driven by the compe-titive interstate environment, as emphasised by economic geographers such as Dicken. Sachs (1992) expresses the dynamic well in his account of debates about the car in early twentieth-century Germany:

What critics of the automobile saw themselves confronted with in the debates of the time could be called the executive syllogism of competition-driven progress: (a) technological development cannot be stopped; (b) escape is not an option, so Germany [or Britain, France, the United States, etc.] must take the lead; (c) therefore, we are called upon to support the automobile and its industry with all the means at the State's disposal ... The world market cast its long shadow over debates about the meaning of motorization on native streets. (Sachs 1992: 27)

But it was not only interstate economic competition which created strong incentives for governments to promote the car industry. After 1918, the increasing military utility of motorised transport meant that a strong car industry was connected in governments' minds to preparedness for war (remember that Mussolini and Hitler first conceived of motorways to accelerate the movement of troops).

As governments have systematically promoted cars over their alternatives they have thus also helped to sustain their own rule. Economic growth has become one of the central indicators of government legitimacy in the twentieth century. Favouring the car has therefore enabled state elites to ensure their own rule because they have been able to promote both the interests of structurally dominant capital and consumerist understandings of individual identity, helped to focus nationalist projects around particular technologies and in specific contexts to promote employment.

Conclusions

The backlash discussed in chapter 3 assumed that the rise of the car can be empirically understood in terms of the interactions of millions of individuals 'autonomously choosing' to buy cars and drive them and then normatively basing this analysis on the presumed moral connections between human autonomy and car driving. This chapter has shown that the empirical side of this argument is thoroughly unpersuasive and misleading. The rise of the car was directly stimulated by a range of decisions by states that favoured cars over their competitor transport modes. States did this because of the way that, for a variety of reasons, cars produced accelerated economic growth and thus secured the conditions for the reproduction of capitalist society and state legitimacy as well as at times enabling states to pursue other goals such as military expansion or defence. The chapter has also shown that this is best understood not as an inevitable, necessary connection between automobility and economic growth but because of the particular way in which a growth regime, known most commonly as Fordism, was assembled during the early part of the twentieth century and then the way in which car firms, and the consumption of cars, played particular roles in the collapse of that growth regime in the 1970s and the transition to something coming 'after Fordism' – however that 'after' is characterised.One of the things this analysis thus enables is a critical look at projects to 'green the car'. This is the subject of chapter 7, but the point from this chapter to be taken up further there is that such projects are almost all posed in technical terms (whether in terms of changes to individual cars, or in terms of promoting other transport *technologies*) and need to take account of the political analysis suggested here concerning the importance of cars to capitalist reproduction, the structural power of car firms and so on.

What this analysis does not adequately enable us to account for is the normative side of the backlash's arguments. In other words, even if this history of cars is right (or, at least, much better than their crude individualist account), it does not get rid of their claims that cars (more or less uniquely, as far as Lomasky is concerned) act as extensions of human autonomy and that to challenge them is thus to be an 'enemy of freedom'. As we have seen, one of the limitations of the political economy frameworks is that they tend (with some exceptions) to focus on the politics of production at the expense of the consumption dimension of capitalist accumulation. A crucial dimension, explored in chapter 5, is thus overlooked. What is also entailed in the development of automobility has been the (re)production of the modern subject as 'autonomously mobile' and thus the intertwining of automobility and the practices of governmental power. It is this which at the same time undermines the essentialist connections made by Lomasky and others about cars as extensions of human freedom. For what was done in the making of automobility was the (re)making of the human subject *as autonomously mobile* through car driving itself.

5 | The car's cultural politics: producing the (auto)mobile subject

> A body in movement, therefore, is not simply
> an immobile body subsequently set in
> motion, but a truly mobile object, which is a
> reality quite new and original.
>
> (Boccioni 1913/1973: 93)

Introduction

The promotion of 'the car' by states, as discussed in chapter 4, has also
entailed attempting to promote and produce a new type of person, a
new subject, oriented towards the sort of movement which cars make
possible. Cars presuppose and reproduce – or, rather, their benefits are
maximised by – an orientation to mobility which regards its maximisation and flexibilisation as a value, as something of positive meaning.
But for such subjectivities to arise, effort was expended. Thus at the
same time as automobility has been at the heart of the reproduction of
capitalist political economies it has also been closely bound up with the
shifts in the operations of power in modern societies, as emphasised by
Foucault, Virilio and others. It is now a commonplace to define modern
subjectivities as existing principally through movement itself, that the
modern subject *is* the mobile subject – or, otherwise put, to *be* modern
is to *be* mobile.[1] This chapter attempts to show how at the heart of
automobility's politics is the production of particular types of subjects.

I thus want here to focus on the way in which the emergence of a car
culture has been crucial to establishing the dominance of automobility.
While the naturalisation of the autonomy/mobility connection is basi-
cally flawed, as shown in chapter 3, it would be nevertheless inadequate and misleading to characterise the rise of the car simply as a story

---

[1] As we saw in relation to IR theory in chapter 1, this is often an uncritical
recognition. See, for example, Bellanger and Marzloff (1996) or Attali (2003).

of economic manipulation and political promotion: to treat, in effect, the emergence of the 'mobile subject' as simply the 'effect' of the dynamics examined in chapter 4. What Gorz (1980) called 'the social ideology of the motorcar' has become deeply entrenched in individual and collective identities; we need thus to investigate the processes by which this has come about. While the symbolisms of cars (speed, freedom, power, individualism and so on) are a common starting point for such analyses (e.g. Sachs 1992; Wolf 1996) I want rather to start with the way that such subjectivities are produced – the symbolisms of cars as evidenced in either people's expressions of self-identity or in advertising and marketing need to be seen as arising out of this history.

The way this is embedded in those identities seems to me, however, not best expressed in Gorz's terms. For Gorz (1980) the term 'ideology' is used in the sense of something which *masks* reality. Cars and their associated symbolisms operate as part of the 'false consciousness' of subordinated classes which prevents them from realising their 'real interests' and thus from working to overthrow capitalism. All that is required is to unmask this ideological cloak and social change becomes possible. This 'false consciousness' interpretation is one which most easily comes out of the political economy perspectives discussed in chapter 4. Similarly, Gartman (1994) and Wolf (1996) both treat the way that cars are embedded in identities as primarily a psychological reaction to alienation in the capitalist labour process: a means by which capitalism displaces the alienation it inevitably produces. The car for Wolf is then a 'substitute satisfaction' (1996: 192) or, for Gartman, an 'ersatz satisfaction' for the degradation of work under Fordist mass production (1994: 12). Outside Marxist discourses, psychologists tend also to adopt a similar image of the attachment to cars as signifying some sort of 'lack'. Cars are thus interpreted as a 'return to the womb' to overcome the birth trauma, or as the expression of power in a world without 'genuine' creativity (Zuckerman 1991: 57–8; see also Marsh and Collett 1986). But the notion of false consciousness, or alternatively, a 'psychological lack', which underlies these interpretations is deeply problematic. While the 'facts' they present (Gorz's argument about the impossibility of everyone owning a car, Wolf's concerning the myth of speed, for example) are not in doubt, it seems to me more useful to take seriously the reality and depth of the identities produced around the car. They should not be dismissed as false consciousness, which implies the manipulation of needs and interests and the existence of 'real interests' outside social construction. As Gartman argues, 'rather than see the needs appealed to by consumer goods as false needs engineered by the culture industry, my formulation conceptualizes them as true needs for self-determining activity channelled by class conflict into the only path compatible with capitalism – commodity consumption' (1994: 11). However, Gartman still relies on viewing mass consumption, notably of the car, as a displacement from the alienation produced by capitalist mass production. This in effect relies on a notion of human subjectivity which predates particular social forms and socio-technological projects; what is actually at stake is rather the way that human subjectivity *per se* – what it is to be 'me' – is produced.

Berman again seems to me to understand the relationship and contradiction better:

This strategy [of the promoters of the 'expressway world'] was effective because, in fact, the vast majority of modern men and women do not want to resist modernity: they feel its excitement and believe in its promise, even when they find themselves in its way. (1982: 313)

As Berman quotes Allen Ginsberg, the forms of identity produced in this process are not false, imposed purely to meet someone else's interests; they are more like 'Moloch, who entered my soul early' (1982: 291). The car is partly constitutive of who it is to be us, not something externally imposed on us through deceit. Understanding the relationship in terms of notions of the cyborg developed in general by Haraway (1991), and invoked in relation to the car by Luke (1996) or Thrift (1996), for example, gets closer to the complexities of the relationship between human identities and the machines through which such identities are shaped. The transformation of those identities cannot be achieved by simply showing their 'false' nature.

A more fruitful starting point might be with the varying ways in which automobility has been conceptualised in social theory. One of the most prominent such accounts is in the work of John Urry, in particular his *Sociology Beyond Societies: Mobilities for the Twenty-First Century* (2000). Urry suggests that rather than start with the concept of society, which suggests spatial fixity ('British society', 'Indian society', etc.), relatively closed social relations and stability over time, sociology should proceed from the concept of *mobilities*. Urry points out that mobility was a central theme within traditional sociologies but that this mobility was presumed to be bounded within a 'society', territorially defined. While there were always limits to this presumption it is now increasingly clear that the mobilities around which social life is organised exceed the spatial limits of territorially bound units. Automobility is for Urry central to the twentieth-century form that mobilities take and despite the appearance that the forms of movement involved are (paradoxically for his general argument) largely bound within 'national' societies, he is clear that for him this is not the case; since automobility is a 'system' which is not just about the act of driving cars, but a complex set of interrelations of six elements – production, consumption, machinic complexes, mobility, culture and environmental resource-use (as elaborated in chapter 1) – it should thus be conceptualised as expanding on a world-wide basis (2004: 27).

For my purposes here, the central question is how we may explain the rise of automobility's dominance. Clearly, a more general reconceptualisation of (modern) social life as fundamentally defined by an orientation to mobility is an important element in this, but an attempt to explain the specific rise of automobility is also necessary. Urry is more interested in describing the different elements which make up automobility as a 'system' and analysing some of its consequences (and possibilities for its transformation, which I discuss again in chapter 7) than in explaining the rise of automobility itself. This is clearest in his article on 'The "System" of Automobility' (2004) which analyses automobility in terms of systems theory. Urry argues that automobility should be understood as a 'self-organizing autopoietic non-linear system' (2004: 27). As a consequence it is difficult to identify a 'cause' in his arguments, partly because this is not the focus of his work. But two sorts of explanation can be discerned. First, the explanation for the rise of automobility is that societies become 'locked-in' to patterns of development which reproduce themselves: 'Once economies and societies were "locked-in" to what I conceptualize as the steel-and-petroleum car, then huge increasing returns resulted for those producing and selling the car and its associated infrastructure, products and services' (Urry 2004: 27).[2] A variant of this 'lock-in' argument is that the spatial structure of automobility – suburbanisation, highway development,

---

[2] For another systems-oriented account, although less theoretically sophisticated, see Schneider (1971: 59–60) who describes what he calls an 'iron law of automobile expansion'.

shopping malls, etc. – becomes coercive and renders car ownership and use necessary. This produces his nicely turned phrases that auto-mobility is 'immensely flexible *and* wholly coercive' (2000: 59), or that automobility '*coerces* people into an intense *flexibility*' (2004: 28). Car-dominated space 'forces people to orchestrate in complex and hetero-geneous ways their mobilities and socialities across very significant distances' (*ibid.*). But this explanation begs the question of how the process started, since the various processes of 'lock-in' occur only after the system has become dominant.

Urry's second explanation concerns the 'multiple desires and forms of inhabiting' for and of cars which 'have produced as unintended effect the expansion of the system of the privately owned and mobilized "steel-and-petroleum" car' (2004: 31).[3] These 'multiple desires and forms of inhabiting' include the instantaneity and flexibility of car travel, the seamlessness of car journeys, the changed forms of social interaction in cars (as opposed to when one is a pedestrian, for example), the intensified importance of visual experience in car driving, or the merging of human and machine involved (Urry 2004: 28–31). But while this may go some way to explaining the attractions of automobility it can hardly be used as an explanation for the investment made in expanding the system before significant numbers of people could even envisage owning a car, let alone actually owning one.

While one problem with Urry's account is the weakness of explaining how automobility came to be so dominant, another (albeit closely related) concerns the ways that politics appears in his account. While there is clearly the sense that automobility itself is coercive – in relation both to coercing people into being flexible and mobile and in terms of the bodily disciplines involved in the act of driving (e.g. 2004: 31), a more 'conventional' account of politics in the sense of how people are governed and how patterns of governance shape social developments (such as automobility) is largely absent from his analysis. Governance in this conventional sense comes purely in terms of the regulation of movement – how do governments deal with the various tensions and contradictions thrown up by automobility and its consequences?[4]

---

[3] He expands further on the notion of and practices of 'inhabiting' the car in Urry (2006).
[4] Tangential for the present purposes is the discussion of governance in Urry's concluding chapter in *Sociology Beyond Societies* (2000: esp. 188–90 and

Back to the problem of movement

But it is necessary to (a) historicise and (b) politicise this sort of account of mobility further. In addition to the contribution of political economy approaches as developed in chapter 4, it is useful to turn to Foucault's notion of 'the problem of movement'. Foucault discusses how in the eighteenth century, 'the problem of movement' became a central concern for governors.[5] By this, he means that they wished to create the conditions for the accelerated and controlled movement of people for a variety of purposes of 'government' (broadly construed). These needs were largely to create 'mobile, productive bodies' who could engage in economic production more effectively, move physically to where labour was needed and serve in the mass armies which were becoming required for military/strategic reasons.[6]

Foucault suggests the problem of movement had a number of elements. On the one hand, certain forms of movement had to be

195–200). He draws on Bauman's (1987) metaphor of 'gardening and gamekeeping' – that states shifted in the modern era from a mode of governance which entailed deciding who to keep in and out, restricting and regulating their movement (gamekeeping), to one which involved more careful 'tending' of subjects (gardening). Urry suggests that in an era of intensified global mobilities states are shifting back to a gamekeeping mode, unable to restrict the mobilities (of people, money, ideas, etc.) across the globe. This particular argument is akin to the 'decline of the state' argument in relation to the political/economic dimensions of globalisation, and like that is thoroughly unconvincing. While states may be unable to restrict certain forms of movement, they nevertheless tend their gardens ever more intensely. The implications of the automobility literature here – especially that, for example, concerning the 'car-driver' as hybrid subjectivity – is precisely that the mode of governance becomes progressively more 'interiorised' or 'biopolitical'. States work to produce particular types of mobile subjects which are productive and manageable, in a manner akin to a Foucauldian argument as developed below (or analogously in political/economic debates, states become 'competition states', rather than 'welfare states', see Douglas 1999; Cerny 2000).

[5] My reading of Foucault here draws heavily and shamelessly on the exegesis by Douglas (1999, esp. 40–147). I cannot see much point in charting a course through this material independently of his exemplary account.

[6] Although it is the modern period which is most pertinent here, the dynamics of statist or imperial domination, road construction and mobility, can be traced back further. For example, Charlesworth writes about the motorway programme: 'The idea of a national road system was introduced into Britain by the Romans, who needed a network of roads, first for military purposes of conquest and the maintenance of Roman authority and, second, as Romanisation spread, for purposes of trade and general communication. It is interesting to compare a map of main roads in Roman Britain ... with the motorway network of 1980' (Charlesworth 1984: 2, quoted in Wall 1999: 19).

proscribed, constrained and limited; in the mode of sovereign power, sovereigns attempted to control populations through a variety of means. Such sovereign conceptions arose out of, or at least occurred alongside, part of a general shift in the sixteenth and seventeenth centuries, with emerging mechanistic accounts of humanity and society exemplified, in different ways, by Hobbes and Descartes (Douglas 1999: 141). The account is more explicitly connected to modes of political organisation in Hobbes than in Descartes, Hobbes' account of the necessity of a Leviathan emphasising the mechanical motion of human bodies in collision with each other requiring a sovereign power to constrain them.[7] This mechanical conception of the body helped to enable accounts of governing which involved constraining and regularising the motions of bodies in society. Foucault, in *Madness and Civilisation* (1967), discusses how political disorder was understood to result from an 'excessive mobility of the fibres', and thus mobility 'must be measured and controlled . . . the cure consists in reviving in the sufferer a movement that will be both regular and real' (Foucault 1967: 172–3; see Douglas 1999: 141).

But at the same time as motion had to be regularised to prevent disorder it had to be promoted in order to make people productive. The tension between these two elements in governors' strategies plays itself out to the present day. Foucault tends to place the emergence of the 'disciplinary' form of power, attempting to shape and regularise movement, as dominant over the 'sovereign' form, attempting to restrict and control movement, in the late eighteenth and early nineteenth centuries. But at least in the seventeenth century some governors saw the value in promoting movement. Vauban,[8] for example, wrote that:

The greatest good that could ever happen to this kingdom would ensue, thanks to easier circulation of foodstuffs, which would produce a

---

[7] See especially *Leviathan*, chapter 13 (Hobbes 1651/1968: 183–8), where the account of the inevitable violent conflict is set up in terms of the notions of competition, diffidence and glory, all of which are understood by Hobbes to operate mechanically as consequences of how it is that humans *move* in the world. Meyer (2001: chapter 4) discusses this claim in detail, suggesting that Hobbes was less successful in practice in sustaining this claim about deriving politics from nature conceived in terms of motion.

[8] Vauban was, variously, commissioner general of fortifications, lieutenant general of the army and marshal of France in the late seventeenth and early eighteenth century (Mattelart 1996: 12).

considerable increase in them, and consequently a rise in well-being and convenience, and a very great ease for the provinces in helping each other in expensive years and in times of war. (Mattelart 1996: 7, quoting Vauban 1843: 139)

Vauban, along with other French officials (notably Colbert) produced elaborate plans to improve roadways, build canals, improve river navigation and so on, in order to improve the 'circulation' of goods and people throughout France (Mattelart 1996: 6–9).[9] These culminated in the mid-eighteenth century with a national policy to develop a road system across the whole country (*ibid.*: 9).

Metaphors of circulation and flow emerged during the eighteenth and nineteenth centuries to guide the principles of urban design in particular, to create the conditions for political order but also to increase the flows of goods and people and to make people productive for both economic and military purposes. These metaphors of circulation again have older roots, going back to Harvey's discovery of how blood circulates through the body, which were then deployed in political and social reasoning by, among others, Rousseau (Mattelart 1996: 16–21).[10]

The eighteenth century saw the emergence of political economy which provides the principal site at which an emphasis on the importance of promoting movement is articulated. The Physiocrats in France were the first to attempt systematically to explain the flow of wealth and think mathematically about production and exchange. François Quesnay, in particular, developed analyses in the 1750s that charted the movement of income through the economy and the first attempts to measure something like a 'national product'. Central to the success of the economy, in this view, is the importance of flows of people, goods and money; Quesnay postulated that only by '"guaranteeing circulation" ... will wealth be perpetuated and reproduced' (Mattelart 1996: 28).

---

[9] In French, this becomes more than a metaphor – while in English the term 'traffic' (originally meaning trade) becomes used in its contemporary sense of numbers of vehicles (reserving the older usage for illegal trade – drugs, etc.), in French *'circulation'* takes on its contemporary meaning – with, of course, the negative connotation that one of the terms for 'traffic jam' in French translates as 'too much circulation' (*trop de circulation*).

[10] Mattelart also notes that it was at this point that the word 'network' was first used in a meaning apart from that associated with lace making – in terms of blood circulation and human skin. See Mattelart (1996: 16).

In practical terms, this meant that the state should engage in aggressive measures to improve transport links (canals, roads; in the nineteenth century, railways), develop communication systems (semaphore, telegraph, telephone ...), reduce restrictions on movement (taxes, tolls, etc.) and work to improve the flow of money through banking systems. Turgot was the government official who carried out many of these activities in the later eighteenth century in France, aggressively developing the road network in particular (Mattelart 1996: 34–9).

The Physiocrats' arguments fell out of favour in the late eighteenth century in France, partly because they held that only agricultural production was 'truly' productive while agricultural interests often opposed free circulation (to protect their interests) and governors increasingly required industrial products for economic and military purposes. But the emphasis on free circulation was then taken up with a vengeance in the work of Adam Smith, who did not assume agricultural production to be the basis of all wealth, as well as by nationalist economists such as Friedrich List (Mattelart 1996: 54–8, 203–9). They differed in terms of whether they thought circulation should be promoted on a nationalist or internationalist basis, but both emphasised the government's centrality in the promotion of the means of circulation.

Warfare provided another impetus to the development of the means of movement. But while the discourses of political economy were more 'passive', in that they entailed a set of practices to *enable* movements to occur (improving road surfaces, etc.), with warfare came a set of practices to *channel* and *shape* people's orientation to movement more aggressively. As Douglas quotes Foucault:

At first, [disciplines] were expected to neutralize dangers, to fix useless or disturbed populations ... now they were being asked to play a positive role, for they were becoming able to do so, to increase the possible utility of individuals. Military discipline ... coordinates ... accelerates movements, increases firepower ... The discipline of the workshop ... tends to increase aptitudes, speeds, output. (Foucault 1977: 210; see Douglas 1999: 144–5)

One of the central transformations is thus the emergence of the mass army in the late eighteenth century, especially during the Napoleonic Wars. This helped to produce a set of disciplines through which populations were perceived less in negative terms by rulers, as to be constrained and ordered, and more in positive terms as being organised to enhance their usefulness. Bodies had thus to be mobilised rather than simply organised, in a practice of government which Foucault calls 'bio-power'.

Once mobilisation had become understood as a goal, the next move was the emergence of notions of acceleration, emphasised more by Virilio than Foucault. Virilio suggests that in the nineteenth century society moved from the 'age of the brakes to the age of the accelerator' (1983; see Douglas 1999). Such a shift at the same time entails an increasing motorisation of movement to enable the accelerated movement of goods, workers and armies. But such motorisation and attention to acceleration simultaneously complicates the legitimation of such governance practices: as Virilio puts it, the 'freedom of movement' attained early on in the French Revolution, quickly became the 'dictatorship of movement' (1986: 30). Mobility, then, became 'simultaneously the *means to liberation* and the *means to domination*' (Douglas 1999: 147).

The central technologies in the nineteenth century which served to mobilise people in this way were the train and the telegraph (Mattelart 1996: 47–53). The forerunners of the telegraph, principally highly co-ordinated semaphore systems, were developed during the French revolutionary wars as a means of sophisticated marshalling of troops in a 'war of movement'. These combined with the use of road networks and reorganisation of military hierarchies and divisions to increase military power: 'Instead of troops formed in rectangles and a compact organization of a troop in depth, he [de Guibert, the principal architect of such new military methods, writing in 1770] proposed linear formations, a firing line, and mobile columns, which, when troops are on the offensive, form a converging network' (Mattelart 1996: 200). Such a mobile form of army required intensified means of communication to co-ordinate itself and highly developed logistics (transport, food, etc.), to enable it to continue its operations successfully. These techniques of warfare were then adopted to great effect by Napoleon and profoundly influenced thought about military strategy in the nineteenth century.

The train fitted well into this military logic. Train systems, in addition to their economic function, facilitated significant acceleration of mobilisation of armies, shipment of supplies to the lines and so on: 'With the steam engine, we are in the presence of a weapon of movement that extends the weapon of war' (Virilio 1978: 24, quoted in Mattelart

1996: 49). But the consequences were also a rearticulation of power outside the military sphere: 'The operating rules of railways would be copied from those of the military. The cult of exact schedules would be that of a strategy of tensions necessitated by the requirements of traffic safety' (Virilio 1978: 21, quoted in Mattelart 1996: 50). The development of the railways, both to create the conditions of military mobilisation and to accelerate the circulation of goods to promote economic growth, simultaneously entailed a greater disciplining of those who travelled. Strict timetables were required for predictability, which required further development of timekeeping methods (and their standardisation across national or regional spaces), to which not only workers in the railways but travellers also had to be subjected. One example of the consequences of this shift is the rapid development of a market for watches in the late nineteenth century as people attuned themselves to the new need for precision in timekeeping (Thrift 1996: 265).

Trains also attuned people to speed, producing a situation where for the first time a significant number of people could move faster than they could walk. They started to produce industries which have become staples of the global economy – tourism as a mass pursuit became possible because of the train. Trains also produced for the first time the possibility of significant distanciation between home and workplaces: at the same time as they produced significant economic shifts, they entailed shifts in sensibility, in people's orientations to movement.

A final important shift in the late nineteenth century is the way in which travel was reconceptualised as *transport* (Bonham 2006). There was a change in the nature of subjectivity, involving an 'increasing sense of the body as an anonymised parcel of flesh which is shunted from place to place' (Thrift 1996: 266). A range of bodies of expert knowledge emerged which encouraged a shift in thinking away from simply travel towards '*transport*: movement from one point to another in order to participate in the activities at the "trip destination"' (Bonham 2006: 58). Movement, especially in urban settings, was increasingly calculated, monitored and planned, but at the same time valued according to its purposefulness and the efficiency with which a particular journey was undertaken: 'Through the late nineteenth and early twentieth century . . . efficient movement was popularised as the principle by which to guide the arrangement of street-space and the ordering of urban traffic' (Bonham 2006: 58). This principle emerges as part of what during the twentieth century become transport planning and urban planning, as both academic disciplines and practices of city governments.

The emergence of automobility

During the twentieth century, automobility became both the dominant form of daily movement over much of the planet (dominating even those who do not move by car) and the prime means through which the 'dictatorship of movement' was legitimised. But the emergence of automobility can be understood in terms of similar governing pressures to those understood by Vauban, quoted earlier: It would enable 'easier circulation of foodstuffs, which would produce a considerable increase in them, and consequently a rise in well-being and convenience, and a very great ease for the provinces in helping each other in expensive years and in times of war': growth in consumption, legitimacy for the state and the means of making war. But the historical moment in which automobility arises is the point at which other forms of mobility start to encounter problems. Two principal areas are worth emphasising.

One is that by around the end of the nineteenth century people started to complain about the rigidities of trains and trams, not only in terms of the structuring of cities around fixed-line transport net-works, or the way that people's lives were subordinated to timetables, but also as a populist reaction against the monopolistic practices of many of the transport companies. Trains in many places became associated with movement as a 'dictatorship' and less as 'liberation'.

In this context, the importance of the way that cars could be linked to freedom and mobility has reflected the way that industrial societies have become increasingly regimented and bureaucratised to serve the needs of industrial production: 'More than any other consumer good the motor car provided fantasies of status, freedom and escape from the constraints of a highly disciplined urban, industrial order' (McShane 1994: 148; see also Ling 1990: 4–5). This fantasy was particularly important since even in the United States, the most motorised country in the world, no one was actually able to commute or even, apart from a very tiny number, travel far (for example) on holiday, until after the Second World War (McShane 1994: 125–7).

It is thus no accident that this was the period at which speed became distinctly valorised and became, in Freund and Martin's terms, 'the premier cultural icon of modern societies' (1993: 89). Berman (1982) makes this explicit in his account of modernity; while for him the central general feature of modernity is that 'all that is solid melts into air', in the early twentieth century this continual change is effected through continuous acceleration brought about by new transportation technologies, primarily the car. Bauman quotes Giedion, Le Corbusier's most famous 'disciple' (Berman's term) in architecture and urban design, relating this explicitly to the car: 'The space–time feeling of our period can seldom be felt so keenly as when driving' (Giedion 1949, quoted in Berman 1982: 302). Berman also quotes Le Corbusier:

On that 1st of October, 1924, I was assisting in the titanic rebirth of a new phenomenon ... traffic. Cars, cars, fast, fast! One is seized, filled with enthusiasm, with joy ... the joy of power. (Berman 1982: 166)

The association is then one from modernity and modernisation, with built-in notions of progress (which are so valorised that they cannot be resisted) to acceleration and increasing speed, and thus the car becomes a primary symbol of modernity itself. The driving experience becomes itself an end, not simply a means.

The second impetus was the experience of the First World War. As noted in chapter 1, one famous account of the war's origins was that it was caused by train timetables (Taylor 1969). While trains had made possible massive increases in the speed of mobilisation, the numbers of troops and weaponry which could be rapidly transported to a front line, they did so in a way which was exceptionally dependent on the strict following of schedules: once mobilisation was started, it was practically impossible to stop it. But even without this understanding, what was clear was that when the war started, the balance of forces in terms of the prevailing weaponry (the heavy machine gun and the shell) was weighted overwhelmingly in favour of defence and this situation was transformed only by technologies of movement, principally the armoured tank (Virilio 1986: 51–5). As in Napoleon's day the decisive advantage came with those who innovated in terms of their ability to move. Hitler, in particular, recognised this; as Virilio makes clear (1986: 25–7) the Nazis developed the 'National Socialist Automobile Corps' in order to get round rules about rearmament while preparing sufficient people to use the mobility of cars to 'increase the Assault Forces' strength by an extraordinary degree' (Virilio 1986: 27).

Automobiles helped to respond to these two blockages to the circulatory system as well as to enhance the possibilities for utility maximisation and 'system maintenance'.[11] But the principal innovation is the way that they did so through articulating individuals into a 'circulatory system' as active participants, makers of their own travel plans, etc. rather than 'passive' recipients of transport services. In the First World War, for example, cars became recognised as progressive, as having enabled the break-up of the rigid trench warfare that had prevailed for much of the conflict and having thus furthered national 'progress'. It also contributed to specific liberations, notably for women in enhancing their range of opportunities outside the 'domestic' sphere (e.g. Scharff 1991: chapter 6; Möser 1998) but also (and in a contradictory fashion) for men whose masculinity was threatened by the decline of physical labour due to industrialisation (McShane 1994) and by the emergence of feminism itself: cars served to reconstitute masculinity around questions of technical competence (Scharff 1991; McShane 1994; O'Connell 1998). Thus, while automobility reflects a longer-standing 'problem of movement', it entails a specific form of power able (apparently) to present itself purely in terms of the *means to liberation*. As a specific mode of organising movement, automobility thus emerges as a set of institutions, discourses and practices through which mobility can again be understood as freedom:

The stroke of genius will consist in doing away with the direct repression of riots, and the political discourse itself . . . the transportation capacity created by the mass production of automobiles (since 1914 with Ford) can become a social assault, a revolution sufficient and able to modify the citizen's way of life by transforming all the consumer's needs. (Virilio 1986: 26)

I will turn later to discourses of automobiles in terms of freedom; for the moment what is important is to emphasise the enormous effort which has gone into establishing the possibility of their appearance as freedom, and also that the consequences of such freedom in fact do serve more general, collective goals: that automobility, in effect, is a perfect example of what Mick Dillon usefully terms the 'strategic orchestration of the self-regulating freedoms of populations' (2003: 135).

---

[11] For example, especially in the United States, an early major market for automobiles was among doctors, enhancing the possibilities of medical services in rural areas and thus increasing the productivity of farmers (e.g. McShane 1994).

We have already seen in chapter 4 that states spent considerable sums developing the road network, downgrading public transport in favour of cars and so on. Here, what is worth emphasising is the attention and resources which were devoted in the early part of the twentieth century to the micro-aspects of these efforts. City and national governments spent much energy (nearly going bankrupt in some cases) on improving road surfaces, drainage, regularising rules to do with traffic (parking rules, which side of the road to drive on, traffic lights[12] and so on) to improve its flow as well as contain its side-effects (crashes, congestion) which might delegitimise the system as a whole. As they re-made surfaces to enable easier travel by car, bicycle and transit, they restructured the nature of the street as a multi-use site to being a thoroughfare – a space for moving through (McShane 1994: chapter 4). Resources were disproportionately devoted to road construction and maintenance rather than transit, even while the vast majority of actual urban mobility (even in the United States) was carried out through walking, cycles, horses and various forms of mass transit. Later, after the Second World War (but with its forerunners in fascist Italy and Germany), constructions of national networks of motorways (or similar title[13]) reproduced the implications of circulatory metaphors by creating a national space of potentially unlimited movement. Such networks all have military origins as well as the more obvious economic and ideological intent, intending either to be able to move military forces in a faster and more flexible manner than trains, and/or (especially articulated in the United States in the nuclear age) to enable rapid evacuation of major cities in response to military attack.

The process of suburbanisation should be seen as a crucial part of this process. This is not only in the sense that the spatial change entailed in low-density development with extensive separation of places of home, work, education and leisure, and the shift from 'corridor'

---

[12] For Berman, the invention of these (in the United States in 1905) was 'a wonderful symbol of early state attempts to regulate and rationalize the chaos of capitalism' (1982: 159).

[13] *Autostrada*, *autobahn* and later *autoroute* emphasise the 'auto', with its conflation of the 'autonomous' self and the 'automation' of the machine. 'Motorway' more unambiguously emphasises its motorised nature, emphasising the differences from other roads which still in 1940s and 1950s Britain had a varied set of users. 'Freeway', of course, has the most immediately ideological content, emphasising both the liberty-producing effects and the lack of charges (although on many, tolls were later introduced).

developments associated with the train or tram to more loosely structured patterns of development rendered public transport increasingly
problematic.[14] This aspect of the governance of automobility – that car
driving increasingly became a mundane necessity as a consequence of
such spatial change – was certainly important. But the process was
more complex still, in that suburbanisation was also a more positive
means by which the set of life-projects of individuals and communities
were produced and reproduced. Ideologies of the value of rural living
or small towns, the desire for space or a 'closeness to nature', at times
infused with racism or class prejudice, were also reproduced through
the process of suburbanisation: they have often appeared (and still do
in, for example, the ideological renditions of Lomasky and others) as
the positive ability of people to realise their aspirations. These aspirations are nevertheless articulated with the interests of land developers,
car and oil firms and municipal authorities in such a way that the
process becomes self-feeding and increasingly difficult to resist, or for
an alternative to be imagined. Suburbanisation has nevertheless
entailed picking up on particular aspirations and organising societies
to enable their (partial and contradictory) fulfilment in a way which
involves producing certain sorts of subjectivities which value suburban
environments and the forms of mobility and sociality which they make
necessary.

These efforts therefore present a significant enhancement of the
regulatory powers of the state in relation to the everyday actions of
individuals. As automobility developed, it was simultaneously ordered.
A first, and relatively obvious element is the way that the regulation of
the use of street-space was reshaped from something of mixed use, with
a range of economic, leisure, social, political, as well as travel activities
going on, to being a place principally of purposive and efficient movement from one place to another: transport (Bonham 2006). Bonham
(2006) shows how in Adelaide in the early twentieth century regulations were introduced which restricted the presence of things (people,
animals, inanimate objects) which would impede the flow of traffic,
and how different sorts of moving bodies (cycles, pedestrians, those on
or with horses, trams, automobiles) were categorised and regulated

[14] As conventionally emphasised by transport planners; see, for example, Newman
and Kenworthy (1999: 27–33).

accordingly. Bonham's analysis is exemplary of processes (and the contestation of these new regulations) in many cities at the time.

But the forms of power went beyond a regulatory balancing of the interests of different individuals or groups; they also entailed producing 'drivers' as particular sorts of individuals who could function success-fully in the new automobile environments, and re-produced other sorts of people who needed to adapt to them. This also simultaneously involved the emergence of a whole paraphernalia of new rules, advice and training for drivers, road signs and so on to prepare drivers for the new driving conditions and the skills and mentalities required to navi-gate them. Drivers' licences were introduced in most places which, as Bonham (2006) notes, 'marks the first time in the state's history that private travellers were required to obtain permission to travel by their preferred means of mobility'. This created a means of distinguishing between those 'fit' and 'unfit' to drive, as well as the possibility of producing, keeping and analysing data about drivers through records of traffic offences, accidents and so on. Projects were developed to educate pedestrians – in particular, about the new dangers and the appropriate means of behaving on newly automobilised streets.

There was then the parallel production of other subjects who must co-exist with cars. One of the principal long-term consequences has been the reshaping of the experience of urban space by children: their reduced independence, the reduced range of places where they are allowed to go alone, their reduced levels of physical exercise. As such, the automobile subject has thus physically reshaped bodies (e.g. Hillman *et al.* 1991; Meikle 2001).

Merriman (2006: 83) analyses the processes associated with the opening of the first large motorway in the United Kingdom, the M1, in 1959, showing the concerns that many had that such a new road would create many problems as drivers would lack the skills and experience necessary to successfully and safely operate on it. He thus shows how through a range of interventions, motorway drivers were 'produced' and emphasises three elements in the governance which aimed to bring this about. First, new objects came into existence – specific forms of road signs, the Motorway Code, enhanced attention to the importance of wing mirrors, the marketing of specific tyres for motorway driving. Second were the deployment of particular experts – he emphasises the role of AA patrolmen and racing drivers – to provide reports on the state of the road, emphasise the new skills necessary to drive on it and so on. As part of their competitive strategy with the RAC, the AA 'perceived their role as being to study, as well as effect and facilitate changes to, the performance of drivers *and* vehicles: studying the behaviour of motorists and vehicles; educating motorists about good driving and vehicle maintenance; and spotting and repairing vehicles that had broken down' (Merriman 2006). Third were the activities of the Road Research Laboratory, which conducted research into the patterns of movement by cars on the motorway, patterns and causes of accidents, how the shape of the motorway (road lanes, hard shoulders, even the landscaping and planting on the verge) could be organised best and the development of service stations, again subtly reshaping the particular ways in which people would interact with the road and others around them.

These governance practices, which shape and produce *new types of people* consistent with automobility's logics, are fundamentally 'dromocratic' in the sense articulated by Virilio in chapter 1. Such 'dromocratic' projects remain a key part of political processes; the TransEuropean Networks, developing corridors of development across Europe, while designed to facilitate economic growth and integration in the manner demonstrated in chapter 4, also operate as a key part of a European political integration project. Corridors and regions are constructed across national borders to support the development of European identities, or at least weaken national ones (as Ek 2004 shows concerning the emergence of Öresund as a region) and to construct people as 'dromocratic travellers' rather than 'democratic citizens' – that is, as 'a politically unquestioning, highly mobile "useful tool", intoxicated by the fascination of speed' (Ek 2004: 18).

This production of 'drivers' as specific sorts of people has involved two other developments. One is the elaborate phenomenology of cars and the spaces they simultaneously inhabit and produce: much of the contemporary interest in automobility in sociology, cultural studies and geography concentrates on the way in which a huge variety of sensibilities, orientations, habits and so on have coalesced around automobiles and the daily routines they effect (e.g. Miller 2001; Featherstone *et al.* 2004). These analyses range from studies on the importance of sound (in particular music) to people's daily use and experience of driving (Bull 2001, 2004), specific car subcultures (Garvey 2001; O'Dell 2001), to those on the way that the 'view from the windscreen' articulates with other technologies which shape visual experience in similar ways (television, cinema) (see the contributions to Wollen and Kerr 2002), to the ways that the car becomes a 'home' (Urry 2006) and to more subtle ways in which automobility has transformed urban spaces – for example Thrift's focus on the illumination of cities to 'facilitate the movement of motor vehicles' (2004: 46, quoting Jakle 2001: 255). These analyses help to understand the transformations in subjectivities brought about by automobility but also the way that such transformations are readily understood as the active participation by subjects in it. They could thus be articulated by Lomasky and others with the uncritical celebration of automobiles as extensions of individual freedom.

This second consequence is that the production of drivers cannot usefully be thought of as a grafting of particular skills and orientations onto pre-existing humans who then are able to control machines which remain separate from them, but rather the production of hybrid subjectivities which are the particular meshing of humans and machines. The ambiguity present in the very term 'automobility' serves as a good way of introduction to this way of thinking about the 'automobile subject'. There is little ambiguity in the noun 'automobile' – an artefact which moves itself. It is immediately connected to the term 'automatic' or 'automation', which again implies movement or action without external force being applied. But at the same time the whole ideological apparatus of automobility serves to emphasise that not only does it refer to the vehicle moving itself but that the person using the vehicle is simultaneously 'moving autonomously' – this is a mobility which serves, produces and makes possible human autonomy. In one mode of imagining, the car is a machine which moves itself; in another, automobility involves a fusing of car and driver which means that the car is a prosthetic and it is the driver who is moving autonomously. This conception is used by many who refer to automobiles in terms of notions of 'cyborg' or 'hybridity', some coining the term 'carson' to refer to the merger of car and person (Luke 1996; Thrift 1996; Lupton 1999).[15] There is widespread recognition and articulation that 'drivers

---

[15] Dant (2004) objects to both the term 'cyborg' and' hybrid' in relation to the 'driver-car' subjectivity, the first because (in his view) it should be reserved for prosthetic extensions of or replacement for body parts which 'cybernetically organise' human bodies, the second because it suggests a permanent (and sterile) merging of two organisms (as in horticulture). As Merriman (forthcoming) suggests, Dant has too narrow a view of how these concepts may be 'mobilised'

experience cars as extensions of their bodies' (Thrift 2004: 47) – a widely quoted comment by a Californian city planner in the 1930s was that 'it might be said that Southern Californians have added wheels to their anatomy' (Flink 1988: 143). The various technical elements in cars (from the simple framing device of the windscreen, rear view mirror or steering wheel to the emergence of 'head-up display' or GPS navigation systems) operate not only as extensions of human agency but transform its nature,[16] while the car's shell becomes a 'second skin' and the interior is increasingly moulded around the driver's body.[17] Invoking notions of hybridity is not simply an abstraction; it has significant and productive consequences for how we understand specific aspects of automobility. For example, Michael (2001) uses the notion to advance the understanding of the phenomenon of 'road rage', by showing how it is the particular ways in which cars and drivers merge to become hybrids which produce the phenomenon, while an account avoiding thinking this way always wants to 'purify' the 'cause' of road rage by blaming 'either' the car (or traffic jams, overregulation, or some other feature of the 'car system') 'or' the driver (as, for example, Marshall and Thomas 2000). Beckmann (2004) shows the utility of the notion of hybrids in interpreting the dynamics of traffic safety politics.

Three principal areas (especially when combined) are currently the principal sites where we can both see at work this (re)production and governance of automobile subjectivities. These concern safety, environmental politics (narrowly understood) and the spatial contradictions of automobility (congestion). Automobility is being reshaped through

and when he states that 'the human remains complete in his or her self' when using a car, essentialises the 'human' and misses the transformations of subjectivity which occur (Merriman forthcoming, quoting Dant 2004: 62). In the end, Dant ends up with an assertion of human agency and independence resonant of Lomasky's libertarianism (if more sophisticated theoretically): 'the car does not simply afford the driver mobility or have independent agency as an actant; it enables a range of humanly embodied actions available only to the driver-car' (Dant 2004: 74).

16 Ihde (1974: 272, as quoted in Urry 2004: 31) describes the process of reversing into a parking space to illustrate the way a driver 'feels' the space and movements required; 'he "feels" the very extension of himself though the car as the car becomes a symbiotic extension of his own embodiedness'.

17 Thrift (2004: 50–1) usefully emphasises the importance of the emergence of ergonomics in the way that cars come to act as extensions of (and transformations of) human agency.

informationalisation: the application of a range of software and communications technology to the body of the car – 'Now software controls engine management, brakes, suspension, wipers and lights, cruising and other speeds, parking manoeuvres, speech recognition systems, communication and entertainment, sound systems, security, heating and cooling, in-car navigation and . . . crash protection systems' (Thrift 2004: 50). This can be an application of software to pre-existing activities or can create new activities and is occurring in ways which extend the intertwining of car and driver in new directions – taking some functions away from drivers, adding others, altering the nature of interaction with others on the road and so on. It also occurs in conjunction with the informationalisation of the street: the intermingling of car and road now goes far beyond the immediate need for reasonably smooth surfaces and regular petrol stations to encompass a range of ongoing communications with satellites, traffic signals, internet traffic management systems and so on. These systems have emerged partly in response to the technological fetishism of consumer markets (DVD players as a technological 'solution' to the 'problem' of bored children and so on) and of course to car firms' search for profits[18] but also partly to 'solve' a range of issues of safety, pollution and congestion. The consequences are to intensify the forms of power operating both through and over drivers (and others). The power of drivers to know about and avoid congestion, to drive into 'wilderness' spaces and know someone can find them, to engage in multiple other forms of communication (phone, internet, etc.) while driving, or simply to have a more immediate and intensified sense of control over the vehicle, is enhanced by such technologies. But this power is nevertheless both highly dependent on the networks within which it is enmeshed (as Thrift notes

---

[18] Thrift (2004: 50) suggests that firms are devising strategies to make software systems a means of ensuring a competitive edge, by assuming that customers will be loath to change manufacturers if it requires in effect learning a new software language. He suggests (2004: 56, n. 20) that this process has already started as the service relationship with a manufacturer is now conducted partly to meet software problems with the car rather than mechanical ones. Certainly, software as a marketing strategy has begun in earnest, most notably in GM's aggressive branding of its OnStar safety system where the car is connected via GPS to a range of security systems which can track it if it is stolen (and, of course, when it isn't), if the driver is lost or breaks down, accidentally locks their keys in the car and then call out various emergency services (or, in the case of the latter, remotely unlock the car).

(2004: 51), the more immediate sense of control is ironic since that sense is produced precisely by a *more* intensely mediated set of perceptions) and also enables drivers to be continuously monitored and controlled. 'The result is that both surveying and being surveyed will increasingly become a norm' (Thrift 2004: 51–2): GPS enables drivers to navigate journeys more precisely, find out where they are, find alternative routes and so on but simultaneously enables them to be tracked and monitored – for example, enabling remote sensing of speeding[19] as well as the more commonplace automated payment systems for 'smart' toll roads.

The emergence and continued reproduction of automobility is thus simultaneously a *means to liberation* and *means of domination* (Douglas 1999: 147). Cars express human freedom but they simultaneously express it through the subordination of the human body not only to the technology of the car itself and the disciplines this imposes (concentration, immobility within the car itself, etc.) but also to the whole panoply of regulatory mechanisms constraining the automobilist's practices as a driver – from parking restrictions and traffic lights to tax regimes or pollution control requirements. People thus participate intimately in the production of their subjection to this order, conceiving it precisely as the realisation of their freedom – what I read the term 'governmentality' to mean: in Douglas' term 'the passing of the command structure to the very constitution of the individual' (1999: 138).

Automobile identities: selling cars

The multiple symbolisms of cars have both reflected and contributed to this historical emergence of the 'automobile subject'. 'The alliance of those whose livelihood depends on a robust automobile-centred

---

[19] Such regulation need not only be by states. In 2001 a car rental company in New Haven, Connecticut, used the GPS tracking system in its fleet to charge renters who travelled over 80 mph at $150 per 2-minute period over that speed, on the grounds of 'excessive wear and tear' (Greenman 2001). A Connecticut court ruled the practice illegal, but the technical possibility clearly exists, and debates about whether it is legitimate for states to use this technology to police speeding are underway in many places. In the United Kingdom, for example, the government's Commission for Integrated Transport (CIT) argued that such technologies could be used both to regulate speeding and as the means for organising payments for congestion charging on busy roads (Dodd 2002).

culture ... also feed[s] on the cultural symbolism of the automobile: freedom, individualism, mobility, speed, power, and privacy' (Tiles and Oberdiek 1995: 137). Such symbolic connections are ubiquitous in the variety of cultural arenas where cars are widely valorised (Baird 1998: 28–35). There is a substantial literature on such symbolisms as they have been constructed in novels (Laird 1983; Howe 2002; Samuels 2002; Miller 2006; Thacker 2006) discussing both obvious novels such as Kerouac's *On the Road*, Ballard's *Crash* and Grahame's *The Wind in the Willows* and a broad range of works where the symbolic connections are less obvious or iconic.[20] There is an even bigger literature on cars and film (Hey 1983; Julian Smith 1983; Eyerman and Löfgren 1995; Ross 1995; Cohan and Hark 1997; Urry 2000: 62; Mottram 2002; Pascoe 2002; Rees 2002; Featherstone 2004: 14–15) and a smaller literature on cars in visual art (Silk 1983; von Vegesack and Kries 1999; Wollen 2002[21]).

Less recognised, but arguably no less important given its importance generally in popular culture since the mid-twentieth century is the place

---

[20] While Ballard's *Crash* (1973) is a staple citation, his *Concrete Island* (1974) is arguably a more interesting commentary on automobility and the alienating urban landscape which its produces. *Concrete Island* concerns a man (Robert Maitland) who crashes through a barrier onto an island in a motorway junction in West London and becomes marooned as on a desert island. The novel is a metaphor for the alienation produced by car-dominated cityscapes and the way in which they become a self-reproducing space both physically and psychically. The island is an enclosed space from which it is possible to escape only by climbing up steep banks and crossing motorway traffic. Maitland starts by making repeated attempts to escape and failing, but then accommodates himself to the island, finds food, meets two others who live there (one of whom has a way of getting out to work and who provides food for the others), explores the island finding remnants of buried earlier cityscapes (old houses, shops, a cinema) under the rubble of the motorway. In the end one of the other people offers to help him escape but he stays, preferring an endless dream of plans to escape than actually leaving. Cars are at times treated in less 'serious' novels, including their contested nature, as in Tom Sharpe's *Blott on the Landscape* (1977), a fictionalised story loosely based on the well-known anti-motorway protester in the UK in the 1970s (John Tyme), or Ben Elton's *Gridlock* (1991).

[21] The book by von Vegesack and Kries (1999) is actually associated with a large historical exhibition at the Vitra Design Museum near Basle on the history and culture of automobility, combined with critical essays from a range of authors including Wolfgang Sachs and Paul Virilio. The weakness of my German prevents me doing anything more than making reference to it, but it has the impression of an interesting set of pieces and the collection of images on the subject is unsurpassed.

of cars in popular music,[22] whose symbolisms range from the celebratory to the critical to merely underscoring the ubiquity of cars. Some celebrate the joy of driving for its own sake, as in Chuck Berry's 'No particular place to go', in Bobby Troup's 'Route 66' (originally 1946, later covered widely, including by Bob Dylan and by the Rolling Stones), The Beach Boys 'I Get Around' or 'Fun, Fun, Fun', or in Madness' 'Driving in my car', where the banality of driving is precisely the point ('I drive up to Muswell Hill, I've even been to Selsey Bill'). Others focus on the car as a means of escape; Tracy Chapman writes 'You got a fast car, and I got us a plan to get out of here' ('Fast Car'), while a car is a means to leave someone in Vince Taylor's 'Brand New Cadillac' (with a later and more widely known version by The Clash). In others, it provides compensation for other problems, as in the Beatles' 'Drive My Car' ('Working for peanuts is all very fine, but I can show you a better time, Baby you can drive my car'), while some more crudely emphasise speed (Deep Purple, 'Speed King'). Others suggest privacy and safety as the key dimensions – 'Here in my car, I feel safest of all, I can lock all my doors, it's the only way to live, in Cars' (Gary Numan, 'Cars'[23]). Others emphasise the connections to sex or sexuality – from the straightforward use of cars to attract women ('I get around', or Bruce Springsteen's 'Pink Cadillac'), to the euphemisms of Chuck Berry ('Can you imagine the way I felt, I couldn't unfasten her safety belt'), to the sexualising of the car itself, intertwined with that of the woman, in Prince's 'Little Red Corvette' or Billy Ocean's 'Get out of my dreams, and into my car', to the direct and misogynist as in NWA's 'Automobile'.[24] Motown itself as a

[22] There is some literature on this theme. See in particular Belasco (1983), Pruett (1990), Gilroy (2001), Field (2002) and Widmer (2002). The coverage which follows necessarily reflects disproportionately the where and when of my teenage years (the United Kingdom, late 1970s–early 1980s), but similar narratives could be constructed from many times and places. Thanks are due to Jo VanEvery, Andreas Krebs and especially Chris Green for extra suggestions.

[23] Numan's song emphasises both the physical safety he feels in cars but also the emotional, even existential security it provides. The second verse is more ambivalent about this: 'Here in my car, Where the image breaks down, Will you visit me please, If I open my door in cars, Here in my car, You know I've started to think, About leaving tonight, Although nothing seems right in cars.'

[24] The sexualisation of the car precedes the rock and roll era: Widmer (2002) gives many examples from 1920s and 1930s blues.

phenomenon is also worth mentioning here (S. E. Smith 1999; Gilroy 2001: 91).

Tom Waits' 'Diamonds on my windshield' combines some of these themes particularly well:

And there are diamonds on my windshield
And these tears from heaven
Well I'm pulling into town on the Interstate
I got me a steel train in the rain
And the wind bites my cheek through the wing
Late nights and freeway flying
Always makes me sing
It always makes me sing.

XTC's 'Roads Girdle the Globe' does the same, as in the epigraph to chapter 1:

Roads girdle the globe
We all safe in your concrete robe
Hail mother motor
Hail piston rotor
Hail wheel
. . .
Oil, iron, steel
You holy three.

Others are more ambivalent, or even critical.[25] Julian Cope's album 'Autogeddon Blues' revolves almost entirely around the problems of automobility as articulated in chapter 2. But he expresses it ambivalently, recognising the pull of cars, as well as focusing on the way they have come to be necessary, as in for example in 'Ain't no getting around getting around': 'Yeah, I'm just one more Polluter, But the Travel-bug has got me, And the buggers all have Taught me . . ., That there ain't no gettin' round gettin' round'.[26] Gang of Four similarly recognised the huge consequences of automobility combined with the normative value of cars: 'A man with a good car, needs no justification, Fate is in my

---

[25] I am not sure how far a historical analysis can be pushed here, but certainly other works which focus on the period before the 1970s almost exclusively contain only celebratory symbolisms of cars (e.g. Belasco 1983; Widmer 2002).
[26] More simply, with religious overtones, was Chris Rea's 'The road to hell', adverts for which depicted a motorway sign showing the M25, which had recently opened.

hands, and in the transmission.' Adam Ant suggested a technologically determinist vision in 'Car Trouble': 'Have you ever had a ride in a light blue car? Have you ever stopped to think who's the slave and who's the master?', as well as commenting on the ways cars figure in people's lives to mark class and status: 'you might have seen them very busy at the weekends, licking and polishing the beep-beeps into shape, and then its proudly up the M.1. M.2. M.3., and keep your feet off the upholstery Ronnie, car trouble oh yeah' and gender politics: 'I used to sit at home silently and wonder, why all the preference is polishing the chrome, while all the mothers and the sisters and the babies, sit and rot at home'. Dave Edmunds writes in 'Crawling from the wreckage' about driving home after too many drinks: 'crawling from the wreckage, crawling from the wreckage, you'd think by now that at least that half my brain would get a message, crawling from the wreckage, crawling from the wreckage, into a brand new car.' Radiohead worry about danger in 'Killer Cars', while Kraftwerk intone for 22 minutes that '*Wir fahr'n fahr'n fahr'n auf der Autobahn*' (We drive, drive, drive down the motorway), effectively creating the sense of monotony in this sort of journey. The cover for the single recreates ideal-typical images of the open road and reflects the middle lines of the verse – '*Die sonne scheint mit glitzerstrahl, Die fahrbahn ist ein graues band, Weisse streifen, gruener rand*' (The sun is shining with glittering rays, The driving strip is a grey track, White stripes, green edge), while that for the album has an image reflecting a motorway road sign.

Others resist the totalising identifications of cars with status, as in William DeVaughan's 'Be thankful for what you've got' (re-popularised by Massive Attack in 1990). Echoing and reversing the sentiment in 'Drive My Car' that the lack of a car is a lack elsewhere in life ('I got no car and it's breaking my heart'), DeVaughan suggests 'You may not drive a great big Cadillac, gangsta white walls and a TV antenna in the back, though may not have a car at all, remember brothers and sisters, you can still stand tall'. As Gilroy (2001) suggests, after quoting the same lines, 'this is a very long way from Missy Elliott's insistent, insinuating request to know "Beep beep, who got the keys to the Jeep?"' (Gilroy 2001: 91).

Many songs are a testament to the ubiquity of cars and their ability to symbolise the staple in pop music lyrics – relationships, anxieties, and so on – and at times stranger subject matters. See, for example, Tom Robinson's '2468 motorway' and 'Grey Cortina', Pearl Jam's 'Many

Fast Cars', Ken Clinger's 'Automobiles' (which has intimations of cars as themselves social agents – 'automobiles meeting in secret, automobiles making their plans, automobiles scanning their future, visions of highways eternal'), Robyn Hitchcock's 'I watch the cars', U2's 'Daddy's going to pay for your crashed car', Ian Dury's 'Billericay Dickie' ('Had a love affair with Nina, in the back of my Cortina', on which see also chapter 6 below), Meatloaf's 'Paradise by the Dashboard Light', David Bowie's 'Always crashing in the same car' (see also Dery 2006), or Bob Dylan's 'Highway 61 revisited'.

These themes are reflected, more or less subtly and with varying sorts of normative reflection, in car advertising. The images of the 'open road' (Sofoulis 2002) in car advertising are well known – images which combine the sense of unlimited freedom of movement, with a variety of positive images regarding 'nature' in ways which normally uncritically represent cars as furthering human freedom. At times the imperialist and nature-dominating aspects of these adverts are explicit, at other times implicit (Paterson and Dalby 2006). It is perhaps more interesting to look at shifts in advertising practice over time, suggestive of how the symbolisms that manufacturers associate with cars in advertising both reflect social change (both generally, and specifically in relation to the car) and attempt to shape such change.

Wernick (1991) suggests that from the 1960s through to the 1980s there were two principal sets of themes around which car advertising operated in response to (and in attempting to shape) the cultural challenges which the car faced (as discussed in chapter 2). One of these was a cluster around the family, gender and patriarchy while the other was around the environment, technology and notions of progress. Car adverts have increasingly had to take into account the environment, and critiques of techno-optimism more generally and have tended to reappropriate nature (Wernick 1991: 77–9; see also Gunster 2004). But these cultural challenges persist, partly because of ongoing tensions between the articulations of cars in advertising and the consequences of mass car use. I shall pick up on two themes here.

The first consists of more or less self-conscious attempts to acknowledge and respond to the critiques of automobility as noted in chapter 2. One instance is a series of adverts in the United Kingdom in the mid-1990s which could be brought together under the heading of 'unnecessary driving'. In a paradigm example, an advert for the Nissan Primera in 1996–7 has a man get up in the morning, dress, leave the house, drive to work and get to work, which turns out to be back at home. As Eagar (1997) puts it: 'A smug yuppy in bed says "I think I'll drive to work today, Mrs Jones." His wife replies: "Fine, Mr Jones." . . . You see, they work from home, but he likes the car so much, this Nissan Primera, that he still commutes' (Eagar 1997). The punch line of the advert is: 'It's a driver's car, so drive it.' When asked the reason for such a slogan the writer, David Woods, said: 'We were looking for an unnecessary reason to drive a car' (quoted in *ibid.*).

This series of adverts was produced at the height of the protests against road building and car culture in the United Kingdom, and the popularity of 'Swampy' as a protester in particular (see chapter 6). These protests helped to create a challenge to the presumption in favour of the motorist in suggesting that driving should be only for necessity and avoided if possible. These adverts make most sense as attempts by car manufacturers, and the manufacturers of car culture, to hit back with an advocacy of the virtue of driving simply for its own sake. Of course, as emphasised earlier in the book, there have always been challenges to the car since its inception but what is interesting is that the value of adverts espousing 'unnecessary' driving become salient at the juncture when mainstream acceptance of the points made by protesters and (perhaps less so) the values they espouse was forthcoming.

As car culture was threatened, advertisers and other manufacturers of car culture shifted the discursive frame within which car culture had to be reproduced. The Primera advert is one such strategic shift: car culture is brazenly espoused – the joy of driving for its own sake is celebrated as the problematisation of the car since the mid–late 1980s is discursively erased. In a later version of the same series of Primera adverts, an environmental connection is at least implicit. A Florida TV weatherman announces that a particular hurricane has switched course and is headed for downtown Miami. He gives instructions that people should under no conditions leave where they presently are. The advert then cuts to him driving his Nissan Primera down a Miami highway singing along to The Troggs' 'Wild Thing', with the 'It's a driver's car, so drive it' slogan rounding off the advert. The image of motoring being about the open road without other car drivers is simultaneously revalorised and satirised – like the Nissan Almera advert (see below), a nostalgia for a past where the car could be presented unproblematically is produced (perhaps reinforced by the choice of music), knowing that it can no longer be portrayed in such a fashion. The advert also hints at the irony of promoting something which causes environmental changes which can then be used to promote further consumption of those products: increases in the severity and frequency of hurricanes are among some of the secondary effects thought by many scientists to result from global warming, itself caused by, among other things, cars.[27]

At times, the response to automobility's critics is blunter. Vauxhall ran a TV advert as part of their campaign for the Vectra in 1998 which had as its general slogan 'For the corners of the earth', focusing on how well the Vectra takes corners while implying how the owner will want to drive everywhere in it. In one of this series, the advert starts in a road protest which aims to prevent a forest being cut down to make way for a road. The roadworks would have straightened out a road which currently wound around the forest. The protest succeeds in preventing the road being built and then one of the protesters (conspicuously in short hair, chinos and polo shirt, as opposed to dreadlocks, combat trousers, etc.) leaves the group and the advert cuts to him driving around the forest on the old road, happy with the windy road because of how well his Vectra 'corners'. To top this audacious appropriation of the road protests with a two-fingered salute, the driver passes one of his fellow ex-protesters who is now hitchhiking, and shouts out of his window 'get a job'.

Similarly, a UK advert for Jeep proclaims: 'So it's massively over-engineered for the school run. And the problem with that is what, precisely?' (see figure 3). The advert recognises a widely recognised problem of automobility in the United Kingdom (the increases in congestion brought about by the massive increases in the numbers of children being driven to school by their parents[28]), and specifically the element in

---

[27] Other car manufacturers have also espoused the joys of unnecessary car driving in their adverts. VW, for example, in early 1999, had billboard adverts for the Bora, which said 'Distant Relatives Beware', and then had a slogan under the VW logo and the name of the car: 'Any Excuse'.

[28] In the United Kingdom, from 1994 through to 2004, the proportion of primary children being driven to school went from 30 per cent to 40 per cent, with a corresponding decline in the numbers walking or cycling (Department for Transport 2005: 46–8). Over a longer period (1971–95), a separate study reported that the number of 7–8 year olds getting to school on their own (walking or cycling) dropped in the United Kingdom from 80 per cent to just 9 per cent (Hillman *et al.* 1990). The moral panic about the school run plays on a number of other aspects, concerning children's health and independence (the walk/cycle to school providing a source of both) and a complicated gender politics with implicit discourses of what cars 'should' be for (to drive men to

3 'So it's massively over-engineered for the school run': advert for the Jeep Grand Cherokee

Source: Reproduced by permission of Daimler Chrysler UK Ltd.

anti-SUV discourse that focuses on the fact that SUV owners virtually never drive off-road but instead use such vehicles for mundane tasks like taking their children to school. On the one hand it brazenly rejects the problematisation of the school run *per se*, but it is is ambiguous as to whether the driver figured is involved in the school run – the image does not show whether children are in the car or not. The predominant image is the rain, and then that we are in an urban setting (buildings in the background, another car behind). It can be read as saying: 'Well you still need to drive your kid to school when it's raining heavily' or alternatively as saying: 'But you can use it for so much more than that' – it's 'over-engineered' character enables you to be safe in driving rain, and so on.

Other strategies, however, have been adopted by the promoters of car culture to respond to, or displace, critiques of automobility. Baird (1998: 152–3), for example, suggests that images of the open road are being dropped as the advertisers recognise that people mistrust them as being increasingly discordant with peoples' everyday experiences of traffic jams. She cites adverts such as one for the Vauxhall Vectra, which is located in a traffic jam itself; where other drivers get furious with frustration, the driver in the Vectra is 'cool and relaxed' (*ibid.*: 152) because of the Vectra's air-conditioning. An advert for the Renault Espace picks up on similar associations; it figures a runner in a large crowded public marathon where the Espace owner has a car-shaped space around him free from other runners, accompanied by the slogan 'Personal Space'. While the name for the car has always been principally used to emphasise the space inside the car, with the associated comfort for passengers, the ability to carry many people and so on, the advert emphasises the additional implication of giving the sense of space in the busy, crowded streets of contemporary traffic. The advert recognises the contemporary conditions of driving and widespread dis-ease with the problems of automobility, and turns them to its own advantage.[29]

work, where taking children to school is somehow 'less important' as (predominantly) women do it) and resistances or complications to those discourses (providing a source of opposition to demonising the school run, but also occasional recognition that men's domination of access to cars combined with the emergence of the school run has produced, for some, significant increases in the amount of time and effort some men spend on/with their children).

[29] This tactic by advertisers is not necessarily new. In the early 1970s, Fiat, Saab and Atlantic Richfield (the oil prospecting company) all ran adverts in this vein. 'The auto industry's troubles are now so well known that one international auto corporation, Fiat, has even tried to use it to sell cars' (Rothschild 1973: 4–5).

Others attempt directly to restructure the car's relationship to 'nature' to take into account explicitly environmentalist critiques. Two adverts running alongside the Primera advert in 1997 – those of the Ford Ka and the Honda Dream II – adopted such a strategy, as do more recent ones – such as that of the Renault Laguna and of the Vauxhall Vectra (the latter already discussed).

In the first of these (actually a series of TV adverts) for the Ford Ka, the car's body is in places almost invisible. In the first of the series the car appears only fleetingly at the end of the advert, being submerged in images of 'nature'. In others, the car is presented through a particular configuration of the themes of nature, technology and progress, where technology and progress are presented in terms of harmony with nature (to the point of literal invisibility within nature's emblems, often trees in these adverts). The Honda advert is perhaps less subtle, certainly less surreal, in portraying Honda's prototype solar car as the car of the future, where technology is again placed at the service of progress in addressing questions of environmental change.

The advert for the Renault Laguna, running in 1998, had well-known (socio)biologist Steve Jones delivering a lecture on evolution and natural selection. In the background earlier models of Renault cars 'evolve' into the current Laguna. Jones intones that evolution is 'not just a theory, it is going on all around us'. The appropriation of nature as evolution serves to represent the car in question as being progressively refined and improved, adapting to its environment as would an organism (or gene). At the same time, this is a classic example of the processes discussed by Haraway (1991) whereby social norms are read onto nature, and then back onto society as naturalising justifications for social practices. Discourses of evolution and natural selection read modernist notions of competition, selection, adaptation and most importantly progress onto nature, and then back – in this case onto car design. Such a move renders car-centred development 'natural', and by implication irrational, if not literally impossible, to resist.

One element of this sort of construction is the widespread interrelation between cars and animals in adverts. One particularly striking advert for the Land Rover Freelander figures the car as a hippopotamus, traversing rivers in the African savannah with the same ease as the mammal. The car is in the river, alongside two actual hippopotamuses, framed in a diagonal line ascending left to right in the manner of stereotypical 'flying geese' domestic displays, connecting the image to standard cultural tropes of the domestication of 'wild nature'. The headlights and wing mirrors neatly mirror the nostrils and ears of the animals while their eyes are mirrored in those of the driver and the windscreen. The advert is part of a series for both the Land Rover Freelander and Discovery which take place in African settings or invoke travels by Europeans in Africa. In another TV advert in the series, the vehicle is 'released' from the back of a truck into the 'wild' somewhere in southern/eastern Africa, watched warily by African game reserve wardens as it escapes in the manner of a newly released rhinoceros.[30] With the immediate connections back to game hunting in the colonial era (in which Land Rovers were used as the vehicles for hunting) and to the politics of game reserves across southern and eastern Africa, the Freelander adverts recall a colonial past (in which nature conservation was closely implicated, see Peluso 1993) which the reader (as upper-middle class consumer able to afford a Freelander) is enjoined, if ironically, to valorise. But at the same time, this colonialist imagery is then transformed, in that the car becomes not only the means to master space but also the animal to be viewed in the mastered space. The imagery, design and symbolism of cars have long involved a mimicry of animals (Shukin 2006). This is obvious, with names such as Mustang, Rabbit, Impala, Bobcat, Cougar, Lynx and so on. It is also, as in this Land Rover advert or in that for a Saturn Vue discussed by Shukin (2006), a prevalent image in advertising (see other examples in Laird 1996: 808, Andersen 2000: 160 and Gunster 2004: 7). Laird (1996) shows that this imagery goes back a long way, discussing a Jordan advert in 1923 which mixed images of the car with those of a wild horse to convey the impression of the animality of the car. Shukin's point is stronger: that this animal mimesis works because 'as nature increasingly ceases to be produced in any form able to meaningfully contend with capital's dual rendering of nature as empty signifier and as material resources – capital rushes to produce a semblance of non-capitalized, wild life' (Shukin 2006).

One final point which Wernick (1991) makes regarding shifts in culture and advertising imagery is that another strategy is to use nostalgia, which he suggests has become a prominent theme in car advertising. He discusses at length a (late 1980s) Vauxhall Cavalier advert in

---

[30] Gunster (2004: 10) gives a number of similar examples in North American SUV advertising.

which a stylised advert from the 1950s is shown, with a Dan Dare/Buck Rogers-style futuristic cityscape, a nuclear family in its car with the father at the wheel, unproblematically taking his family 'for a spin'. The two-page advert shows all the features which car in the future might have. On the opposite page is a photograph of the Vauxhall Cavalier against a backdrop of grass and trees and some (unspecified, but again futuristic in design) industrial building in the background. There is no family or people present, but nature is represented. The caption reads: 'Who said tomorrow never comes?' The point of nostalgia is to concede the ground that the car can no longer be conceived of unproblematically, but to encourage people to hark back to an age when it could be. In the Cavalier advert 'tomorrows-car-of-the-future-today is presented as fulfilling a technological dream which in crucial respects, the promotion for it also disavows' (*ibid.*: 88).

In 1997, a prominent ad for the Nissan Almera also used such a strategy. This was a pastiche of the 1970s action detective series 'The Professionals',[31] similar in format and style to the American 'Starsky and Hutch' programme. The advert involved much screeching of car tyres, driving through puddles and market barrows full of fruit, shouting and so on. The billboard version is shot in blue-black and white. Although 'nature' or the environment is nowhere present in this advert it clearly fits with Wernick's argument that nostalgia as a discursive

---

[31] The force of this advert may have been helped by similar nostalgic constructions of 'The Professionals' by Comic Strip Productions, who wrote two spoofs of the series (and whose member, Peter Richardson, directed the advert, see Baird 1998: 141), one in the mid-1980s, called The Bullshitters, and a follow-up produced in the early 1990s. The latter focused on the death of a TV detective and three different sets of TV detectives fought over which era's style (from the flamboyant, crushed velvet-wearing late 1960s/early 1970s, through the all-action mid-1970s [The Professionals/Bullshitters], to the laconic, austere mid-1980s [Spender]) in which to go about investigating the murder. Perhaps importantly in terms of making the discursive link, the actor in the advert is also in the second of these two shows, although playing a different character. The place of cars in detective TV shows could be a focus of inquiry itself. While there is a long tradition (paradigmatically in 'Starsky and Hutch') of using the cars to illustrate the rebelliousness and machismo of the detectives, the contrast with the contemporary equivalent, CSI, is striking. In CSI, the cars of the detectives (notably the Hummer in the Miami version of the show) are rarely in car chases and stereotypically move smoothly and effortlessly along a freeway, reflecting the construction of policing throughout CSI as produced by efficient surveillance rather than macho heroism.

strategy responds to challenges to car culture (see also Baird 1998: 141–2).

These adverts responding directly to automobility's critiques serve, in various ways, to reproduce the normative status of the driving subject. But at the same time, adverts can signal ongoing shifts in its character. In some senses these adverts entail a recognition that the automobile subject is now required to adapt to the consequences of automobility to which s/he was previously blissfully oblivious. The ongoing changes in the character of the automobile subject can be seen more fully in considering the role of 'technology' in car adverts.

Wernick (1991) starts his account with a discussion of how when IBM first brought out personal computers they invoked the shock people would have felt when cars first came along. The adverts functioned to reassure, to suggest that while the emergence of personal computers would revolutionise people's lives, this would be for the better, and to do so by reference to something which had once been revolutionary but was now commonplace. They also served to identify computers as progressive by reference to something more widely recognised as such. The reverse has now become true. Cars, no longer able on their own to signify progress in either technical or social terms, attain their symbolic value through their connection to other, now more prevalently 'progressive' technologies.[32] In an advert for the Peugeot 106, the car appears, plan view, literally as a computer mouse, with a cable coming out of the back of the car (figure 4). The slogan 'Unlimited Access' uses the sense of the whole world being accessible at the click of a mouse to remind the reader that the car can give a similar sense of accessibility. The reputation of the 106 as a small car enhances this sense perhaps, as the slogan also presumes that readers no longer assume that cars do provide this access to the world – the car's size and flexibility enables it to reach places in cities that other cars cannot. In another advert in the same series, the car appears as a computer mouse with a small aerial appearing out of the front of the

---

[32] At times this cars–communications connection is resisted. In 2001, an advert for the Ford F150 ran (in Canada) which contrasted the car as symbol of rugged masculinist independence (the truck owner is putting up a fence on his midwestern land, establishing his dominion) with those of the feminised communications technologies (the voiceover discusses the romantic comedy film 'You've got mail' with Tom Hanks and Meg Ryan; the gendered point of the advert is precisely that the male truck owner has not seen this movie).

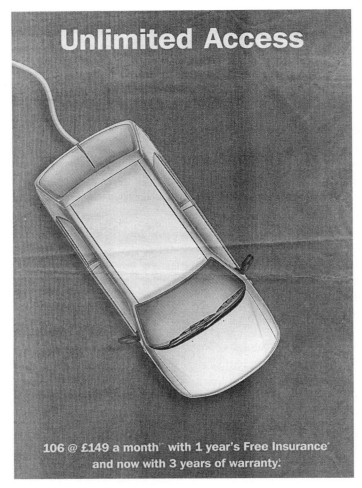

4 'Unlimited access': advert for the Peugeot 106
Source: Reproduced by permission of Peugeot Motor Company plc.

car, with the slogan 'mobile from £6,495'.[33] On top of simply emphasising the two principal symbols of mobility and autonomy (the car is

---

[33] One interesting, if speculative, thought is that in North America the term is
'cellphone', while in the United Kingdom 'mobile phone' is used. (Similar trans-
atlantic differences occur in French, with '*téléphone portable*' in France and
'*téléphone cellulaire*' in Canada). The term 'cell' emphasises the technical aspects

called the '106 Independence' in this advert) the text plays with the
interrelations of these two forms of mobility. By emphasising the cost
of the car (cheap for a car, orders of magnitude more expensive than a
mobile phone) the advert suggests that while the forms of mobility are
clearly different, the car somehow makes you more 'really' mobile,
since otherwise why would you pay so much for it? But at the same
time, the advert depends for its force on the valorising of mobility
underpinning both technologies, on a recognition that phones – and
in the advert shown, computers and the internet – have become somehow more genuine symbols of mobility and, through it, progress.

Some of the best expressions of this intertwining of communications
technology and cars in advertising appear in BMW adverts.[34] One for
the BMW 5 Series in the United Kingdom advertises the car via its use
of 'head-up display'.[35] The advert suggests that 'you receive vital
information without having to look down'. The technology itself is of
military origin, having been developed primarily to enable fighter
pilots to navigate without having to look away from what is directly
in front of them. The advert's images reflect this military heritage, with
one distinct image on the left-hand side containing a screen with a
military plane circled as in a target, and another directly below that of
contour lines (a rectangle and cross) again suggesting targets for delivery of weapons systems. Alongside three different images of the car
itself, and one showing the top of the dashboard with the head-up
display above it saying the middle-ring road is 500 m away and the
car is travelling at 38 km/h (a screen image then reproduced at a larger

of the phone – that it relies on a technology which parcels up space into cells and
is then able to identify the location of the phone within a cell and keep it
connected as it moves across cells. It positions the user in a network which relies
on sophisticated forms of surveillance (which can, of course, also be used more
self-consciously to track people) in order to work. 'Mobile', as with cars, has the
ambiguity that the phone can be moved with the person, but it also enables
another form of movement – as do 'landline' phones. (*'Portable'* in French does
not, however, have this ambiguity – meaning just that it can be carried around.)
Levinson (2004: xiii) rather optimistically suggests that 'cell' also invokes its
potential to 'generate new communities, new possibilities and relationships'.

[34] Most of what appears below also appears in Paterson and Dalby (2006); the
images of the adverts also appear in that paper. That piece is centred on the
notion of 'Empire' as it appears in these adverts; this analysis is focused differently, however, and has been rewritten accordingly.

[35] 'Head-up display' refers to elements of the display projected from the dashboard
onto the windscreen so it is visible at eye-level.

scale subliminally across the whole advert), the image is marked by four strips of male eyes running across it.

These eyes are intended to emphasise the importance of vision and concentration in driving activity (and by extension how head-up display helps this) but also serve to connect the car symbolically to a set of technologies of surveillance which the head-up display exemplifies. The overall image presented is one where such technologies enable an orientation to both the car itself and the outside world predicated on control and mastery. But while this is closely related to the images of rugged outdoor heroism in most SUV adverts, the crucial difference is the way in which a range of technologies – GPS, head-up display, on-board computers – are the condition of possibility of this control. The masculinist subject here is therefore not the warrior but the technocrat – or, perhaps more precisely, it is the hybrid subjectivity of the two, in which the civilian consumer is figured as inhabiting a quasi-militarised world in their daily life – quotidian driving being analogous to airborne targeting. But as with the Peugeot advert above, the BMW 'itself' cannot achieve this subjectivity; it does so rather through a set of surveillance and communications technologies with which the advert connects it, and the intended driver.

BMW present the car as engendering a network-subjectivity in another advert for the 5 Series, but this time without express military imagery. The connections to the notion of networks rather than surveillance are given more prominence in the way these technologies are figured, in both the images and in the slogan: 'Active steering. You don't need it like you didn't need a mobile phone.' The slogan has a number of possible readings. At its most basic, it renders the car (and its active steering) as progressive by virtue of the connection to the mobile phone, now understood as a more 'advanced' technology but one which is made to appear older than active steering, as in the Peugeot 106 advert. But the slogan also refers to the way that novel consumer items first appear as fripperies but after a time become understood as indispensable. It also, in conjunction with the image, connects the two as both enable successful navigation through the complex network-space of the road, with one enabling successful cornering, the other enabling contact to be restored and directions found once one is lost.

The imagery of the collage itself constructs striking associations. The car is figured in terms of its position in a network of roads – or, perhaps more appropriately and suggestively, in a collage of re-presentations of such a road.[36] This re-presentation mirrors the spatiality of mobile phones with each image as a cell. The re-presentation takes the car through the standard set of images – from airport carpark through clover-leaf intersections and highways, through forests, mountains, deserts, fields, ending in a city (although the ending is not 100 per cent unambiguous – the driver has to choose, to be 'active', in order to attain his subjectivity). Once again, the subject attains his (despite the absence of a visible driver in the car, the overall coding of the advert as masculine is clear enough) mobility, control and autonomy through his participation in the network. Indeed, the contrast with dominant SUV images is striking – the subject's freedom here is to be attained only through participation within the road network, not through his rejection of it. But it is nevertheless a narrative of control – 'This intelligent system augments what is already a highly responsive set up, by seamlessly adapting the steering response from agile to ultra-agile and back again according to driving conditions'. Not only is the subject therefore conditioned by its relationality with other subjects and the network within which it operates and which constitutes its subjectivity, the conditions of control are about responsiveness and agility as opposed to toughness and domination.

A further extension of this logic of network or relational subjectivity can be seen in a series of Honda adverts for the Jazz.[37] With 'touchy-feely' cartoon images (resonant of the Yellow Submarine cartoon style) and music (in the TV versions) the advert suggests two possible forms of sociality engendered by the driver's participation in the road network. Recognising that a dominant form is one where cars don't 'get on', where cars do 'cut each other up' and so on, it exhorts the reader/driver to create a more hospitable/friendly form of driving and interpellates the reader as Jazz driver and thus as sociable participant in

---

[36] A similar TV advert, in Canada in 2004–5, pictured a SUV driving on a hillside road, superimposed with a map image of the same space, with contours, graphic representations of trees and so on. The image merges the 'real' and its 'representation' in a way which works precisely because people's experiences are permanently mediated in this way. The advert works through the way the car can be figured as a part of the virtual networks with(in) which intended consumers are presumed to be familiar and with which they are assumed positively to identify.

[37] Note for North American readers: the Honda Jazz in Europe is a mid-size 'family' car not a small motor scooter.

the network. The name Jazz, supported by the random, 'free-form' of the cartoon road, combines with the advert's message to create an image of the car's freedom as flexibility, adaptability and accommodation with others. A more explicit rejection of the car as domination/conquest is adopted in favour of a subjectivity based on recognition of others and our interdependence with each other and dependence on the successful functioning of networks. It also has rather different cyborg images than those of the BMW, suggesting that it is 'cars' which don't get on and which cut each other up, and 'humans' which have the potential agency to 'turn the other cheek' or let others pull away first.

The 'technology at the service of sociality' image is given a different twist by adverts for the Nissan Micra. A series of Micra adverts involves various neologisms – simpology, modtro, funamic and the like – which combine two words for effect but more importantly project the Micra as new, innovative and progressive precisely because one needs new words to encapsulate its 'essence'. This is not only, however, about figuring the car (the advert suggests 'it takes a whole new language to describe it'), but gives the sense that the Micra requires a new subjectivity on the part of its driver ('Do you speak Micra?'). These neologisms are each given dictionary-like phonetic spellings and definitions after and alongside the 'Do you speak Micra?' slogan are accompanied by the phrase 'SHIFT_expectations', emphasising the progressive character principally by the underscore, which suggests an e-mail or internet address.

These tactics are overlaid with a relatively crude form of imagery. In one advert where the neologism is 'simpology', defined as 'the perfect balance between *simp*licity and techn*ology*', the car is shown simply facing the viewer, in front of a row of wind turbines. The imagery is obvious: to present the car as benign in ecological terms, through its (misleading) association with renewable energy and through the analogous combination of the two components of the neologism. The effect is then given a social twist as the headlights are on (although the car is empty) and the text at the bottom reveals them as 'Friendly Headlights' which 'stay on long enough to see you to your front door'. Combined with the image of wind turbines there is a presentation here of a discourse of security predicated on subtle shaping of the world around – lighting a space to render it safe, working with the forces of 'nature' – rather than on the images of sheer power and domination prevalent in SUV adverts.

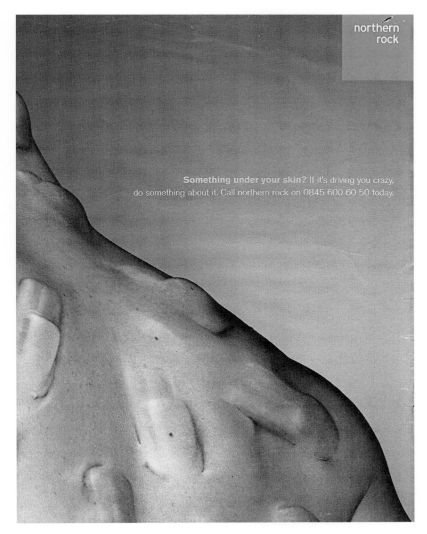

5 'Something under your skin': advert for Northern Rock building society
Source: Reproduced by permission of Northern Rock plc.

Each of these adverts, but in particular the BMW ones, figure the car-driver as a hybrid subject as emphasised in contemporary sociologies of automobility. Technology and humanity merge in specific ways to produce not only the car-driver hybrid but also particular versions of it – militarist, surveillance-oriented, sociable and so on. This merging is demonstrated most completely in the advert for Northern Rock, a building society, where the car becomes internalised to the body of the figure in the advert, the hybrid becomes almost a cyborg. This imagery is combined with a more straightforward account of how cars are 'under your skin' in the metaphorical sense of an object of intense consumerist desire which is 'driving you crazy' (figure 5).

To emphasise that cars figure heavily, and in particular ways, in advertising, popular music, novels, films and so on, does not of course imply some straightforward claim about the 'effect' of this on the subjectivities of those who drive. At one level, these images can be seen simply to reflect cultures of automobility, the way in which cars have been valued and manufacturers have attempted to use these values to their commercial advantage. Without making such causal claims about 'consequences' of advertising, films, etc. it is reasonable to suggest that such images contribute not only to the market advantage of particular firms but also to the broad reproduction of norms about the values which societies attach to cars in general; in other words to the production of subjects who value cars and driving and the legitimacy of automobility *per se*.

Conclusions

This chapter has tried to show that alongside its political economy the success of automobility has been in its ability to articulate with one of the central problems for government since the eighteenth century (at least) – how to *mobilise* people in order to accelerate consumption and, in particular, create the means for war. One of the central claims is thus that automobility was successful because it could construct that impulse, that pressure for mobilisation, as an expression of individual freedom. Cars emerged precisely at the point where movement was again (through, for example, the rigidities of train timetables) being experienced as domination – the 'dictatorship of movement'. We have also seen in this chapter two principal sites, popular music and advertising, where the symbolisms which have sustained this articulation of cars as freedom have been expressed and at times contested. But *contra* Lomasky, this freedom cannot be understood as an articulation of an ahistorical expression of some 'natural human drive' for freedom/ movement, but rather the concrete historical production of particular types of freedom-/movement-oriented humans – or, even more precisely, of particular types of human/machine hybrids. As noted in the conclusion to chapter 3, therefore, the appropriate response to automobility is neither simple celebration nor condemnation, but *ambivalence*. Berman (1982) is particularly useful here. He begins his book: 'To be modern is to find ourselves in an environment that promises us adventure, power, joy, growth, transformation of ourselves and the world – and at the same time, it threatens to destroy everything we have, everything we know, everything we are' (Berman 1982: 15). Our experience of automobility is emblematic of the simultaneous joy and fear that modernity produces. In this context, the backlash discourse discussed in chapter 3 appears as part of 'modernity's struggle against ambivalence' (Bauman 1991: 15). For Bauman, 'ambivalence' refers to the inability accurately to assign items to a specific linguistic category, while modernity entails the deliberate effort to separate and identify everything according to its precise characteristics. Thus modernity struggles against ambivalence but its efforts to purify simply produce new forms or sites of ambivalence (Bauman 1991: chapter 1).

Ambivalence also extends to the types of people which automobility helps to produce. To bring this out, it is worth returning to the earliest period of automobility where its discursive field was being configured. While the automobile subject is most frequently articulated as a 'free' subject – their mobility is connected normatively to their freedom – it is worth recalling that there were and are competing notions of the automobile subject at play. A classic early articulation was by the Italian Futurists. The Futurists were pre- and proto-fascist thinkers, artists and activists who articulated automobiles as one of the principal things to be celebrated and aggressively pursued a vision of the future based around speed, machines and violence. 'We affirm that the world's magnificence has been enriched by a new beauty: the beauty of speed. A racing car whose hood is adorned with great pipes like serpents of explosive breath . . . a roaring motor car which seems to ride on grapeshot, is more beautiful than the *Victory of Samothrace*' (Marinetti 1909/1973: 21). But this speed is celebrated as beautiful precisely because of its potential for domination and violence (hence the comparison to machine-gun fire and military victories). Other points in the manifesto expressly 'glorify war – the world's only hygiene', and 'sing the love of danger, the habit of energy and fearlessness' (Marinetti 1909/1973: 22, 21). The narrative which surrounds the manifesto points concerns the joy of violence ('crushing beneath our burning wheels ... the watch dogs on the steps of the houses'), the contempt of the valuing of the past (mostly about how Italy is a museum) and the contempt for the slower – 'suddenly there were two cyclists disapproving of me and tottering in front of me ... their stupid swaying got in my way. What a bore! Pouah! I stopped short, and in disgust hurled myself ... head over heels in a ditch' (Marinetti 1909/ 1973). The narrator's disgust reads best as both with the cyclists but also with himself for failing to live up to the automobile's logic, to crush the cyclists as he had the dogs.

While we can certainly exaggerate the importance of the Futurists they have contemporary echoes in SUV advertising and in a broader culture of driving that they sustain. It is precisely this association of technology, sexuality, domination and violence – an alternative reading of the auto-mobile subject if you like – which is the target of Ballard's widely cited *Crash* (1973). As automobility's chief ideologist in the United Kingdom (Bennett 1999 terms him 'our motorist-in-chief'), Jeremy Clarkson writes (on what is for him the ignominy of owning a bicycle):

Now before you dismiss me as a damned traitor to the cause of performance motoring, I must stress that I will continue to drive as I always have done; in other words with no regard whatsoever for those who use the roads without paying tax. I am fully aware that every time I mount the mighty Raleigh [the brand of cycle] ... I am a guest in the motor vehicle's territory and must learn to get out of its way. (Clarkson 1996b: 58)

Just in case this seems like a one-off, here he is a few years later, more graphically, as recounted by Catherine Bennett:

He [Clarkson] confessed that he was particularly impressed by footage that shows 'what happens when a big off-roader hits a normal car, and it was incredible. It just rides up the ordinary car's bonnet, ripping the roof clean off and severing the heads of anyone inside'.

As Clarkson points out, the aim of the footage was to deter people from buying a turbo-charged guillotine. 'Nancies! I was jumping up and down on the sofa shouting "I have got to get me one of those! You can keep your Land Rover Uzis and your Shogun AK47s. It's a war zone out there and I wanted a Toyota Howitzer"'. (Bennett 1999, quoting Jeremy Clarkson)

Similarly, in designing SUVs for Daimler-Chrysler, Clotaire Rapaille carefully researched the psychology of SUV buyers and the construction of their identities and developed designs that appealed to (and rein-forced – Rapaille later resigned his position as ethically untenable) an orientation to the car that 'If there's a crash, I want the other guy to die' (as quoted in Bradsher 2002: 100). Note – not 'I want to be safer', but 'I want to impose violence on someone else'. In other words, one can just as easily read the history of the automobile subject as a history of violence and domination as a history of freedom and equality. In this context, the rise of the SUV or the rise in the consumption of armoured protection for cars (Palad 2004) can be read as much as the rise of this particular form of automobile subject (Gunster 2004), where the pre-dominant association is with the overcoming of fear through physical prowess and the understanding of such insecurity as irreconcilably antagonistic: to be secure, I must impose myself on you.

The general point to revisit from this chapter is that the automobile subject which is the condition of possibility of automobility (as its principal daily agent) is something which has been produced, has multiple forms and is continually being reproduced through a complex interplay of popular cultural forms, daily practice, regulatory interven-tions, surveillance and resistance.

6 | *Swampy fever, Mondeo Man*

As cars have increasingly been contested one of the consequences has been a complex and at times contradictory set of projects to re-form subjectivities in relation to the car. Such projects reveal the depth to which the modern subject has become the auto-mobile subject, as discussed in chapter 5, and some of the particular forms and consequences of the development of this subjectivity. This subject is also constructed as a *citizen* and a participant in formal political processes such as voting, with knock-on consequences for how politicians competing in this electoral arena behave and are limited in their freedom of action. These projects also entail attempting not only to reconstruct the subject of the car-driver but also of those who engage in protest activity to oppose automobility. Dealing with such opposition rarely involves engaging directly with the concrete arguments of protesters but more commonly operates through constructing the protesters as particular types of people with (or against) whom others might be able to identify (or differentiate) themselves. This chapter deals with two such instances in the United Kingdom, the first covering the way which protesters against a road project in the south west of England were treated in the media in 1997 ('Swampy fever') while the second deals with the articulation of electoral identities as car drivers in and after the 1997 general election in the UK ('Mondeo Man'). In between, I show how opposition to automobility also entails performing alternative subjectivities to those entailed in 'the automobile subject'.

Swampy fever

In early 1997 British politics produced a most unlikely hero, known as Swampy. For the first few months of that year Swampy was one of the most talked-about figures in British political debate and his popularity endured throughout the year. Swampy was one of five protesters against a road building scheme on the A30 in Devon who had gone to ground down an extensive network of tunnels that they and others had constructed when their protest camp, Fairmile, was evicted. Swampy was the last of the tunnelling protesters to be pulled out of the ground by 'rescuers' employed by the bailiffs to clear the way for the road, seven days after the five had gone underground.

Swampy certainly had his fifteen minutes of fame. 'The Fairmile five are media darlings. Frost wants them, Lawley wants them, Sky, The Big Breakfast, Radios 1, 2, 3, 4, 5, Reuters, the Germans, Aussies and Czechs want them. Poised in the wings are film, record companies and chat-shows' (Vidal 1997a). For nine weeks Swampy had his own column in the *Sunday Mirror*;[1] he appeared on the TV news quiz comedy show *Have I got News for You* (2 May 1997). Some of the more bizarre episodes included the *Daily Express* paying for a photo shoot with Swampy dressed in Armani and Paul Smith suits (*Daily Express*, 3 February 1997, see figure 6, p. 174); a (failed) attempt to get him to record 'I am a mole and I live in a hole' for a record company ('Pass notes', *Guardian*, 18 March 1997); and a rumoured plan to make a film about him, starring Matt Dillon (on the last of these, see *Sunday Mirror*, 30 March 1997). Swampy became a byword for environmental direct action and youth disaffection from formal politics, often being used in headlines of articles where he as a person never appeared.[2] He also became a particular sort of sex symbol, with *Just 17* (a teenage girls' magazine) proclaiming him 'alternative totty' (Bellos 1997) and *Cosmopolitan*'s editor declaring him to be 'so much more sexy' than 'lads' (Raven 1997). He was the subject of the *Independent*'s Dilemmas page, where parents write in about their worries concerning their children; one contributor had a daughter who 'has a crush on Swampy', and wanted to go to Manchester to join the anti-second

[1] According to Vidal (1998) this was ghostwritten by a fellow activist at the Manchester airport protest which immediately followed the A30 demonstration.
[2] Bernard Crick (1997) proclaimed Swampy 'King, for a day'. (Crick later became New Labour's chief adviser on 'citizenship'.) A review of A. N. Wilson's book about St Paul suggested that the author 'downgrades Jesus to the role of first century equivalent of Swampy, a flash-in-the-pan political activist within Judaism of symbolic rather than real significance' (Stanford 1997). Andrew Moncur (1997) suggested that Swampy should play rugby for England. An interview with a professor of English at Liverpool University in the *Times Higher*, who writes about ecology and literature, was entitled 'Swampy's Smart Set' (Wallace 1997).

runway protest (Ironside 1997). The Manchester airport protest camp had a sign saying that 'Swampy groupies' were not wanted (*ibid.*). A Hull businessman trademarked Swampy's name in order to cash in on his fame (and lack of interest in matters entrepreneurial) (Penman 1997). In 1998, a character (Spider) in the soap *Coronation Street* was based on him (Wall 1999: 3). Swampy's reported response to his fame was: 'Bollocks!' (quoted in Gibbs 1997; see 'Pass notes', *Guardian*, 18 March 1997). The commercialisation of Swampy and the other A30 activists was satirised in *Do or Die* (the Earth First! UK magazine) with a cartoon advertising a 'Swampy Action Figure™ with 'realistic digging hands', 'Authentic iron-on Fairmile mud' and a quote from Muppet Dave, another of the 'Fairmile five': 'When I'm worried about being turned into a youth icon I ask them if they know about DBFO. They vanish!' (*Do or Die* 6: 142).[3]

Although a certain proportion of the media construction in the A30 case was negative, portraying the protesters as unemployed outsider activists rejecting the values of 'normal' people,[4] what was interesting was that most of the British press and TV discourse had a largely positive slant (see also Wykes 2000). The predominant image was constructed through discourses of youthful active heroic idealism, as widely noticed both by activists themselves and by other journalists (e.g. Vidal 1997a). This marked a significant change in the

---

[3] DBFO stands for Design, Build, Finance, Operate, and refers to the principles underlying road construction as organised through the Private Finance Initiative (PFI). The A30 scheme was one of the first constructed under this policy initiative, designed to bring in private finance to fund roads schemes and widely criticised for involving a privatisation of the roads system which would ultimately be more expensive than direct building by the state.

[4] 'Adrian Rodgers, prospective Tory MP for nearby Exeter, is demanding that the tunnellers be "gassed out" or "starved"' (Vidal 1997a; see also Griffiths 1997b; *Guardian*, 8 May 1997: 18, letter from Addrian Hutson (father of Animal, one of the other Fairmile tunnellers)). Later, during the Manchester airport protest, John Watts, the Roads Minister, declared that he wanted to 'bury Swampy in concrete' (Margolis 1997; see also Brown 1997). Before its appropriation of Swampy as a popular hero, the *Daily Express* had highlighted the way that the protesters were receiving social security benefits (criticised much more vehemently by Norman Tebbit in the *Sun* (see n. 6). Although less strident in their critique than Tebbit, both the *Daily Express* and the *Daily Telegraph* used the clearance of one camp on 24 January 1997, while protesters were in the pub spending dole cheques received that day, to portray protesters in a negative light – engaging in protest 'at the taxpayer's expense' in the *Daily Express*' words (Rees 1997; see also O'Neill 1997).

constructions of protesters in previous actions against road building at Twyford Down in Hampshire, Solsbury Hill in Bath, the M11 Link road in East London, the M77 extension in Glasgow, or the Newbury Bypass. There, most media construction was negative, of a small minority of extremists rejecting 'normal' society's values and undermining democratically approved decisions.[5] While the press tried to associate the violence there with the protesters, by the time of the A30 protest we were shown photos of a protester 'tickling' a climber who is trying to bring her down from a tree (O'Neill 1997). Wall (1999: 131) suggests that the failure to successfully portray the protesters as violent was one factor in the shift in construction outlined here.

Central to the construction of the protesters in a positive light was a process of 'normalisation'. Given the clear popularity of the A30 protesters, the tabloid press were faced with a need to be able to accommodate this in their coverage. But this had to be done within the discursive frames available both to them and their audiences; the effect was to 'normalise' the protesters, to construct them as normal, regular members of society, in other words to make them 'safe for *Express* readers'. This is an extension of the processes by which modern subjects became mobile subjects as discussed in chapter 5. Such processes of government entail producing certain sorts of people as normal and others as deviant, but this process of governing is always contested.

What was perhaps bizarre was that this construction reached the staunchest of right-wing newspapers (Bellos 1997), notably the *Daily Express*, which gave the protesters easily the most coverage of any of the UK tabloids.[6] One commentary by Radio One DJ (and regular *Daily Express* columnist) Mark Radcliffe stated: 'I'm speechless with

---

[5] Representative of this is the announcement of an RTS event in Birmingham in 1996. The headline on the front page of the *Birmingham Metro News* (15 August 1996) screams 'Tarmac Attack Threat'. It continues: 'A massive army of environmentalists are [*sic*] threatening to lay siege to Birmingham's roads this Saturday. Over 2,000 campaigners are today adding the final touches to a cloak and dagger plan that could trigger gridlock in the huge anti-car demonstration.'

[6] The *Sun*'s only coverage was a column by former Conservative Minister Norman Tebbit complaining about how it was they were able to claim social security benefits and about the police and bailiffs being too liberal and 'making such a meal of clearing them out of the way' (*Sun*, 31 January 1997: 9). The *Daily Mail* gave only a small amount of coverage to this protest compared to the *Daily Express*; the *Daily Mirror* gave more and the *Sunday Mirror* featured a 'The World According to Swampy' column, from 9 March to 20 April.

admiration for Swampy' (*Daily Express*, 1 February 1997: 9). The paper
also included an article by Bel Mooney, prominent protester at an earlier
protest against the Batheaston bypass over Solsbury Hill in 1994,
entitled 'Right or wrong, the young at least show some guts' (Mooney
1997). (Of course, while the young may have guts, youthful idealism is
often easily understood as 'just a phase', again making it safe.)

The normalisation process in the *Daily Express'* construction is
fairly overt. A leader entitled 'Suburban guerrilla' on the day the
paper had him dressed in designer clothes (see figure 6, p. 174) sums
up the construction well:

He went from Swampy to Smoothie in a few short minutes. Britain's favourite anti-roads protester was transformed from sweaty guerrilla to male model
with surprising ease.

Perhaps this is why so much of the country – especially the furry-animal-loving
vegetarian section – has taken him to its bosom. They could already see what
we [the *Daily Express*] have now proved. Beneath the encrusted grime and
matted hair beats a respectable suburban middle-class heart. (*Daily Express*,
3 February 1997: 10)

It is extremely difficult to conceive of the *Daily Express* or other
conservative newspapers approving of actions such as those involved in
the roads protests. Their capacity to make such actions acceptable
occurs through a combination of discourses of family, class and
nation.[7] Use of these themes permitted the papers to make the protesters appear familiar and safe. The *Daily Mail*'s main coverage was a
page-long article on Animal, the next most famous of the five tunnellers
after Swampy (Mollard 1997),[8] making much of her as a sixteen year

---

[7] I should perhaps at this point emphasise that I am not suggesting that the journalists involved sat down and consciously articulated these discourses, and this social
construction of the protesters, as a deliberate strategy. Their intentions as they
wrote their articles, and while editors worked on them to give them a particular
spin, are not particularly important. They may have been aiming simply to sell
copy, to please their editors/proprietors, report 'objectively' according to their
understanding of their professional code, or whatever. My aim is simply to offer a
reading of the social/political symbolism embedded in the texts themselves. As
Gitlin points out, the journalists need not consciously articulate news discourse in
terms of hegemonic projects for us to be able to understand them in terms of
hegemony (1980: 257–8). I am grateful to Chris Rootes for raising this point,
although I am not sure he will agree with this answer to his question.

[8] The other three, who received less coverage, were Ian, Muppet Dave and John
Woodhams.

old young woman. We are informed that Animal is 'the eldest daughter of middle-class, if unconventional parents, [who] gained good grades in 10 GCSEs last summer', and is 'a member of MENSA'. The *Mail* continues:

So why has this talented and articulate young woman decided to risk her life in a smelly tunnel?

What is the attraction when your parents have a perfectly nice semi-detached home, albeit with cabbages growing in the front garden? (Mollard 1997)

Clearly, the *Daily Mail* cannot quite bring itself to normalise her fully, harping on as it does about her 'unconventional' parents, the cabbages in her front garden and the use of 'smelly' invoking notions of femininity which in the *Daily Mail*'s view Animal was transgressing (boys are allowed to be smelly, not girls). But the support of her parents is crucial in the way that the *Daily Mail* communicates to its readers the acceptability of her actions in its eyes and takes up much of the rest of the article. The references to class, both direct and through the emphasis on her membership of MENSA, also serve to make her feel more familiar to aspirant middle-class readers. The *Daily Mirror* similarly expressed this in its portrayal of 'Animal Magic' (29 January 1997: 4–5), homing in on Animal's statements that her parents were proud of her, as well as on her MENSA membership. The *Daily Mirror*'s profile of Animal was on the 'Mirror Woman' page, emphasising Animal's gender (it referred to her blushing when asked about boyfriends) and her being a teenager, implicitly underlining the importance of family (teenagers become relevant in part by reference to their relationship to their parents). At the other end of the journalistic spectrum, the *Guardian* also made similar constructions of Animal, with a lengthy article (on its 'Parents' page) on Animal's family, illustrating the importance of their support to enable journalists' or popular support for the protesters to be given (Brooks 1997). The *Telegraph* offered similar accounts (Leonard and Barwick 1997; O'Neill and Davies 1997). In the latter, however, the *Telegraph* blacked out Animal's eyes, claiming that she could not be named for legal reasons because of her age. Whether or not this was correct (all of the other papers named her) the blackout of her eyes served also to construct her as subversive.

Family and class are also important in the *Daily Express*' construction of Swampy, where he is pictured predominantly with his mother, under headlines such as 'Short history of Swampy, a nice middle-class boy' (1 February 1997: 20–1).[9] This goes across the spectrum of the newspapers: 'Daniel Hooper, aka Swampy, … kisses his mother, Jill, after a court fined him £500 for damaging equipment at the Newbury bypass last May. "I support Daniel all the way", she said. "He deserves to be a hero."' The title of the *Independent* article is worth quoting here: 'Swampy the digger fined £500, but his mum still loves him' (*Independent*, 2 February 1997). The editorial in the *Sunday Mirror* on the first day of Swampy's column in the paper also emphasised the family theme: 'Today on PAGE 9 he starts his eco-diary. But leaves one vital question unanswered: Does an eco-warrior give flowers on Mother's Day? I certainly hope I get MY bunch of daffs!' (*Sunday Mirror*, 9 March 1997).

The other major normalising theme in the protests' coverage was that of nation, of patriotic heroes saving the British (sometimes explicitly English) countryside. This occurred more prevalently in the broadsheets, particularly in the *Guardian* and the *Independent*. The *Daily Express* did regularly refer to Swampy as 'Britain's favourite anti-road protester' (e.g. 3 February 1997: 10). But more was made of the theme in the broadsheets. The *Independent* had a leader entitled 'The nation digs you, Swampy' (30 January 1997), followed by a series of letters headed 'Why we should hail Swampy and friends as patriotic heroes' (*Independent*, 1 February 1997). Their actions were, in the words of one letter, 'a spirited defence of our land, our country' (*ibid.*). John Vidal, in the *Guardian*, suggested that they should be thought of as doing 'active citizen service' (and invoked, as elsewhere, notions of 'Middle England', see Vidal 1997b). Radio 4, appealing to a similar audience as the broadsheets, referred to him as a 'symbol to crystallize the nation's changing mood' (Vidal 1998).[10]

---

[9] Alex Bellos picks up on this theme in his review of the 'Swampy Fever' (1997). Class also plays an important role in Wykes' analysis (2000: 79–80).

[10] Although I did not find any instances of this in the A30 protest, the invoking of nationalist imagery was taken up more critically and reconstructively elsewhere in the roads protests, whose impact frequently relied on images of the specifically English countryside, and worked with the romanticised and at times nativist rural politics. But it also worked with, and reworked, images of nationalism, partly by revisiting histories of radical politics in English history, in particular the Diggers and Levellers of the seventeenth century and William Blake, and also by reworking images such as the flag, as in the production of the 'Union Jill', a union flag in rainbow colours, or to 're-enchant' the human relationships to countryside through the development of tribal identities and writing of tribal histories as in the Dongas. See on this McKay (1996: 134–41), Barry (1999: 80, 82) and Wall (2000).

The protesters themselves by and large fairly actively complied with the construction. Populist/nationalist expressions abound in their public proclamations (or at least how they were reproduced in newspapers themselves; the assumption that this is a reasonable representation of what they said is a rather problematic one). Muppet Dave (a former soldier) said: 'I will continue in my efforts to fight against the needless destruction of my country' (quoted in Jury 1997). Swampy, in various parts of his 'The World According to Swampy' columns in the *Sunday Mirror*, made similar populist appeals. 'Police helicopter circled camp for four hours. What a waste of taxpayers money', he wrote on 16 March, and on 23 March wrote: 'My bail conditions are outrageous. I shall ignore them. The police should be catching muggers, burglars, murderers and crack dealers.'

Perhaps the starkest image of normalisation is the Armani suit episode (*Daily Express*, 3 February 1997: 4–5). The piece is a two-page spread, with a general headline 'Look what emerged from the Swamp'. On the left hand side, there is the caption 'Swampy the eco-warrior', alongside a photograph of him in stripy jumper and baggy trousers tucked into Wellington boots. On the right, three photographs surrounded by the caption 'Swampy in designer Armani', dominate the page, with his hair neatly groomed and adopting men's clothing catalogue poses (presumably as directed by the photographer) – legs apart, one hand in pocket one adjusting his tie, for example. In a small box at the bottom, the ubiquitous interview with his mother has her stating that the transformation 'just goes to show that underneath he's a normal lad from a normal family' (*Daily Express*, 3 February 1997: 5; see figure 6). Middle-class clean normal masculinity was literally inscribed on Swampy's body, leading him to say that he felt 'like a model, or worse, like I was selling my body' (quoted in Griffiths 1997b), and that it was 'pornographic' (Vidal 1997a).

In 'Performative States' Weber (1998) analyses an advert for the US edition of *Men's Health* in the business section of *The New York Times* which involved a full-length photo of drag artist RuPaul in a leotard with a Stars and Stripes flag design, juxtaposed with the byline of the magazine, 'Tons of Useful Stuff for Regular Guys'. Weber uses the work of Judith Butler (1990, 1993, see also Maples 2000 in relation to direct action protest), particularly the notion of performativity – 'the ways that identities are constructed iteratively through complex citational processes' (Weber 1998: 79; see also Parker and Kosofsky

Swampy the eco-warrior

Look wha
emerged fr
the Swam

EXCLUSIVE He came out of a hole in the g
Britain's most talked-about, worst-dressed pr
GERARD GREAVES persuaded him to have a

HOLE NEW LOOK: Main picture, Swampy in Armani, taking him from tree-dweller to city slicker. 'Not very durable material, though,' was Swampy's verdict

LIME-LIGHT: Left, Swampy stays true to his colours with this dazzling creation from chic British designer Paul Smith, although it had "very weird pockets"

GLOWING UNDERGROUND: Above, Swampy's Armani anorak would get him spotted in the darkest tunnel, but he says: "Somehow I don't think these jeans would keep their colour for long"

MUM'S VIEW OF HIS NEW LOOK ...

PROUD: Jill Hooper thinks her son looks 'lovely'

6 'Swampy in Armani'
Source: *Daily Express*, 3 February 1997.

Sedgwick 1995: 2) – to shows that it is precisely the discursive construction of RuPaul's body which helps to reproduce hegemonic forms of heterosexual masculinity and at the same time hegemonic forms of US *national* identity. In other words, rather than understand the identity of 'Swampy' as pre-existing the media constructions of him, his identity is produced through those discursive constructions. As with RuPaul, clothing is important. It is the business suit which is attached in the article to the 'natural' Swampy, existing 'underneath' (to use the phrase attributed to his mother) his more common appearance. Weber emphasises how processes of normativity are bound up with performance and performativity, but that this involves 'processes whereby "regular subjects" and "standards of normality" are discursively co-constituted to give the effect that both are natural rather than cultural constructs' (1998: 81). The construction of Swampy dressed in particular clothing was important to the way in which the *Daily Express* could normalise him. Swampy in the suit is presented as the 'natural' Swampy, while Swampy in boots and grimy jumpers is 'performing'. Following Weber and Butler, we should regard his identity as being one which is continuously performed, but one which needs to be stabilised in order to make him conform to particular 'standards of normality'.

From contestation to human interest stories: taming radical protest

News is fundamentally a discourse of morality, procedure and hierarchy, providing symbolic representations of order. (Ericson *et al.* 1991, cited in Anderson 1997: 128)

Most work on the mass media and environmental politics concentrates on the processes surrounding particular environmental issues. The intention in general is to understand the way in which relationships between the media and environmental groups facilitate or hinder processes of mobilisation and resolution of particular environmental problems (see, for example, the various contributions to Hansen 1993, Anderson 1997, Allan *et al.* 2000, or Joe Smith 2000). Social constructionist analysis focuses on the discursive constructions of 'nature', or of particular places, embedded in news media and environmentalist discourse. In this case, however, the form of media content was rather different since the focus of coverage was not an environmental issue but rather the people involved in environmental protest, and their personalities.

Tabloid journalists in particular are apt, as evidenced above, to cover such protests in terms of the people engaged in them rather than the issues raised by them. The protest became a human-interest story, with much of the coverage involving biographies of the protesters, particularly Swampy and Animal;[11] even much of the *Guardian* coverage contained primarily human-interest stories. While there was much more coverage of the issues, such as DBFO, the destruction caused by road building, and so on there was much 'profiling' of protesters as individuals and fascination with the practical aspects of tunnelling. One episode illustrates this nicely: 'When he [Swampy] wakes, he starts to describe life underground. "We did some interviews for radio people when we were down the tunnels and we said, 'We want to talk about the road scheme.' They said, 'So what's it like down there?' We said, 'We want to talk about the road scheme.' They said, 'So what's it like down there?' 'We're drinking our own piss, what do you think?'" He pauses. "And they believed us." ... So what's it like down there?' (Griffiths 1997b). The *Guardian* journalist can't help asking the human-interest question he knows Swampy has been trying to avoid.[12]

For the media, the intention is to produce a 'symbolic package' (Anderson 1997: 35) and such packages operate within prevailing cultural 'frames'. 'In choosing among possible stories, journalists, sources and consumers reveal the cultural templates of their understanding' (Ericson *et al.* 1991: 356, quoted in Anderson 1997: 124). Such frames are not fixed, and shift over time and across different media sources, but are also not completely fluid, 'since they are constrained in important ways by the market and format considerations' (Anderson 1997: 124). There are a number of ready-made such packages with which to construct environmentalists: doom-mongering scientists, scruffy hippies, technocrat hustlers, to name but three. Constructing the protesters within these frames means that whatever else covering the protests does in terms of helping to set political

---

[11] See also Wykes (2000), who gives a particularly good example in relation to the Manchester airport protest, focused on a couple who conceived a child while in one of the protest tunnels.

[12] Jay Griffiths was also involved in the protests, as well as sometimes writing reports on them for the *Guardian*, perhaps complicating this point. I am grateful to Brian Doherty for this information.

agendas surrounding road building it will also play a part in social reproduction, by stabilising norms about 'normal' people, giving the readers a clear sense of who they are by defining who they are not. What is interesting here, of course, is that journalists predominantly chose to construct Swampy *et al.* as 'us', not 'them'.

This is partly because of dynamics specific to print journalism. As Anderson makes clear, print journalists are often much closer to their audiences than are TV journalists through the letters' pages (1997: 174) which provide for two-way communication between readers and editors/journalists. (Anderson specifically quotes a *Daily Express* journalist in this regard.) In addition, readership of daily newspapers is significantly more homogeneous in its social make-up than are TV audiences, with readers being familiar with the attitudes and politics of the paper(s) they read.[13] Print journalists would thus have reasonably clear notions of the sorts of interpretive frames their readership would have wanted to see so that Swampy *et al.* were not viewed unfavourably by their readership. The *Daily Mirror* conducted its own reader survey on the question, and stated that 80 per cent of its respondents supported the protesters (30 January: 11); however imperfect their survey methods might be from an academic point of view this clearly gave their editorial line the appropriate push (see also Longrigg 1997).[14] This created incentives to produce the sort of interpretation outlined above. However, it does not produce the specifics of that interpretation. Swampy *et al.* still had to be 'made safe for *Express* readers', to be made to appear as 'normal'. This is where discourses of family, class and nation come in.

The effect of such a framing of the roads protest is in stark contrast with many of the protesters' senses of their own identity and strategy. While clearly the positive construction of the protesters in terms of youthful idealism – 'at least the young have guts' – undoubtedly reinforced a broad public understanding that opposition to road building

---

[13] 'Politics' should be read broadly here – readers often do not know which party their paper supports.

[14] It is, however, also backed up by more systematic evidence. The 1997 *British Social Attitudes* survey revealed a broader tolerance for protest than in earlier years (Curtice and Jowell 1998). Vidal (1998) also suggests that this personalisation of the protest 'neutered or trivialized' it. He also shows the consequences for Daniel Hooper, whose personal life was affected deeply by the unwanted attention that he received.

programmes was legitimate, and therefore perhaps contributed to the scaling back of the road programme (on which, see more below), it had other less positive consequences. The connections between roads building and broader social and political questions, and thus deep opposition of the road protesters to modern forms of social organisation and power, were erased. The question of contemporary legal reforms, notably the Criminal Justice and Public Order Act (CJA) 1994, one of whose targets was roads protesters, was absent from tabloid discussions of the protests, and the contradictions in *Daily Express* readerships' and journalists' views were ignored (as Carey 1998 shows, these papers provided much of the moral panic around protesters, squatters and travellers which facilitated the CJA's passage). But at the same time, as will be developed further below, this strategic sense of the goals of protest is closely intertwined with a sense of the importance of performing and developing a subjectivity which is radically different from that to which the press is attempting to 'normalise' them.

Fundamentally, perhaps, there is a contradiction between the *Daily Express'* construction and radical environmentalists' self-constructions. Environmentalism, like the media, is heavily dependent on symbols. In Melucci's words:

Contemporary movements operate as signs, in the sense that they translate their actions into symbolic challenges to the dominant codes ... In this respect, collective action is a *form* whose models of organization and solidarity deliver a message to the rest of society ... Contemporary social movements stimulate radical questions about the ends of personal and social life. (Melucci 1989: 12; Anderson 1997: 207)

The symbolic codes of radical environmentalists, and thus forms of collective action and preferred social organisation, or 'the ends of personal and social life' are, however, fundamentally at odds with those of tabloid newspapers and (their assumptions about) their readership. In the particular constructions made by those newspapers of environmental protest such contradictions are discursively erased and the challenge posed by Green politics neutralised.

So while, for tactical reasons, the media is widely acknowledged by most environmental groups as vitally important (Negrine 1989: 163–78; Gamson and Wolfsfeld 1993; Hansen 1993; Anderson 1997; McKay 1998: 9), many simultaneously recognise the tension created by this dependence. As Gitlin puts it:

Mass media define the significance of movement events or, by blanking them out, actively deprive them of larger significance. Media images also become implicated in a movement's self-image . . . The forms of coverage accrete into systematic framing, and this framing, much amplified, helps determine the movement's fate. (Gitlin 1980: 3)

This was clearly understood by the protesters in the A30 protest. Swampy, in his *Sunday Mirror* column, wrote that despite misgivings about journalists, 'the attention is welcome so we can raise and discuss the issues and the environmental damage done in the name of "progress"' ('The World According to Swampy', *Sunday Mirror*, 9 March 1997: 9). But if the media is important in this way then so is understanding the effects of mediated messages if we are to appreciate how they can (or cannot) be used for environmentalist purposes.

Given that both media and protesters operate at the level of symbolic codes, which are ultimately antagonistic to each other, this tension is high. What the analysis above of press coverage of (one of) these protests suggests is that the coverage is never *only*, if it is at all, about the issues which campaigners want to see covered and promoted but is always interpreted in the light of prevailing frames of understanding which the journalists, the owners of the paper or TV station have, the assumptions about the readership and so on. In this case, it seems to have been more about neutralising the critique offered by Swampy *et al.*, by showing them to be in fact 'normal' middle-class suburbanites whose mums love them. The issue for the media was not the pros and cons of DBFO or the impact of road building on the environment, and the process of constructing the news 'contributes to *decontextualising*, or removing an event from the context in which it occurs in order to *recontextualise* within news formats' (Altheide 1976: 179, quoted in Hannigan 1995: 60). Such a recontextualisation neutralises the impact of the protesters' intentions.

This recontextualisation involved focusing on the lives and (media-constructed) identities of the people involved rather than the political processes associated with road building and the environmentally and socially destructive nature of road building schemes. Gitlin (1980: 146–79) shows how in relation to the New Left in the United States the media converted leaders into celebrities, in the process neutralising their political message. In the A30 and in other direct action protests, certain people had to be converted first into leaders and then into celebrities, since roads protests were organised on a direct action model which eschewed divisions into 'leaders' and 'followers'. Organisations associated with roads protests such as EF! on principle deliberately tried to avoid a politics which promotes 'personalities' (Wall 1999: 92) but this intent has been effectively subverted by the media's need for such personalities on which to hang stories.

Environmentalist recognition of the importance of the media is therefore frequently tempered with an understanding that it tends to reproduce existing forms of social power, not destabilise them (e.g. DPPW 2003: 675–6). UK owners of newspapers often regard this as an explicit part of their purpose and have routinely intervened in editorial policy to ensure that a particular line is promoted (see, for example, Curran and Seaton 1997). But this reproduction does not simply involve promoting certain political agendas – it also involves governing by 'a specific, a permanent, and a positive intervention in the behavior of individuals' (Foucault 1988: 159), as evidenced here in the A30 case. The media have thus become part of what Foucault (following the meaning which emerged in France and Germany in the sixteenth/eighteenth century) refers to as 'the police'. This is a much broader set of practices engaged in by the state than that of the 'police' as the term is understood in English, and explicitly involves the governing of the 'moral health' of the population, something which can easily be recognised as a practice carried out by the media in the late twentieth century. One sort of response, facilitated by technical change – the development of hand-held cameras, digital camera technology, mobile phones and the internet – has been the development of 'alternative media' sources such as Undercurrents and IndyMedia as part of activists' strategies (Holloway 1998).

Resisting cars, resisting the auto-mobile subject

What the attempt to normalise protesters reveals is that for many activists working against automobility, or one or other of its specific consequences, the immediately strategic nature of their action – to stop this or that road, to highlight how an intersection between roads would be much better as a meeting place for communities than a simple thoroughfare and so on – is intimately connected to the performance of identities at odds with those produced as part of the development of automobility. The protesters attempt to shape their own subjectivities in terms of, variously, a shared, collectivist orientation to communities which they are in the process of creating, a resistance to the surveillance-oriented politics of automobile modernity, an emphasis on the importance of place over movement in individual and collective identities and so on.

The roads protests, stimulated by the 'Roads for Prosperity' programme announced by the Conservative government in 1989 as well as a generational shift with the appearance of a new generation of activists who regarded the 1970s environmentalist organisations (principally Greenpeace and Friends of the Earth (FoE)) as having become too professionalised and losing their radical edge, provided one of the key controversies of the early-to-mid-1990s and peaked in the period shortly before the 1997 election.

The roads protests were marked by the extent to which many protesters were prepared to engage in direct action to protect places threatened by road construction. At the principal protest sites – Twyford Down, Solsbury Hill, Newbury, the A30, Pollok Park and East London, in particular – protest involved both significant tactical innovation (Doherty 1997) and the willingness of protesters to put themselves in considerable physical danger, usefully referred to by Doherty (2000) as 'manufactured vulnerability'. The innovation involved the construction of walkways between trees, treehouses, the use of 'lock-ons' (arms of protesters sunk into concrete and held in place with bicycle D-locks) and the construction of extensive but unsupported tunnel structures to prevent earth-movers from entering a space safely (Doherty 2000). Many of these produced dangers for the protesters, but this was a deliberate part of the strategy and a means by which it became both tactically successful and politically powerful. The walkways worked to prevent the felling of trees (as protesters in or between trees would be endangered) and to create work (and thus cost) as specialist climbers (in combination with cherry pickers) had to be employed to get protesters safely out of the trees. Lock-ons created a situation where there were real possibilities of breaking protesters' arms if security firms or police attempted to move them. The extreme in terms of vulnerability was the tunnelling system, used to some extent at Newbury (Doherty 2000: 69) but most extensively at the A30 protest, where protesters would be underground in tunnels deliberately built so they might collapse easily, killing them.

These tactics were often used in conjunction with more conventional forms of protest or direct action – mass trespasses, attempts to sabotage machinery, court injunctions, petitions, media stunts and so on. The protests received widespread media attention and in most instances popular support. The original roads programme envisaged in 'Roads for Prosperity' was subsequently drastically scaled back. There were, of course, many other elements to explain this: the fiscal crisis produced by the recession of the early 1990s; the small parliamentary majority after 1992 and the siting of some roads in constituencies with slim Conservative majorities; the official shifts in transport planning philosophy which accepted the concept of induced demand – that building roads creates traffic (see SACTRA 1994; Robinson 2000: 207–8) and that urban air pollution from cars was important in causing significant health problems (Robinson 2000: 206–7). Yet, it would be difficult to explain the decision entirely without the political pressure and legitimacy crisis produced by the protests themselves (even though all of the actual roads which saw significant direct action protests were in the end built).

But to focus solely on the strategic or tactical elements of the protest – whether, why and how, they 'succeeded' or 'failed' – would be to miss an important dimension of the protests themselves. As well as seeking to produce certain goals they can also be interpreted as important sites of cultural resistance and the articulation of alternative ways of life and forms of identity. Much of the social movement research on the anti-roads protests emphasises this (e.g. McKay 1996; Wall 1999; Maples 2000; Seel and Plows 2000; Szerszynski 2002, 2003). Doherty (1999) shows persuasively that models of 'political opportunity structures' (e.g. Tarrow 1994) cannot account successfully for the emergence of anti-roads protests in the United Kingdom in the 1990s. While this might help to explain the external conditions which favoured a radicalisation of activism (the professionalisation of environmental groups, disappointments concerning the fate of the Green Party after the 1989 electoral success, the roads programme itself), it cannot account for the agency of the activists. This was not determined by 'the relative chances of success' of one strategy over another; but 'direct action seemed to be essentially expressive, based upon immediate concerns: sites for protests were chosen based on the need to oppose the imminent destruction of valued locations rather than based upon an instrumental calculation' (Doherty 1999: 287). McKay (1996) interprets the protests in terms of a long lineage of cultures of resistance in the United Kingdom (sometimes specifically England) against materialism, individualism, domination and in favour of community, diversity, ecology and so on. McKay situates the roads protests in terms of a history of resistive identities involving the peace movements, punks, travellers and so on. Central in this view was that the identity of the protesters became itself a means of protest; by bodily signifying an alternative – or, more precisely, alternative (plural) – way(s) of *being*, protesters showed that existing societies could be resisted and alternatives pursued. McKay quotes Donga Brian: 'protesting is not a way of life, but your way of life can be a protest' (1996: 148).

Emphasising the protests' theatrical, performative nature is central to understanding this dimension. Many activists self-consciously understood their activity as a theatrical or artistic event (McKay 1996; Szerszynski 2002), which served not only to create a spectacle around which public attention could be drawn, but to manifest ('demonstrate', in Barry's useful (1999) reading of the double meaning of this term in relation to the Newbury protests) that alternatives to specific acts of destruction, or specific problems of automobility, required different forms of subjectivity, of being in the world and with others. This was elaborated in the roads protests through the development and adoption of particular styles of dress, hair, often tattoos and body-piercing, which invoked a range of counter-cultural styles but went beyond simple 'fashion statements', expressing the identity of protesters with each other. At the extreme, in the Dongas, groups became identified by themselves and more broadly as Tribes, with a similar logic of performative subjectivity as outlined above, drawing on Weber (1998). Szerszynski (2003: 198–203) brings out the logic of this adoption of such forms of identification and bodily performance of identity as part of the protest activity. He poses the question that why, if they wanted in effect to 'speak *for* the planet' would environmentalists 'want to mark themselves out as different?' (2003: 198). While part of the answer is that such 'marking-out' serves to produce a group identity and reinforce sentiments of solidarity, another dimension is the manner in which it communicates to 'wider society' (2003: 201). For Szerszynski, this 'works by trying to recode oppositions or paradigms so that this zero degree[15] shifts – the natural and taken-for-granted becomes

---

[15] Szerszynski draws here on Barthes (1967), for whom the 'zero degree' refers to the 'unmarked' categories of subject against which difference is being contrasted, or 'marked'.

denaturalised and problematised' (2003: 201).[16] But I would add to this, as Szerszynski emphasises elsewhere (2002: 56), that when connected to the broader 'lifestyle' elements, especially around protest camps or street parties, what is being 'performed' is not only the dramatics of the protest but a vision of an alternative life with which those watching might identify. The 'wider society' is being drawn in not only by a negative problematisation of existing society but also by a vision of something else. In this context, then, a contrast between an 'instrumental logic' and an 'expressive logic' of social movement practice, as emphasised by Rucht (1990: 162; Doherty *et al.* 2000: 12) is misplaced; it is rather that the expressive dimension to direct action politics is simultaneously the performance of a subjectivity which is somehow 'authentic' *and* an enactment with strategic benefits in terms of its intended demonstrative effect. As Szerszynski puts it, it operates as a 'politics of prefiguration, which offers utopian moments, partial glimpses in the here-and-now of another possible way of being' (2002: 56).

Mondeo Man: the consumerisation of citizenship[17]

The roads protests can thus be seen to show that the logic of opposing car-dominated societies is also to oppose the subjectivity which is entailed in automobility itself – the 'automobile subject'. What is involved in the sort of backlash politics discussed in chapter 3, therefore, is not only to attempt to denigrate alternatives but to contain such challenges by a rearticulation of the automobile subject in positive, normative terms. But this operates in a subtler manner than that

---

[16] Although only occasionally articulated self-consciously as a performed and resistive identity (some cycle couriers have been part of RTS or Critical Mass networks) the position of couriers in public discourse is also instructive here. They frequently simultaneously demonstrate (in the technical sense as emphasised by Barry 1999) the chronic contradictions of car-based automobility (by being simply faster than cars, but also by breaking the rules of the road which exist precisely because of car-dependence), combine it with a subcultural style which is similar to those of anti-roads protesters and, of course, complicate it with a (problematic) performance of 'a more authentic automobility'. (On cycle couriers, see Fincham 2006).

[17] Again, while the United Kingdom is taken as an example here there are analogies elsewhere. Gerhard Schröder of Germany, for example, was known as the '*autokanzler*', because of his close ties to the car industry.

adopted by Lomasky or the US right-wing think tanks. Rather than assert a taken-for-granted 'consumer citizen' or 'citizen-driver' connection (see, for example, Dunn (1998: 3)) and then assert the 'rights' of such pre-existing subjects, it involves projects consciously to shape drivers *as* citizens.

During the run-up to and aftermath of the UK 1997 general election (and thus at the same time as 'Swampy fever'), most of the principal signifiers of different sorts of voter were defined through their relationship to particular cars. An aphorism was repeated throughout the press concerning Tony Blair's self-understanding of New Labour's journey and became part of the campaign's mythology. In campaigning during the 1992 general election, Blair canvassed a man in Telford who told him frankly why he was voting Tory. In a speech to the Labour Annual conference in October 1996, Blair drew out his implications from the encounter thus:

I can vividly recall the exact moment that I knew the last election was lost . . . I was canvassing in the Midlands, on an ordinary, suburban estate. I met a man polishing his Ford Sierra. He was a self-employed electrician.

His Dad voted Labour, he said. He used to vote Labour, too. But he'd bought his own house now. He'd set up his own business. He was doing very nicely. 'So I've become a Tory', he said. He wasn't rich. But he was doing better than he [his dad] did, and as far as he was concerned, being better off meant being Tory too.

In that moment, he crystallised for me the basis of our failure, the reason why a whole generation has grown up under the Tories. People judge us on their instincts about what they believe our instincts to be. And that man polishing his car was clear. His instincts were to get on in life. And he thought our instincts were to stop him. (Blair, quoted in *Daily Mail*, 3 October 1996: 3)[18]

So it started with Sierra Man, with a mythology of New Labour's journey to the 1997 election by its leader told through a focus on a particular type of voter, defined by the make and model of car they owned. But this is no empty signifier; it is not simply that a particular car can be used to create images of people with particular class and gender positions from which their voting practices can be read, but that these voting practices themselves arise to a significant extent out of their orientation to consumption in general, and specifically to cars and

---

[18] For other newspaper accounts of this story and its role in legitimising Labour's political shifts see, for example, Haynes and Leake (1996); Grice (1997).

the freedoms they (allegedly) provide. Sierra Man is someone who votes *as a car driver*.

There is a longer history of politicians *identifying themselves* with cars – Hoover with his election slogan (chapter 4), Hitler travelling in an open car (satirised in Charlie Chaplin's *The Great Dictator*, see Zuckerman 1991: 16–21), UK Prime Minister Attlee deliberately choosing an 'unpretentious Austin' to symbolise his Labour credentials (Younge and Glancey 1999), the 'Popemobile', the car fetish of Soviet leaders (Brezhnev had 'two Rolls Royces, a Cadillac, Mercedez-Benz, Citroën, Maserati and a 200-mpg Matra-Bagheera' according to Ward 1991: 12) and so on. But it is another thing to identify *voters* as people who vote *as* car drivers.

During the run-up to the 1997 election, these car-based signifiers multiplied. Blair is reported as saying a week before the election that he was convinced he would win when he saw 'obviously well-to-do people in new cars' supporting Labour (Eason 1997; Woods and Nuki 1997). Having perceived that they had successfully captured Sierra Man they turned their attention to 'Galaxy Man' (e.g. Woods and Nuki 1997).[19] 'Mondeo Man' also gets an occasional look-in and some other mentions prior to 1997 (e.g. Clarkson 1996a; Massey 1996), but these references have no direct connection to the election. Their indirect connections are, however, revealing. The references are usually to the class and geographical connections to particular car ownerships, but the specific positions of the Mondeo are not agreed on despite its clear intent when it becomes a political signifier. Writing in the *Daily Mail*, Massey (1996) suggests that its home is in the North where people are fans of 'traditional and thrifty models'. Eason, in *The Times*, suggests similarly that Sierra Man represents the 'garages of working class Britain' (1997). Another article in the *Daily Mail* (22 October 1996: 16) has a rather different image, suggesting that the archetypal Mondeo driver 'is a regional sales manager and lives in Milton Keynes or another new town with his wife and two children'. For Giles Smith, it is similarly the 'berth of a salesman' (Smith 2000). There are a couple of

[19] Note for non-UK readers (especially North Americans): the Mondeo replaced the Sierra in Ford's range in the mid-1990s. It is a 'mid-sized' car in North American parlance, the equivalent of a Taurus. The Galaxy is a minivan equivalent to a Windstar, but marketed less simply as a family van and more as facilitating an outdoor lifestyle somewhat akin to the marketing of SUVs in North America (Eason 1997).

fairly weak references in the run-up to the election (Cohen 1997; *Guardian* 1997),[20] but as a political signifier Mondeo Man comes into his own a year or two later, and then becomes hegemonic as the signifier of Labour's target voter. After the election, the new Tory leader William Hague continued the identification of key voters with cars. When told by a taxi driver on the way from Newcastle upon Tyne to the airport that he would not vote Tory again, having voted Tory for much of his life, his response was: 'We have to win over that taxi driver and millions like him' (Hastings 1997).

At one level, this set of connections between cars and voting patterns could be taken as simply a byword for a particular psephological category. Colin Hay uses the phrase as a synonym for the median voter as outlined in theories of electoral behaviour (1999: 97); it is used, both by Hay and other commentators on New Labour and in general political usage, to signify a certain political/economic location – C2 floating voter, 'middle England' – and thus a position along the left–right continuum.[21] In Hay's book, the phrase appears in the middle of a discussion of the application of Downs' economic theory of democracy to New Labour's modernisation – the moving of Labour to the political middle or even to the right of centre. Hay suggests (1999: chapter 3) that Labour had moved from an assumption that voting behaviour was principally 'bi-modal' – with a group of working-class Labour voters and a group of middle- and upper-class Tory voters – towards a distribution of voters

[20] The *Guardian*'s 'Pass notes' column on 29 April 1997, two days before the election, was on Galaxy Man, and suggests that 'Tony Blair has decided that Sierra Man and Mondeo Man are in the bag; the target for the last week of the campaigning is Galaxy Man'. Cohen (1997) has a different target, and suggests that 'Mondeo Man is the real threat to John Major's Arcadia', principally reading this to mean that the 'middle England' voter who is synonymous with Mondeo Man may defect in sufficient numbers to the anti-European Referendum Party to cause Conservative candidates to lose to Labour.
[21] Journalists commenting on the 1997 election frequently refer back to the 1980s and Thatcher's invocation of such electoral categories. For them, the 1980s equivalent was 'Essex man' (e.g. Deans 1997) and in the 1992 election there was the phenomenon of 'Basildon Man', referring to the key Labour target constituency of Basildon in Essex which the Conservatives famously won. In the current context, my preferred equivalent category for that era would be Ian Dury's 'Billericay Dickie', complete with the appropriate class and aspirational connotations – 'I'm not a blinkin' thickie, I'm Billericay Dickie, and I'm doing, very well' (Dury 1977). Billericay Dickie, of course, drives a Ford Cortina ('I had a love affair with Nina, in the back of my Cortina'), the forerunner of the Sierra and then the Mondeo.

around a 'normal distribution', as Downs had classically argued (1957). In this context, party competition is organised around capturing the 'median voter' and, as Downs shows, Labour came to accept this conception during the early 1990s (Hay 1999: 97).

It is reasonably common to assert that citizenship has been transformed away from a 'classical' account concerning the duties and obligations of citizens in relation to a well-defined public, collective sphere of life, and towards a form of citizenship arising out of an individual's orientation to consumption (e.g. Scammell 2000, 2003; Bennett 2003). Consumption becomes at the same time the signifier of membership in society and the orientation to one's membership in it (as a bearer of rights and consumer of collective services and politicians' programmes).

But the Mondeo Man example also signifies how certain consumptive practices are privileged in political discourse. Neither the invocation of median voter theory nor the construction of 'consumer-citizens' tell us much (if anything) about the question: 'Why cars?' Why were cars used to describe this category of voter in the run-up to the 1997 election?[22] The signifying capacity of cars has been used in political debate in relation to class, gender and overtly political subject positions. A political 'middle' defined by the ownership of a (particular brand of) car reflects the privileging of car drivers as a group and car use as a mode of consumption and mobility. At the same time that New Labour has done what Hay says it has in moving to the right politically, it also has done so in part by connecting certain forms of political identity to certain forms of consumptive identity and thus to certain forms of socio-ecological practice.

It is no accident that Sierra/Galaxy/Mondeo Man appeared as political signifiers (for convenience, I shall simply use Mondeo Man from now on) after several years of sustained, radical political activism centred on the social and ecological destruction wrought by a car-dominated society. Like some of the adverts discussed in chapter 5

---

[22] There are, of course, a set of other questions which in other contexts would receive more emphasis: 'Why the Mondeo?' 'Why "Man"'? This would take us in the direction of the gender and class dimensions of the electoral category and its chosen signifier. We could also speculate on the choosing of a car which signifies 'the world' – Ford's attempt to revive the world car project (a car to be manufactured the same everywhere, except in North America) abandoned by most manufacturers in the mid-1980s. For the present purposes, however, it is the simpler question of 'Why cars?' which occupies me.

(the project to celebrate 'unnecessary driving', the deliberate attempt to use the protests to the advantage of the car which prefers 'the corners of the world'), Mondeo Man emerges precisely in a context where 'the car' and its drivers were under threat and which produced a discourse where the popular press felt the need to celebrate (while normalising) the activities of these protesters.

Enter Mondeo Man, stage right. Mondeo Man operated as discursive reframing. Rather than seeing cars as 'the problem' they become seen as the source of identity through which a subject's political identity can be understood. The legitimacy of car driving had revived and 'normal' politics resumed.

Of course, once put into practice, the problems created for transport policy in such a framing have been serious. As Andy Jordan notes, 'Much to his[23] annoyance, Blair has intervened on more than one occasion to pacify the anxious car drivers of Middle England, personified by the archetypal "Mondeo Man" who bore him to power in 1997' (Jordan 2000: 270; see also Coward 2000). Having legitimised car driving, it then became more difficult to engage in the 'attacks' on car drivers widely believed to be necessary to achieve other goals in terms of congestion or meeting emissions targets. The Labour government came in, in formal policy terms, with ambitious goals in relation to shifting transport use from the car to public transport. Prescott famously stated shortly after the 1997 election that he would be very surprised 'if in five years' time there are not many more people using public transport and far fewer journeys by car' (quoted in Wolmar 2001). There was a recognition that in order to deal with congestion and air pollution, as well as to meet the targets for greenhouse gas emissions at the time being negotiated in what became the Kyoto Protocol on Climate Change, it would be necessary to develop policies to reduce car use.

Substantial investment was put into the modernisation of the rail network, with an approximate doubling of annual investment between 1991 and 2001.[24] Other aspects of urban transport consistent with an environmental agenda were promoted more aggressively – for

---

[23] That is, to the annoyance of John Prescott, the Deputy Prime Minister, and after the 1997 election, in charge of a 'superministry' combining 'environment, transport and the regions' (DETR).

[24] This was increased from a low point of under £2 million in 1993–4 to around £6.5 million 2002–3. It includes, however, a significant increase in policy-induced private investment in rail during this period. (See DfT 2002, Annex 1.)

example, trams/urban light rail, cycle ways, 'safe routes to school' pedestrian schemes, reduced speed limits, 'showcase' bus routes, or park and ride schemes, in effect many of the elements which make up a broad 'ecological modernisation' of socio-transport systems, as discussed in chapter 7. Goals were set to reduce urban car use by 10 per cent and the Road Traffic Reduction Act 1997 required local councils to draw up plans to meet traffic reduction targets: the government introduced measures to enable local authorities to use fiscal disincentives such as congestion charging or taxes on workplace parking places, to meet such goals. As well as the obvious environmental arguments such schemes have been legitimised in terms of the costs to the economy of congestion and air pollution, and specifically the imperative to enable rapid and flexible mobility in urban areas to meet the needs of an informational, networked economy.

But the discourse of Mondeo Man created two specific contradictions for New Labour's transport strategy which undermined its successful implementation and the commitment of others in the government (particularly Blair) to Prescott's vision. The discourse of Mondeo Man had created an image of a particular constituency to whom the government frequently felt it had to bow; policies would be judged according to how individuals would react as *car drivers*. Commentators noted that in the transport policy which emerged in 1998 the goals would be met with 'minimum pain to Mondeo-polishing Middle England' (*New Statesman* editorial, 24 July 1998). As a consequence alongside the various measures to promote public transport were expanded and revitalised road building projects (Clark 2002b). But this contradiction can be seen not only in the area of road building: New Labour spent considerable efforts early in its first administration (especially in 1999) focusing on what it called 'rip-off Britain', where one of the principal targets was the high prices of cars in the United Kingdom relative to those in other European countries, the effect being that the cost of car purchase declined, and with it the overall cost of motoring (Gibbs and Milner 2003).

But strongly supporting the first contradiction is the fact that having created the subject of Mondeo Man in order to position Labour with particular voters *vis-à-vis* the Conservatives, it then conjured up a set of expectations concerning policy (that the 'needs' of car drivers would be responded to, the road building programme of the Conservatives having been radically scaled back in part because of the anti-roads protests), which then, once Labour failed to deliver, helped to produce the collectivities and discourses which were seen in chapter 3 as part of the backlash. The notions of a 'war on the motorist', the emergence of organisations like the ABD and, in particular, the fuel protests of 2000, all emerged in this period as expressions of frustration with transport policy which can be partly attributed to the legitimation of the driver-citizen which Mondeo Man represented. This crisis in late 2000, and the broader inability to shift transport policy away from cars as much as many desired, was thus brought about at least in part by the discursive reframing of political interests involved in the 'Mondeo Man' discourse three years earlier. For *Farming News* (14 September, 2000: 9), at least, the protesters were quintessentially 'Mondeo Man'; having framed the question of political identity in terms of an orientation to consumer interests or identities, New Labour got its comeuppance. The legitimacy of the automobile subject is precisely the limit on practical political action on transport, and a politics of automobility must thus deal with this mobility/subjectivity connection.

7 | *Greening automobility?*

> The modern economy is likely to go on
> growing, probably in new directions, adapt-
> ing itself to the chronic energy and environ-
> mental crises that its success has created.
>
> (Berman 1982: 347)

What, then, does the analysis of the chapters 1–6 say about the possibilities of transforming automobility in an ecological direction? Can
the critiques of the car outlined in chapter 2 be reconciled with the
defence of the car discussed in chapter 3? There are numerous discourses – of industrial ecology, smart growth, eco-efficiency, sustainable transport(ation), sustainable mobility – all attempting to articulate
a number of elements of public policy, firm strategy, market change,
changes in consumer behaviour and (above all) technological innovation which might contribute to a 'greening' of automobility. Broadly,
these can be grouped (conceptually at least; in practice, they are usually
mixed in some form or other) into those which focus on 'the car', taking
its dominance for granted and attempting simply to change the ways in
which cars are made and used to reduce their environmental impacts
and those which attempt to shift socio-transport networks away from
'automobile dependence' (Litman 2002).[1]

  Most of these discourses, and the specific policy proposals or technical fixes involved, are couched in largely technical terms (whether or
not the technologies exist, whether they are adequate to the task set for

---

[1] Each could be thought of as a variant of 'ecological modernisation' – a broader
discourse concerning political/economic transformations towards sustainability
(e.g. Mol 2001), noted in the discussion of Eckersley (2004) in chapter 1. This is
an enormous literature, and my aim in this chapter is not to provide an exhaustive
survey. For a small selection, see Centre for Sustainable Transportation (1998),
Newman and Kenworthy (1999), Black and Nijkamp (2002) and Low and
Gleeson (2003).

them) or narrowly economic (whether they are cost-effective, whether there is a 'market' for them, how the economic incentives to take them up might be shaped by policies such as taxes, subsidies, etc.). Urry (2004), for example, extends his system-theoretic analysis of automobility in this direction by invoking the notion of 'tipping points' – a series of interlocking developments which permit the transformation from one system to another. But this chapter shows that what I have suggested are the two principal structuring elements of automobility – its political economy and cultural politics – provide the principal forces shaping the possibility of *either* version of this greening. It will be clear that the 'strong' version of greening – of moving away from automobile dependence – is in my view more persuasive as an account of what might meet the conditions of sustainability. But even if one is persuaded that simply 'greening the car' is sufficient – that one can imagine that new fuel sources, engine and vehicle design will produce a dramatic and sufficient reduction in fuel consumption, materials consumed and emissions produced – then it is the capacity to articulate this transformation of the car as part of a 'regime of accumulation' (as outlined in chapter 4), and the capacity to connect it to prevalent forms of 'automobile subject', which are the conditions of possibility of the success of the project.

After outlining some of the elements of these current projects in more detail, I then revisit elements of the environmental politics of cars that have been a part of automobility since at least the 1950s. In a mode of analysis drawn from chapter 4, such politics can be characterised by the ability of large firms to resist attempts by states, pressured by scientists and social movements, to regulate cars, principally in relation to their production of air pollution. From this perspective, the structural power of capital constitutes the principal constraint to acting on the environmental problems produced by cars. The normative implications are thus in terms of either finding means of resisting this power, and/or of thinking of dealing with cars less as regulation of particular side-effects and more as the promotion of an alternative accumulation regime. The current transformations in and of automobility can thus be seen as driven by this overall structural constraint. But then, drawing on the analysis from chapter 5, such politics has also at the same time entailed a gradual and continual reconstitution of the automobile subject. The automobile subject *itself* provides significant resistance to attempts to limit car use but at the same time, as environmental problems from cars are addressed (if tentatively, given the power of capital), it entails reshaping peoples' relationships to cars – what *sorts* of automobile subjects they are. From this perspective, the normative prognosis suggests, on the one hand, the need to attempt to detach automobility from dominant forms of subjectivity but, on the other, to accept that further 'greening' necessarily involves *governmentality* – a reshaping of what sorts of people people are.

Towards a green car?

The project to 'green the car' involves two principal elements.[2] The first consists of technical shifts in the way that cars are designed, the fuels they use and how efficiently they use them, and the second entails the application of information technologies (IT) both to aid the first two developments but also to alter the environmental performance of cars 'in use'.

Improving the car's performance

The first development concerns the technological possibilities for improving the ecological performance of cars themselves; these are principally technologies that attempt to improve the fuel efficiency of cars.[3] While fuel efficiency improved noticeably after the oil crises of the 1970s, this improvement slowed everywhere as oil prices fell during the mid-1980s and beyond but much more sharply so in North America than elsewhere as European and Japanese governments increased fuel taxation dramatically to maintain high consumer prices and stimulate efficiency gains to limit oil imports, while the US government relied on CAFÉ standards and failed to (or didn't really want to) overcome industry opposition to improving the standards, or to close the loophole in the standards which contributed to the rise of the SUV.[4] As a

---

[2] For reasons of space and priority I ignore here questions concerning the greening of the process of *producing* cars. On this, see Graedel and Allenby (1998).

[3] For general treatments of this, see Greene and Plotkin (2001) or Plotkin (2001).

[4] The loophole is that in the United States (and, following the US lead, Canada), there is a regulatory distinction between 'cars', on the one hand, and 'light trucks', on the other. When CAFÉ regulatory system was introduced, different standards were imposed on the two types of vehicle, reflecting the assumption that light trucks were work vehicles. However, manufacturers were then able to produce

consequence the fuel economy of North American cars declined during the 1990s while that of European cars at first slowed from the mid-1980s onwards but then started to improve again after the mid-1990s. New cars on the market are now around 28 per cent more efficient in Europe than in North America[5] as a consequence of this shift, as well as a preference for smaller cars in Europe given city and street size differences. There are significant technical possibilities for improving fuel efficiencies further even with the ICE. As Mytelka (2003) points out, technological developments in engine design since the 1980s have been principally oriented (especially in North America) towards increasing power. Power, vehicle weight and efficiency work in a relational manner and as vehicle weight has been increased because of a decline in concern for efficiency and an increase in concern for safety (and a dubious assumption about the weight/safety relationship) technological development has been oriented to increased power to compensate for the increases in weight, with further knock-on effects on efficiency. But this cycle is not immutable and there are technologies, particularly in Mytelka's view to do with the manner of injecting fuel into the engine, which can still substantially improve fuel efficiency in cars. The existence of cars on the market which already use less than 4.5 l per 100 km (over 60 mpg) (such as the Smart car or the current model of the Vauxhall/Opel Corsa), even without hybrid engines (see more below), compared to a North American average of around 10 l per 100 km (combining both cars and SUVs/trucks) and a European average of around 7 l per 100 km, shows that significant possibilities still exist (figures approximated from IEA 2004: 130).

Alongside measures to improve fuel efficiency are those to improve further the emission of a range of pollutants from cars. This is an area where, despite industry opposition, substantial improvements have been made; emissions of lead, NOx and others have declined not only per km travelled but also absolutely. But given the constant increase in km travelled and remaining concerns about exhaust pollution, in terms of the generation of VOCs in particular, there is continual pressure to

vehicles for passengers which were defined as light trucks for regulatory purposes. This reduced the costs of construction (as fewer regulatory constraints needed to be met) and meant that the costs of such vehicles were relatively low while the profits for manufacturers were high.

[5] Calculated from Orecchini and Sabatini (2003: 33), who give CO_2 emissions per km for new cars on the market, which is a direct correlate of fuel use.

improve this aspect of performance further. Research and development (R&D) was stimulated in particular by the California 'zero-emission' legislation enacted in the early 1990s. One effect has been to split the oil and car companies, traditionally locked together in a strong coalition. The zero emissions legislation made car manufacturers realise that they had been bearing the brunt of the costs of dealing with the car's environmental side-effects, while oil companies had had to do practically nothing beyond removing lead from petrol. During the 1990s car manufacturers shifted their stance to getting regulators to put more pressure on oil companies (a move resisted by most oil companies, especially again in North America given the more adversarial nature of the political system there) to improve the petrol being produced in terms of the emissions that would result from its use in cars. The introduction of ultra-low-sulphur petrol is one outcome of this process.

What is also clear is that there are limits to the possibilities of simply incrementally changing engine design and the specific chemistry of petrol fuels. Significant improvements in fuel efficiency with ICEs are possible, but the most important element in producing these improvements involves new forms of car design and materials involved in their production that dramatically reduce the weight and (significantly but less importantly) improve the aerodynamics of cars (Lovins and Barnett 1993; Hawken *et al.* 1999: chapter 2; Neale 1999). To give a sense of the possibilities, a prototype car that is capable of 280 miles per gallon has been produced (Lovins and Barnett 1993; Neale 1999), but for Lovins and his colleagues production cars which do 80–200 miles per gallon are perfectly imaginable using existing technologies (Hawken *et al.* 1999: 25).

While there are some gains, possibly significant ones, to be had from improving the way the existing 'steel and petroleum' car performs, there are more important gains to be had (especially in combination with changes in design, etc.) from the introduction of new fuels and engines. More important than continued improvements to petrol and to the ICE are the range of alternative fuels and engines developed aggressively since the mid-1990s. Some of these are old technologies squeezed out by the ICE in the early history of the car's development (this applies to both hydrogen and the electric car) while others are new. They also depart from the existing technological model in varying degrees, from the simple replacement of petrol with other fuels (ethanol, 'biodiesel', liquified natural gas (LNG)) through to the replacement of the ICE (fuel cell, electric cars) with 'hybrids' combining elements of both. The environmental improvements of such changes also vary, with liquified petroleum gas (LPG) and LNG principally helping only with those pollutants involved in urban air quality issues and not dealing significantly with questions such as climate change or resource depletion, while others have more far-reaching benefits.

The aggressive introduction of such technologies is clearly *technically* possible; the technologies to improve the performance of individual cars significantly for the most part already exist. Indeed, the transformation since the early 1990s is dramatic; alternative fuels for use in conventional engines – such as biodiesel, LPG and natural gas (LNG or compressed natural gas (CNG)) – are already on the market in a number of places, able to take advantage of relatively low costs of conversion of existing car engines to enable their use and their technical compatibility with the already existing network of petrol stations to enable the delivery of fuel. Uptake has been significantly affected in some places by their adoption by fleet operators – for example, the uptake of LNG in bus fleets in many cities. While, for a variety of reasons, electric vehicles have not yet made significant inroads, car manufacturers have quickly commercialised 'hybrids' with both ICEs and electric engines; the Toyota Prius and the Honda Insight were followed by others including a high-profile launch of a hybrid version of the Ford Escape in 2004.[6] Hybrids have a less dramatic impact on fuel efficiency than might be imagined, however. The Toyota Prius on the market in Europe in 2004 scored 65.7 mpg (*Guardian* 27 November 2004, 'Cars' special report: part 3) while those in North America scored around 55 mpg,[7] presumably reflecting weight differences. This makes a North American Prius around 80 per cent more efficient than the next equivalent-sized conventionally fuelled car on the market (a Hyundai Elantra), but only roughly 10 per cent more efficient than a similar car on the market in Europe (for example, the Ford Focus whose 2004 model scored 57 mpg).

---

[6] For a list of the hybrids available, see http://www.hybridcars.com/cars.html, viewed 26 May 2005.
[7] The Prius scored 60 mpg in city driving and 51 mpg on the highway, see DoE/EPA (2005: 9). The DoE/EPA report does not give figures on vehicle weight.

Most medium-to-long-term attention has been focused on the fuel cell. According to Mytelka: 'by the late 1990s the main question was no longer whether the Fuel Cell could supplant the ICE as the dominant design in the automobile industry but when this would likely occur' (2003: 12). Fuel cells are in effect batteries which reverse the process of electrolysis, converting hydrogen and oxygen into water and in the process releasing electrical energy. In environmental terms they have no immediate exhaust fumes, producing only water, although their overall impact depends on how the hydrogen or methanol used is produced. However, even if the hydrogen is produced electrically the efficiency of fuel cell engines is roughly double that of ICEs so losses in the production of fuel will still be outweighed by gains in the efficiency of the engines.

The chemistry of fuel cells has been known since the 1830s and was used in other contexts – for example, in powering spacecraft – but it was only in the early 1980s that the Canadian military stimulated their development in relation to cars by granting a research contract to a Vancouver-based company, Ballard (Mytelka 2003: 10; see also Koppel 1999). Over the next decade Ballard developed fuel cells which could produce energy at comparable levels to ICEs. An operational bus was working in Vancouver from 1993 and in 1996, according to Mytelka, there was 'a major turning point in the emergence of the PEM[8] fuel cell': a range of major car manufacturers (Daimler–Benz, Ford and also Shell) started to build relationships with Ballard and/or to develop their own R&D programmes to work out how to make fuel cells the basis of a means to power cars (Mytelka 2003: 11; see also Hawken *et al.* 1999: 26–7). By 1997 all the major car manufacturers had fuel cell R&D programmes, amounting to $18.4 billion in 1997 (Mytelka 2003: 15; Office of Technology Policy 2003). The focus of efforts is now which source of fuel to use – whether to use pure hydrogen or an intermediate source of hydrogen such as methanol – and the debate is about whether they will be commercially available by 2010 or 2020 (Mytelka 2003: 12).

These improvements would clearly mitigate a number of the significant environmental impacts of cars. They would address many of the emissions-related problems – to differing degrees depending on the

---

[8]   PEM stands for Proton Exchange Membrane, which refers to the specific type of fuel cell.

alternative fuel chosen – and some of the materials use problems. It is, of course, important to be careful to avoid confusing the *efficiency* improvements (emissions per km travelled) with improvements in *environmental* impact (which depend as much on the km travelled as the efficiency with which travel is carried out).[9] More importantly, these technical developments ignore many aspects of the environmental impacts of cars – the use of space, in particular.

Informatic automobility

There is also a range of technological developments to do with the application of IT to cars. This again has a number of elements. One is the continued development of IT in car production and the contribution this can make to industrial ecology;[10] second is the introduction of IT into marketing/planning with its potential for reductions in waste and overcapacity. Car firms are already starting to use such technologies for online buying and ordering.

The most important element here, however, has to do with the development of informatics in car use. These effectively create patterns of interaction between car, driver and road which monitor the performance of the car and which can, in Timothy Luke's words, operate as a 'surveillance device for forcing car owners to "drive green"' (Luke 2002: 29), ensuring the optimal performance of the car. There is a range of potential economic and environmental benefits in the use of the internet in travel planning (e.g. Kenyon *et al.* n.d.) and in the introduction of 'smart' highways and cars. The former enables the

---

[9] There is, of course, the standard 'rebound' problem with energy efficiency improvements, in particular. If fuel efficiency improvements lower operating costs this may simply mean people drive further and overall consumption does not decline. If driving does decline (it may, of course, in many instances by now be 'saturated') and savings accrue to individuals, it does not necessarily follow that overall energy consumption will decline as it depends what people do with the money saved – if it releases cash for an overseas holiday this would produce a dramatic rise in overall energy consumption via the air travel involved. (On rebound problems, see the special issue of *Energy Policy* (2000).) I agree with White's overall assessment (2002: 7) that while rebound effects clearly exist the potential for dramatic improvements nevertheless also exists – the scale of improvements made possible by existing technologies is such that they would not be completely undermined by rebound effects.

[10] Luke (2001: 313) suggests that this has been a central element in the 'greening' of Ford's operations, enabling it to exceed expectations in this regard.

integration of a range of transport services and can thus improve the use of public transport. It can also aid in the provision of access to services by those with reduced physical mobility (Kenyon *et al.* 2002), involving a range of technologies installed both in cars and on the roadway.

One of the most important of these is the set of technologies using GPS systems, which enable car users to plan journeys, receive information on likely congestion problems and devise alternative routes. Most of these are now becoming commonplace installations in new cars but there are also plans for integrating them further. At the most ambitious, these enable 'driverless cars', with the car being driven by a computer networked into an 'intelligent vehicle highway system' which enables a dramatic reduction in the distances between cars (and thus in congestion problems) and a smoothing out of acceleration, braking and so on, which also improve the car's environmental performance. This set of technological developments might therefore not only improve performance in terms of emissions, fuel use and so on but also address congestion and space problems.

These technologies clearly constitute a significant site of accumulation for car firms. Luke (2002) reports that electronics now constitute over '80 percent of all innovation in car technology', and that the 'dollar value of electronic systems has jumped over the past twenty-five years from $100 in 1977 per vehicle to $1,800 in 2001 on average' (Luke 2002: 7, quoting *Electronics Business News*, 9 April 2001: 42).

Beyond the car: greening transport

But there is also a broader project which recognises the limits of simply improving the way that cars are made, used and disposed of. For many, there are two dangers of this 'weak' approach. One is that the efficiency gains at the level of individual cars need to be able to *continually* outstrip increases in vehicle miles travelled and while there are clearly technical capacities in the short term to enhance such efficiency substantially (although it is still important to recognise that, as emphasised later, social and political conditions are determinants of the uptake of these potentialities) it is unclear that this can be continually achieved in the face of constant growth in consumption. The second, perhaps more substantial criticism, is that the focus purely on changes in the body of the car, the fuels they use and so on deal only with a relatively narrow range of the environmental problems with which the car is associated. Taking the most optimistic view it is possible to envisage such an approach dealing with the major air pollution problems, with climate change (at least concerning the energy in use, much depends on how the hydrogen in fuel cells is produced), with materials use (through substantial recycling of materials and reduction in weight of cars), with some aspects of space use (through maximum use of 'smart highways') and perhaps a reduction in the numbers of people killed and injured on the roads (through weight reductions and design changes). But it is unlikely to deal with most of the problems of space use – parking, congestion and so on and fails completely to deal with the questions of hyperindividualism, inequalities, or other social critiques of automobility (partly perhaps because its proponents by and large do not accept or recognise them as problems). And, like other historical technical changes (including ones expressly developed to deal with environmental problems), it is likely to produce its own environmental consequences – from the energy involved in hydrogen production for fuel cells to the toxics involved in the increased reliance on electronics and so on – which are largely unacknowledged.

Reducing car use; reshaping cities

For many writers, addressing the socio-ecological problems of automobility thus tends to involve two specific sorts of transformation, exemplified perhaps by Sachs' aphorism of 'slower speeds and shorter routes' (1992: 221). One is the promotion of forms of mobility which involve reductions in car use. Reductions in a range of environmental impacts involved in car use cannot usefully be envisaged without the expansion in use of non-car sorts of mobility – mass transit, walking, cycling, in particular.[11] Even hyperoptimists about the possibilities of technical innovation in the building of cars, such as Hawken *et al.* (1999: 40–7), accept that such innovations will be insufficient without strategies to reduce car use and reshape cities. Newman and Kenworthy (1999) provide the fullest overview of the dynamics of sustainability in urban areas, with a substantial study of thirty-seven

---

[11] Many environmentalist pronouncements on transport policy provide evidence for the arguments of this general approach. From the huge range of these materials, see Brown *et al.* (1979b: chapter 6); Renner (1988: 46–56).

cities across the world. One of their core points is that even substantial variations in cars themselves are relatively unimportant in explaining the overall patterns of transport energy use in cities; by far the most important determinant is the proportion of journeys taken in modes other than a car.

Newman and Kenworthy usefully divide strategies to reduce car use into 5 different types:

1. Traffic calming – to slow auto traffic and create more urban, humane environments better suited to other transportation modes.
2. Quality transit, bicycling and walking – to provide genuine options to the car.
3. Urban villages – to create multimodal centers with mixed, dense land use that reduce the need to travel and that are linked to good transit.
4. Growth management – to prevent urban sprawl and redirect development into urban villages.
5. Taxing transportation better – to cover external costs and to use the revenues to help build a sustainable city based on the previous policies.
                                            (Newman and Kenworthy 1999: 144)

At the most general level it is the case that while Dunn (1998) grossly exaggerates the power of the 'anti-auto' lobby in the United States, there has been a shift in the pattern of infrastructure spending across most western countries, with a decline in highway construction and maintenance (although this still accounts for the major share of spending) and towards support for public transport. Newman and Kenworthy (1999) give extensive case studies of cities around the world which have been the most progressive and successful in this regard (Curitiba, Portland, or Stockholm, for example) and others which have been less successful (Perth, Australia, for example) and show that it is the combination of these strategies which works best.

Most of these policies are fairly obvious and need little detailing but the important point to emphasise is that, on their own, simply promoting transit, cycling and walking is of relatively little value. Some cities which remain automobile-dependent but which have focused in this way, such as Perth (Newman and Kenworthy 1999: 233–7) have seen some success in shifting commuters to rail, but much less than in cities which have combined this with other strategies. What is also required is a *structural change* in planning systems and philosophies. Moving away from the car is recognised (at least in principle, there remain many contradictions in practice) to entail not only the provision of more public transport, cycling facilities and so on but that the possibility of promoting these transport modes fully depends on reshaping urban forms. Newman and Kenworthy, for example, cite a study of communities in California which showed that vehicle km travelled fell by a quarter with a doubling of population density while they fell by only 8 per cent with a doubling of transit provision (1999, quoting Bernick and Cervero 1997: 83). Just as the city was remade by and for the car it will have to be remade again to move away from the car. At its crudest level, this entails reversing the trend towards decreasing urban densities, to create the proximity of residences, workplaces, schools and services, thus enabling people to access them without cars. This is what Newman and Kenworthy envisage in the concept of an 'urban village'. This entails rather more than merely increasing density but more specifically creating nodes of concentrated, mixed-use development which are walkable or cyclable within the urban village and permit good public transport connections to the rest of the city. Such urban reorganisations facilitate substantial reductions in car use.

A significant element in recent discourse has articulated these shifts in urban planning and transport policy through the notion of 'smart growth',[12] which is useful to elaborate how the 'greening of transport' may be constrained and shaped. In order to deal with the problem

---

[12] On smart growth, see Maryland State Highway Administration (2002), Urban Land Institute (2003), Wagner (2005) or Ruth (2006). On New Urbanism, its related planning concept, see Lehrer and Milgrom (1996). The idea of 'smart growth' is largely absent from European discussions, in part as the population densities of European cities are significantly higher and the 'donut' effect of suburbanisation more or less absent, urban congestion orders of magnitude worse and thus the transport/economic development/environment problems rather different to those in North America. But there are instances where the dynamic has been fostered. A number of US cities and regions now highlight the importance of network organisation for the success of clusters of firms, especially in the 'new economy', and thus the importance for promoting corridors or clusters of growth with specific implications for transport. Many European cities are also acting to redevelop urban cores and increase the population density in city centre areas. This has sometimes been understood in terms of the changing role of city authorities, developing what are called 'entrepreneurial cities' – acting as agents to attract investment from outside and reshaping the city to facilitate this. Solving transport problems becomes a key element in these strategies, creating opportunities for 'smart growth' focused on density and public transport, but also contradictions – such as promoting the development of air transport. See While *et al.* (2004), on Manchester and Leeds, for example.

posed by the political economy of automobility many have recognised the need to articulate policies to reduce car use precisely as a strategy for economic growth. It is not just a question of attempting to put in place a set of policies to promote public transport and higher density; this needs to be articulated not only as an environmental but as an economic need. Smart growth emerged during the 1990s in the North American context, expressing this ecological modernisation in relation to transport, growth and urban form. Smart growth is widely contested as a viable form of development for North American cities but these, with their very low population densities, are beginning to experience significant economic dysfunctionalities[13] and at the same time high levels of environmental degradation. Smart growth does provide a useful sense of how, if one were to think about applying ecological modernisation ideas to the question of transport, one would begin. Of course, as a number of critics of smart growth suggest, this would indeed have significant impacts for the 'car industry', but promoting the interests of car manufacturers and the development of a national/regional/city economy need not be the same thing.

Political economy and the greening of cars

Structural power and environmental politics

If we look at the attempts which started in the 1950s to regulate cars to meet environmental goals, a persistent feature has been the structural power of car firms in relation to environmental regulation. The attempt at regulation has had to be pushed by social movements of varying sorts, other businesses threatened by car pollution and technocratic scientists. These attempts have at times arisen within the contradictions of automobility/capitalism/the state itself and at times have worked to undermine the hegemony of the car. I will illustrate this in relation to two prominent examples: the debates about air pollution in the United States from the 1950s onwards and the strategies of car firms regarding climate change.

---

[13] For example, advocates of smart growth tend to suggest that the costs (even in narrow economic terms) of the provision of infrastructure are beginning to outweigh the benefits of such low-density development, or that the social and economic costs of inner-city decline and the social instability such decline produces are significant.

Urban air pollution became a significant political issue across the industrialised world in the 1950s. While in some places the most important element was coal-burning in urban areas (as in the famous 'pea-souper' smogs in London in the late 1940s–early 1950s), in most US cities pollution from cars was the biggest problem. State and city officials first started to point the finger at cars during this period and a pattern of engagement by car firms with those pursuing environmental regulation was set up which in the United States at least has persisted ever since.[14] Car firms started by funding other research to cast doubt on the state's analyses, they then suggested that no technologies existed which could mitigate the problem without prohibitive costs and that consumers would not buy cars which had features which minimised pollution; at times they threatened litigation for business lost through 'unreasonable' regulatory measures. These tactics were successfully used to slow down regulatory action – from the initial measures to deal with smog, to the phasing out of lead from petrol, to dealing with particulates in the Clean Air Act, to the mandatory introduction of catalytic converters, to improvements in fuel economy, to measures to promote alternative fuels, to California's zero emissions legislation and to policies to respond to climate change (Gayle 1993; Doyle 2000; Luger 2000).

Underlying this success is the widely recognised importance of the car industry to capitalist economies (at its most extreme in North America, but also elsewhere), which confers on car firms a structural power in relation to regulatory proposals. This has a narrow structural element in terms of the car industry's role in creating cycles of accumulation; but it is also legitimised more broadly. The routine response to proposals to regulate the car industry in North America is a mantra about 'one in seven jobs' being tied to the success of car firms, while a discourse about a 'threat to consumers' rights' is usually close behind.

This structural power can be seen most recently in debates about climate change which has entailed a globalisation of US car firms' strategies but also involved more strategic diversity. Car firms for the most part joined the GCC, formed in 1989 as the principal industry lobby group to protect the interests of industries heavily dependent on

---

[14] Doyle (2000) provides the most comprehensive account of these struggles from the 1940s to the present day.

fossil fuel consumption (Levy and Rothenburg 2002: 178–9) – car firms, oil and coal companies, electricity generators, steel firms and so on. They organised to protect their (perceived) interests which were seen to be threatened by measures to limit CO_2 emissions by increasing fuel costs and thus reducing consumption, by requiring higher fuel efficiency and thus limiting sales of high-profit SUVs, or through other measures which would have the effect of reducing the amount of driving and thus people's 'need' for their cars. The strategy is frequently presented in ways which can be understood as a hegemonic project – attempts to represent the sectional interests of particular firms as the interests of all. While the GCC presents itself as 'a voice for business in the global warming debate' (itself a hegemonic project within business interests, since it represents only certain sorts of firms) many of the arguments made are attempts to suggest broader impacts across society (US society, in particular). Arguments are presented both that acting on climate change will be costly – 'reducing greenhouse gas emissions by the amount demanded by the Kyoto Protocol would require new taxes on gasoline equal to 68 cents a gallon or more' – and that it would also entail more intrusive regulation dictating how motorists would have to behave: 'a wide array of new regulations would be imposed on car owners, such as mandatory car pooling, new emissions tests, and financial penalties on the owners of trucks and sport utility vehicles' (GCC n.d., quoting Heartland Institute 1999).[15]

Along with their allies car firms have been highly successful in defending these interests, especially in the United States but also elsewhere. Globally, they have been able to limit proposals to reduce greenhouse gas (ghg) emissions, initially (through their support from the US administration under George H. W. Bush) by preventing the inclusion of quantified targets on ghg emissions in the UN Framework Convention on Climate Change (FCCC) (Paterson 1996: chapter 3) and then later by limiting the extent of emissions cuts agreed to at Kyoto in 1997 to an average of 5.2 per cent across the industrialised countries (as compared to the 15 per cent cuts proposed by the EU, the 20 per cent cuts proposed by the Alliance of Small Island States, or to a 'small fraction' of current emissions levels that the International Panel

[15] On the GCC, see Gelbspan (1997); Newell (2000: chapter 5); Mayer (2002: 612); Lacy (2005: chapter 4).

on Climate Change (IPCC) suggests are required to stabilise the climate) and creating sufficient loopholes that even this goal will not strictly be required.[16] In the United States, their ability to defend these interests has been even stronger (and this has thus affected their international success since most other countries and commentators believe US participation in the international climate regime is essential since the country produces about 25 per cent of global ghg emissions). Car firms funded US politicians and used their long-standing relations with them (built up through decades of lobbying on a range of issues) to ensure that measures to limit CO_2 emissions would not be pursued in the United States (e.g. Gelbspan 1997; Doyle 2000: 355–88). They successfully prevented CO_2 being defined as a pollutant under the Clean Air Act (limiting the right of the Environmental Protection Agency (EPA) to regulate it) and prevented Clinton's proposed energy tax from coming into effect. This culminated in the Byrd–Hagel Resolution in the US Senate in 1997, which stated that the United States 'should not be a signatory to any protocol' that would:

(A) mandate new commitments to limit or reduce greenhouse gas emissions for the Annex I Parties, unless the protocol or other agreement also mandates new specific scheduled commitments to limit or reduce greenhouse gas emissions for Developing Country Parties within the same compliance period, or (B) would result in serious harm to the economy of the United States. (Byrd–Hagel 1997)

The resolution passed the Senate 95–0 and effectively meant that even if Clinton had agreed to anything at Kyoto later that year he would know that any agreement would not be ratified by the US Congress. Clinton did agree to a deal at Kyoto but never submitted it to Congress

[16] The principal loophole is in the combination of the introduction of the emissions trading system with 1990 as a date for an emissions baseline against which reductions are measured. Since shortly after 1990 the USSR (and the states which came into being as it collapsed) and other Eastern–Central European states experienced a sharp economic decline and simultaneously a sharp decline in ghg emissions, but are allocated emissions permits under Kyoto on the basis of their 1990s level, this creates possibilities for other industrialised countries to simply buy up spare Russian credits rather than reduce their own. At the time of writing (August 2006), few countries are on track to meet their Kyoto targets and will thus have strong reasons to make use of this opportunity.

for ratification and George W. Bush stated even firmer opposition to Kyoto in March 2001, shortly after his election.[17]

The ability of car firms and their allies to withstand pressure from a range of social movements, activist regulators and scientists is evidence of their structural importance, which I interpret principally in relation to the role of cars in reproducing capitalism, as outlined in chapter 4. The picture is, of course, more complex than the narrative presented above. The 1960s and 1970s, as Luger (2000) persuasively shows, were a period where the car firms' hegemony was effectively challenged by what he calls 'public interest' social forces, principally concerning questions of safety, fuel economy and emissions, revealing the contestable nature of corporate hegemony (Luger 2000: chapters 3 and 4; see also chapter 2 in this volume). Doyle similarly concludes (2000: 452–4) that constant public pressure has at times been able to force the car industry to make concessions and enable (or force) the state to regulate the industry. The GCC has been unable to keep the coalition together in terms of strict hostility to action on climate change; a number of oil companies (in particular, BP and Shell) as well as car firms (most publicly, Ford) left the coalition during the late 1990s to take up more 'constructive' activities in relation to climate change. European firms have broadly been significantly more accommodating to climate change concerns than US ones (Levy and Rothenburg 2002). Ford under Bill Ford, Jr. attempted to repaint itself as a 'green' company committed to environmental action (e.g. Doyle 2000: 11–16; Luke 2001). A lot depends on the interpretations of these shifts. While making radical noises (at varying points, Bill Ford has predicted the end of the ICE and the end of car ownership) Ford continues to make most of its profits from SUVs with very low fuel efficiency, to take just the simplest target. But even if the shift were genuine and significant in terms of ghg emissions, it would make sense as a form of what Gramsci called 'passive revolution': the appropriation by ruling forces of elements of the discourse of subordinate forces to secure their continued rule. But whether or not such power creates possibilities for 'greening', the analyses focusing on structural power tend to overlook an

---

[17] Bush did not, in fact, as is often stated, 'withdraw' from the Kyoto Protocol fully, as the United States is still a signatory, although it has not ratified the protocol. The semantics of diplomacy aside, Bush's moves did mark a final victory for the interests of GCC firms.

important element of automobility politics. The power of car firms to resist regulations to limit their environmental impact has not only to do with their financial size, concentration, the jobs they create and so on but also with the whole regime of automobility whose principal managers they are. It is the role of cars as consumption items, regarded increasingly as 'necessary', which serves as an implicit ideological support for the car firms' strategies. Luger (2000), for example, has a properly radical political agenda but does not question 'the automobile' itself, just as it is the corporate power of the car *industry* which limits the force of the analysis in concrete policy terms.

Towards a green regime of accumulation?

The other pertinent dimension of chapter 4's analysis is that automobility plays an integral role in an overall regime of accumulation. As automobility has been integral to both Fordism and flexible accumulation the attempts either to 'green' cars or to move beyond automobility need to be articulated as an element in an overall accumulation strategy, which will enable either a transformation of the structural power of car firms to become an ally rather than an obstacle in the greening process, or require finding a set of other business groups which can serve to overcome continued opposition from car firms.

We would expect one of the principal constraints and 'driving forces' to be the way that these projects intersect with imperatives for capital accumulation in general and the specific contexts of the contemporary dynamics of capitalism. While a crude argument here would tend to emphasise the way in which accumulation tends to exceed ecological limits and the power of capital operates as a brake on progressive policy and political development, the picture is perhaps more complex.

One of the determinants of the ability to transform the way cars work is the ability either to couch such changes in terms of the interests of big car firms, or to be able to legitimise a set of policies to overcome their opposition. They still continue to lobby against many measures, fund politicians to support their positions and so on; this can be seen regarding California's emissions legislation since the early 1990s, for example. But the position is contradictory, as the car firms also seek to legitimise themselves with consumers (and regulators) through the development of alternative fuels and other measures to deal with specific problems of the cars they produce. While there is little evidence of a fully developed 'green consumerism' in relation to cars (in contrast with some other sectors), the pursuit of good 'green PR' by firms is still regarded as a necessary tactic. In addition, and perhaps more importantly, to the extent that new fuels and engine technologies will be required by government regulation or by the exigencies of oil prices, firms are placed in a situation of needing to position themselves for first-mover advantage in the technologies which will replace the ICE. GM has come under much criticism (from shareholders and commentators on firm strategy as much as from environmentalists) for resisting since the 1990s investment in the fuel cells seen as the most likely to succeed the ICE in the long term (Mytelka 2003).

One of the implications therefore is that it is the design of regulatory mechanisms which will determine the success of policies to promote the transformation of the car business. Three elements are important here. The first, and most straightforward, are policies to shape car consumerism in 'green' directions. Many of these are fiscal in nature, involving changes in tax and subsidy regimes, and the crudest are to do with petrol taxation, in terms of either generally high taxation to stimulate fuel efficiency and (as they become technically viable) alternative fuels, or of differential taxation rates to promote particular developments (e.g. differential taxation on unleaded fuel which has been used in some countries to accelerate the phase-out of lead in petrol and more recently to promote diesel and ultra-low-sulphur fuel in some countries). For Hawken *et al.* (1999: 38–9), some of the most effective are those operating at the point of purchase of the vehicle (the point at which the future environmental impact of the car's use is decisively affected) such as 'feebates' – a combination of fees/taxes to be paid and rebates to be given, depending on the fuel efficiency or other measures of the car's impact. These, of course, impose costs on consumers (including businesses) but there is no persuasive general evidence that they have any significant overall effects on GDP growth rates: the growth rates of those countries with low fuel taxation compared to those which since the early 1970s have developed high fuel taxation regimes are broadly comparable.[18] There is a whole range of other tax measures; these

---

[18] This is obviously overly crude as an assessment – it does not deal with more subtle effects of such taxes on growth, or on the more general claim that fuel taxes may harm growth. But it cannot be in general claimed that countries with low fuel taxation (e.g. the United States) have had significantly higher levels of

include incentives to scrap old cars with particularly bad emissions problems, taxes to create incentives to make 'industrial ecology' processes more viable, differential taxes on cars to favour fuel efficient, small-engined, or alternative fuel cars and so on.

The second, and more complex, element is the regulatory mechanisms which shape the incentives of firms in relation to their business model. One potential driver of a transformation in consumer behaviour is a change in the way that car firms do business and depends on transforming on a daily basis the incentives facing firms. While some of this is to do with regulatory change, it can in part be pursued by firms themselves. Broadly, the shift consists in moving from an economy of products to an economy of services and flows (Jackson 1996: 133–5; von Weiszäcker *et al.* 1998; White 2002: 11), where firms make their money through the provision of services surrounding a particular product (finance, maintenance, upgrading, etc.) rather than through an initial sale. A prototype business model often cited is that developed for photocopiers where the product is almost universally leased rather than bought and where the money is made through rental agreements and maintenance contracts. In such a situation the incentive for manufacturers is to produce long-lasting reliable products rather than engaging in planned obsolescence.

Such a model, of course, already exists in some sectors, with large-scale lease systems for company cars, but the market is principally dominated by sale to private owners. One of the areas highlighted by Bill Ford in his statements declaring green intentions for Ford cars was: 'The day will come when the whole notion of car ownership is antiquated' (e.g. the *Independent* (London), 6 October 2000). While much of Ford's 'greening' so far (Luke 2001) has, as we have seen, been oriented around combinations of technical advance, industrial ecology and informatics there is a clear recognition that in the longer term the capacity to keep such developments going is dependent on the development of a different business model. Ford's quote does not imply there will not be cars, but rather that people's use of them will not be on the basis of ownership, but on lease arrangements. The structure of incentives for firms can (in principle at least) shift away from a rapid

growth than those with high fuel taxation (e.g. Germany, Japan, the United Kingdom) over the last thirty years, and it is thus a legitimate basis for arguing that taxes can be used to stimulate improvements in environmental performance which do not harm growth but rather 'ecologically modernise' an economy.

turnover in sales of new cars towards provision of a range of services to car users.

The third element concerns more general regulatory mechanisms which are 'market enabling' rather than 'market restricting'. This is found in ideological arguments about environmental regulation under neoliberalism, but is pertinent here in particular since there is a continuing understanding by car firms themselves that regulations are only one way to restrict their markets and/or profitability. Equally important is a range of possible R&D regimes to stimulate investment in ecological modernisation technologies and processes. Examples of these already abound, with Clinton's Partnership for a New Generation of Vehicles being perhaps the most high-profile. These can involve direct partnerships between public and private institutions, through to tax incentives for R&D development and so on.

But such regulations (and tax regimes) are often simultaneously carrots and sticks. Regulations on both production processes and product can be used clearly to shape the environmental performance of the industry and its products by restricting certain sorts of markets and technologies while favouring others. A range of regulations on allowable additives to fuel or things which must be removed (lead, MMT, sulphur, etc.) exist across OECD countries in particular, as do regulations concerning safety, engine power, fuel economy (CAFÉ – however weak such regulations are in terms both of their absolute level and the SUV loophole) and so on. The most well-known range of regulations on production processes are national origin rules specifying minimum nationally produced components and the ISO14000 series concerning environmental management systems which are essentially self-regulation by the industry (on the ISO14000 series and cars, see Orecchini and Sabatini 2003; on its uptake by Ford, see Luke 2001: 328).

In examining these elements of the 'ecological modernisation' of the car industry I am not suggesting that regulations are simple to apply or that the ecological modernisation approach is unproblematic in its application. It does suggest that a growth/environment or (more precisely) an accumulation/environment contradiction inevitably means that 'ecological modernisation' or similar approaches will face insurmountable difficulties.

When we return to the 'stronger' version of greening automobility, the notion of 'smart growth' serves as a useful starting point. Smart growth exemplifies that it is not merely a set of policies, planning processes and so on which will reduce car use and its associated problems but that such measures are articulated as an *economic* strategy, responding to the needs of the 'entrepreneurial city' (While *et al.* 2004). Smart growth is an *accumulation strategy* at the level of the city, suggesting that increased urban concentration, clustering, advanced public transport, the promotion of cycling and walking can be a growth strategy by creating new growth sectors, reducing costs to business (principally of congestion) and facilitating business networking central to contemporary firm needs. Smart growth can also be taken to represent the power of capital in the structuring of the greening of automobility – in order to 'sell' car-reduction policies politically such arguments need to be articulated as a growth strategy. The 'Moving the economy' group in Toronto is a good example here; founded and directed by members of Transportation Options (an NGO lobbying for better transit, cycle facilities, etc.) and in particular by Sue Zielinski, co-editor of the anti-car book *Beyond the Car* (Zielinski and Laird 1995), Moving the economy has brought together a broad coalition of NGOs, the city government, unions, businesses and other agencies to promote 'smart growth'. Moving the economy is a particularly ambitious and creative set of projects that simultaneously reveals the strength of capitalism in structuring alternative transport projects.[19]

Limits to greening cars?

The way that anti-car or alternative transport policies have been shaped towards the needs of capital in the discourse of smart growth is suggestive of big question marks as to whether or not this process of transformation can be realised within contemporary capitalism. The role of 'globalisation' in affecting the emergence of policies to 'green' automobility is key here. Discourses of globalisation figure prominently in many of the arguments about how regulation can stimulate innovation, but also about the pressures which favour 'smart growth' strategies. Globalisation is held by Porter (1990) (among others) to be a set of pressures which means that environmental regulation can stimulate patterns of technological investment which make firms more competitive (by reducing costs, creating first-mover advantage and so on):

[19] For details of Moving the economy, see its website at www.movingtheeconomy. ca, viewed 16 February 2006.

Stringent standards for product performance, product safety, and environmental impact contribute to creating and upgrading competitive advantage. They pressure firms to upgrade quality, upgrade technology and provide features in areas of important customer (and social) concern ... particularly beneficial are stringent regulations that anticipate standards that will spread internationally. These give a nation's firms a head start in developing products and services that will be valued elsewhere. (Porter 1990: 74–7, quoted in Ekins 2000: 172)

Globalisation is also held by Vogel (1995) and others to be the condition under which diffusion of new technologies can be facilitated – as in the 'California effect'. Local regulation (in strategically important sites) such as zero emission regulations in that state had world-wide effects as car firms sought to maximise the profits from investments made to meet California's requirements. A more complex argument suggests that since for many states globalisation creates pressures to attract investment in 'high-value', 'innovative' and 'leading-edge' sectors (especially when the discourse combines with arguments concerning a 'new economy') globalisation has in many countries in fact essentially led to the development of a new industrial policy (e.g. Palan and Abbott 1999). This policy is in many ways precisely the forms of intervention which could promote processes consistent with ecological modernisation (Barry and Paterson 2003). Clinton's Partnership for a New Generation of Vehicles is best interpreted in this sort of light.

Many suggest that the more common fear that globalisation produces a 'race to the bottom' (Karliner 1997: 12) in environmental regulation is largely misplaced. Kirton, in particular (1998: 193–9), argues forcefully that the integration processes stimulated by NAFTA have stimulated an 'upward harmonisation' of environmental regulation in the three countries (the United States, Canada and Mexico) involved. Similar assessments have been made concerning the EU (Arp 1993) while Vogel (1995) has advanced a similar argument about the 'California effect' in global contexts. In both cases, the general argument is that such upward harmonisation has not had significant economic impacts, and in some instances has benefited firms (Kirton 1998: 204). Of course, one could suggest that this is because the level of the regulations is not particularly stringent, and it certainly does not necessarily follow that just because it has so far been possible to promote both environmental regulation and economic growth it will remain possible to do so as standards get tighter. But, in principle, the possibility exists.

The two key elements in such a dynamic are a concern in the industry for 'level playing fields' and national strategic assessments of 'competitive–first-mover advantage'. The former is the more straightforward – as integration projects proceed (the EU and NAFTA being the most advanced) they create incentives for firms to have the same level of regulation across the emerging single economic space. The cost reductions provided for by harmonisation, as firms have fewer and fewer variations in regulatory schemes to deal with, in turn enable an upward tightening of the regulations in environmental terms. The accounts of both Kirton (1998) on NAFTA and Arp (1993) on the EC/EU are exemplary. The second element is perhaps more prevalent in the EU than in North America, where it is clear that Germany in particular has used environmental regulation in the car industry (the emerging rules for manufacturers to take back cars and recycle them are a good example, but earlier cases concerning unleaded petrol or catalytic converters are also exemplars) in such a way as to gain competitive advantage in the EU market. By acting first to design regulations Germany could then argue for such standards at the EU level, modelled on its own regulations with which its firms were already familiar and thus well positioned in the EU market.[20]

But this account of globalisation's implications is at the very least contested and, for its critics, highly misleading. While it may be the case that in some instances competitive pressures create dynamics favouring innovation in more efficient technologies, curbing of sprawl and so on, it is far from clear that this is a uniform tendency. As Palan and Abbott (1999) point out, globalisation has not produced a uniformity of economic strategy but rather a diversification of 'niches' in the global

---

[20] The classic international-level example of this in environmental politics is the emergence of the Vienna Convention and Montreal Protocol to deal with ozone depletion. The initial lobbying for a convention on ozone depletion came from the United States, where producers were already restricted in their use of CFCs, which had been banned for aerosol use in 1977. US firms declined in international market share, to the benefit principally of European firms, and this persuaded the US government to act diplomatically for an internationalisation of US rules. While the Montreal Protocol which resulted predictably did not totally follow the US rules, it did disproportionately benefit DuPont, the world's largest CFC producer, which subsequently regained market share in the replacements for CFCs (see Benedick 1991).

economy. From the point of view of an argument for smart growth, or for the regulatory stimulation of innovation, this suggests that these strategies may not be available in all states, as they may lack a 'fit' with the overall economic strategy. As I have argued in other contexts (concerning climate change strategy), one can extend this argument to suggest a broad distinction in strategy between the United States and Europe, the former opting for a continuation of 'carboniferous capitalism' while the latter pushes for 'ecological modernisation' (Paterson 2001; Matthews and Paterson 2005). Such strategies respond to certain globalising imperatives, but in very different ways, partly structured by the particular history of their distinct economies.

Related to this problem is the dependence (explicit in Porter 1990, implicit elsewhere) on a Schumpeterian account of growth. The basis for arguing that growth and profitability can be pursued at the same time as reducing the environmental impacts of growth is rooted ultimately in a particular conception of economic growth, going back principally to that articulated by Joseph Schumpeter. In opposition to both classical economics, with its account of growth based on the efficiency of 'free' market exchanges, and at the same time to Marxist political economy, whose explanation focuses principally on the particular way that surplus value is appropriated under capitalist social relations, Schumpeter (1943) suggested that growth was driven mainly by particular socio-technical developments. Comparable to the notion of Kondratieff waves, Schumpeter suggested that growth in capitalist societies went in 'long cycles' driven by the efficiency gains and new economic possibilities produced by particular combinations of technologies. Most of these have been energy-related technologies; waves of growth have thus been driven by coal and steam, then by the development of the train, then by the combination of oil, automobiles and electricity. In each instance, the new energy technologies both improve the efficiency with which existing tasks are carried out but, more importantly, make new sorts of social and economic tasks and connections possible. They typically intensify the possibility of concentrating energy in a single place and also make dramatic leaps in the possibilities of long-distance transport.

The ecological modernisation discourse exemplified in the current context by the notion of 'smart growth' depends on overcoming economy/environment contradictions. It also depends on the idea that globalisation creates powerful impulses to promote technical innovation. For most writers from this perspective ecological modernisation consists principally of identifying patterns of investment (and state intervention to promote those patterns) which will stimulate the technological change which creates markets but at the same time reduces the overall ecological metabolism of the economy. The standard account from neoclassical models, as well as from most Marxist arguments, however, is that economy/environment contradictions are more fundamental. Neoclassical models typically predict that intervention to ameliorate environmental problems *must* reduce GDP since they assume (in practice in their models, if not in their more subtle theoretical formulations) that economies operate optimally.[21] But for ecological modernisation discourse, growth depends rather on the capacity to facilitate combinations of technological innovation which create virtuous cycles of accelerating investment, production and consumption, which Schumpeter famously termed 'gales of creative destruction'. A lot depends, however, on the acceptance of this model of growth.

Overall, then, there are reasons to be both cautiously optimistic and also sceptical, from political economy perspectives, about the possibility of transformations occurring in automobility.

Green governmentality

As we saw in chapter 5, the production of automobility has been a project which entails the ongoing production of human subjects, involving not only regulatory effort to restrict and channel their actual movements but broad discursive practices which produce a certain orientation to movement, acceleration and so on. One of the current contexts in which this subjectivity is being re-produced is that of environmental tensions within automobility itself.

Rajan's *The Enigma of Automobility: Democratic Politics and Pollution Control* (1996), about the politics of air pollution control in California, analyses from this perspective what happens when activists, scientists and policy-makers challenge particular aspects of automobility and attempt to 'green' it. He suggests that it is the lack of a

---

[21] Debates about climate change policy are the starkest example of this. The routine accounts of GDP losses from action to limit greenhouse gases stem almost universally from an assumption built into the economic models that the economy already works optimally and therefore any intervention (to raise energy prices, the modellers typically assume) will reduce GDP.

challenge to automobility itself and a public political debate about the
car which has led to technocratic resolutions of automobile-related air
pollution questions.

As developed throughout the book so far, rather than refer to 'the
automobile' as an object Rajan refers to 'automobility' as a social
institution, comprising 'automobile use and everything that makes it
possible – roads, highways, parking structures, and traffic rules – in
short, the very abstraction of urbanized distance' (1996: 7). For Rajan,
the 'enigma of automobility' is that, on the one hand, cars are taken as
symbols of modernity – 'the pleasures of the open road, speed, power,
and personal control', combined with 'the functionality of covering
distance, managing time, and maintaining certain forms of individua-
tion' (1996: 7). On the other, they produce a whole range of risks and
dangers which require intrusive governance: 'The vast enterprise of
privatized transportation generates serious risks to human health and
social welfare from accidents, pollution, and the wasteful consumption
of energy and resources – risks that even individual drivers ordinarily
face in the form of congestion, mishaps on highways, and the increasing costs of owning and maintaining vehicles' (1996: 7). This is the
enigma of automobility: 'cars serve to create privatized spaces for
individual drivers, but driving propagates socially shared effects that
could quite conceivably undermine the individualist credo of personal
vehicle use' (1996: 8).

This creates a predicament for regulators (which Rajan narrows to
pollution control regulators, a point to be revisited below): 'Where
driving is ubiquitous, cars also tend to turn into essential, even prosthetic, machines for negotiating urban space. Thus, if limitations on
automobile use to control air pollution seem to require an extraordinary degree of public acquiescence and social mobilization, they are
in reality constrained more severely by the problems of having to
remake the urban environment and the institution of automobility
itself' (1996: 9). In other words, the choice for regulators is either to
intervene progressively more intensively in the manufacture, maintenance and operation of cars, or to remake urban landscapes to limit
actual automobile use.

Rajan then shows how the complication of automobile use is that
those who suffer from the effects of automobiles (accidents, pollution,
etc.) are simultaneously bound up in the institution through which such
risks are produced: 'Unlike the typical case of industrial environmental

control where there is a clear distinction between polluters and potential victims, no such demarcation is possible for adjudicating among an entire citizenry caught up in the adverse effects of automobility' (1996: 9). The consequence of this dilemma is that regulators adopt 'risk management' strategies that resemble strategies of insurers, to spread the costs of limiting the risks of automobility across all users – 'by placing broad limits and emission standards on various classes and models of vehicles' (1996: 9). But this form of regulation is increasingly unable to achieve its results because of diminishing returns (1996: 10): 'Instead of promoting serious public debate on the culture of automobility, they attempt to spread the already limited controls on use across an array of vehicle categories and turn even more aggressively to better technological controls for new vehicles' (1996: 10). The crisis of existing regulation only produces more risk management techniques, and regulation becomes progressively more intrusive.

Rajan opens his book with an account of an advert placed on a shopping bag in California: 'Is it anti-social to drive your car? Air pollution control agencies use these arguments to justify mandatory car pools and to subsidize public transport. It's more productive to think of automobile pollution in another way. Some cars are sick. Sick cars cause air pollution' (1996: 3). Rajan uses this to (among other things) show the contrast between professional discourses and popular consciousness. The shopping bag advertised an infra-red sensor device developed by scientists at the University of Denver for use on the side of the road to measure pollution from individual cars. Pollution control agencies construct a collective problem about forms of mobility. The shopping bag seeks to re-individualise the problem, as part of the extension of risk management techniques. Rajan is worth quoting at length:

My argument [is] that administration of automobility requires the creation of a space of effective policy making that is legitimized by elaborate ideological mechanisms that confer special status upon both technology and individuality ... Widespread complacency toward the efficacy of privatized mobility is seen in the ubiquitous and casual use of the car, representing modernity's remarkable achievement in giving the individual means to 'freely' pursue personal goals and interests. But even the most fiercely independent projects carried out on the highway are under the strict supervision of a public power that operates through a plethora of traffic rules and regulations. The endurance of these projects is, indeed, a testimony to the actual and ideological power of a technology that keeps the political questions of automobility at bay while bearing the commanding insignia of individualism. (Rajan 1996: 63)

But at the same time, Rajan shows that many of the side-effects of cars, particularly air pollution, have been very highly contested in the United States. From at least the early 1950s the emergence of smog problems in Southern California, and later in other areas, provided a substantial and continuous impetus to the formation of environmental movements, political lobbying by such movements as well as by car manufacturers and the development of an elaborate regulatory system to deal with exhaust emissions from cars which were regarded as the cause of much of the smog problem (e.g. Krier and Ursin 1977; Rajan 1996; Doyle 2000). The political debate around such regulatory schemes was highly charged and public, especially during the 1970s, and the attempts by environmental movements, some US senators (particularly Ed Muskie) and regulators from the EPA (particularly its first administrator, Bill Ruckelshaus) to introduce stringent pollution control requirements caused a fierce backlash from the car manufacturers (see especially Doyle 2000).

These developments have resulted in two sorts of technologically-oriented policies.[22] First, from the early 1960s onwards states (led by California) regulated the manufacture of cars for sale in the United States, often with what was called 'technology forcing' legislation mandating use of crankshaft devices, catalytic converters and so on. Second, and beginning in the 1980s, Inspection and Maintenance (I&M) regimes were used to ensure that the pollution control technologies adopted in car manufacture were maintained properly so that they worked to maximum effect (Rajan 1996). Disciplinary regimes using remote sensing technology have developed to diagnose 'sick vehicles', further individualising and technologising responses to the car's environmental impact: 'A politics of interest group pluralism coupled with technocratic governance tends to produce increasingly sophisticated actuarial techniques of risk management that call for greater surveillance over driver-citizens rather than their active participation in formulating policy' (Rajan 1996: 31). All of these are

---

[22] As well as Rajan, see Doyle (2000) for an exhaustive overview of these policies, and the struggles to get them adopted.

intended to limit the air pollution problems associated with cars without limiting driving.

One of the principal consequences of Rajan's argument is thus to undermine the sort of individualism of the backlash writers discussed in chapter 3. But the point is stronger: it is not only that individualism provides the ideological basis on which a rejection of anti-car arguments is articulated (*à la* Lomasky) but that the very production of what the individual *is* in the late twentieth- or early twenty-first-century world is comprehensible only as a product of the development of automobility. The tensions in the governing of automobility to respond to its problems are thus as much about the production of *what types* of individuals, and between *what different models* of individualism (rights, responsibilities, etc.) should be advanced, as between 'individualism' and 'collectivities'.

The processes which Rajan analyses can be seen much more widely than in air pollution governance in California. While the politics of mobility continues to emphasise the production of subjects who are favourably disposed towards movement and acceleration, those concrete movements which result, as well as the investments and developments which are put in place to enable them, create a range of consequences which are articulated in negative terms. Policies and practices emerge which seek to control consequences while facilitating ongoing mobility: these start with simple technological devices but increasingly entail surveillance techniques and end up with wholesale management down to the level of individual journeys, driving techniques and practices and so on. The politics of greening cars thus entails a reshaping of the types of driving subject which exist, while the politics of moving beyond automobility involve a more thoroughgoing resistance to the dominance of the 'automobile subject' itself.

Cultural limits to 'greening the car'

Those arguing for transformations away from a car-dominated system, or even transformations within automobility, are often (not always) naïve about the way in which the attachment to cars provides an important source of sustenance to a sense of self, autonomy and so on and thus ideological support for forces wanting to resist moves away from the car.

This is perhaps most evident in the contradiction between Ford's attempts at 'greening' and its ongoing reliance on (and exploitation of) the expanding SUV market (Luke 2001). At its root, then, this contradiction arises partly because of the regulatory loopholes in the CAFÉ standards and the perverse economic incentives to build and market SUVs, but more deeply because of the forms of subjectivity and discourse around SUVs which have sustained their growth. The ability to tap into, reproduce and reinforce notions of freedom (through the emphasis on 'off-road' capability, even while around only 5 per cent of SUVs are actually driven off-road) and the associated images of 'wilderness',[23] and the more recent discourse surrounding 'security' (through which personal security is to be pursued through the brute size and force of the SUV)[24] both serves to generate its rise, with associated increased emissions of pollutants, increased mortality on the roads and so on and to provide significant limits on the abilities to 'green' the car system. Ford's introduction of an Escape with a hybrid engine is a manifestly inadequate compensation for this development, despite its greenwash marketing using Kermit the frog saying 'I guess it is easy being green'.[25]

This sort of contradiction also militates against attempts to shift the business model towards one more conducive to sustainability. One of the principal obstacles to shifting business models from products to services is precisely the cultural attachment to ownership as a value in and of itself, which has been particularly strongly expressed in the West and increasingly globally through cars. White (2002: 11) demonstrates this as a key weakness in the more technologically centred accounts of

[23] I say 'wilderness' as it cannot be granted the ontological status given to it by dominant versions of both US culture generally and US environmentalism specifically. 'Wilderness' operates to code spaces as 'outside human impact' which as a discourse was always both empirically false and false in a racist manner – indigenous peoples in the Americas become part of 'nature' rather than humanity in order for wilderness to be 'outside humanity' and the production of particular landscapes and ecologies by indigenous Americans is similarly denied.

[24] There are two discursive moments here. One is the casting of security as a source of value for car users – the world outside the car becomes insecure and the car becomes the means of 'being secure'. This is multidimensional – security in collisions, but also security from carjackers, muggers, rapists, in short from 'dangerous others'. But security is also to be pursued through size and physical power, as opposed to technical acuity (roll bars, side impact protection systems, crumple zones, etc.) or reduced systemic danger on the roads (speed limits, traffic calming, increased surveillance of drink driving and speeding, reducing the weight of all vehicles and so on). In the 1990s 'big cars are safer' won the discursive war decisively, despite the facts to the contrary.

[25] Thanks to Andreas Krebs for sending me a copy of this advert.

ecological modernisation (von Weiszäcker *et al.* 1998; Hawken *et al.* 1999; see also Low and Gleeson 2001 on the need to understand the ecological modernisation of transport in such cultural terms). Bill Ford appears to recognise this when he stresses the need essentially for manufacturers to play a part in a cultural shift in attitudes in relation to environmental questions (Luke 2001).

But cultural contradictions also abound in relation to broader themes. While there are political/economic questions about the viability of 'smart growth' as an economic strategy for cities, the more important constraint is perhaps the ideology of suburbanism. If it can be successfully pursued, 'smart growth' not only entails shorter commute distances and times, more efficient circulation of goods and services, better networking among businesses and so on, but it also means more terraces/row homes, smaller houses and gardens, more parking problems (for car users), more social diversity (in terms of class and ethnicity) and the like. Much of the backlash against cars, as analysed in chapter 3, asserts forcefully that the objection to 'anti-car' measures is not only that people like driving their cars but that they like living in low-density, relatively homogeneous areas. Books such as those of Holtz Kay (1997) and Alvord (2000) provide evidence of this, demonstrating that greening automobility entails a personal odyssey to remake one's identity and re-engage others according to different social logics.

Greening the car, governing the subject

While both 'greening the car' and a broader transformation of socio-transport systems are possible to envisage (and, indeed, elements of both are already unfolding), both also produce a complex politics of subjectivity not well understood by their respective protagonists but which affect both their possibility and their operation. What is not usually recognised is that getting people to move from cars to buses, trains, bicycles, walking and so on is not simply a technical change but frequently a deep re-shaping of their daily habits and routines, their assumptions about 'normality', their attachments to suburban low-density living (especially in North America) and ultimately their sense of *who they are* in the world. Providing cycle lanes is a condition of possibility of getting more people to cycle but for many cycling is a *deviant* activity while driving is *what normal people do*. Such a politics of subjectivity acts as a significant and widely underappreciated constraint on shifting away from cars.

The politics of subjectivity is equally complex for the narrower project of 'greening the car'. An approach which attempts simply to change the specific technologies (fuels, engines, etc.) in cars and their design (materials, weight, aerodynamics, etc.) tends to work in such a way as to progressively require more and more of drivers, to govern their practices as drivers ever more intensively and progressively to remove their agency as drivers, to replace their decisions (about acceleration, steering, braking, navigation and so on) with those of automated systems in the car and on the road. 'Informatic automobility', discussed above, is at the same time a set of technical means by which congestion can be reduced, fuel economy improved, emissions of particulates reduced and so on, and a remaking of who the 'automobile subject' *is*. But as Rajan (1996) points out, this produces an ongoing problematisation concerning the *autonomy* of the driver. While automobility derives one of its principal ideological supports from this notion of autonomy (even while it is fundamentally contradictory or at least ambiguous, as already argued) this ideological support is progressively called into question more deeply at the level of the daily experience of 'automobilists' as they are increasingly governed in their driving practices and their decisions about driving are moved to the automated systems of the car/road.

8 | Conclusions

> The truth becomes visible that . . . the unleashed powers of life, be they mere vehicles, have to be escaped.
>
> (Adorno 1974: 162)

> Thus, everywhere, the mobile mass' vehicular power is repressed and reduced; from limits on speed or fuel to the pure and simple suppression of the personal auto, the myth of the car is condemned to disappear.
>
> (Virilio 1986: 124)

In this book, I have tried to do a number of things. At the most immediate level, concerning the politics of cars, I have sought to show that attempts to 'green cars' are highly problematic and are likely to be impossible. To move towards sustainable social and political forms a significant downgrading of the economic, political and cultural importance of cars, and the broader regime of automobility, is likely to be necessary. This is partly because of the limits to the possibilities of 'technological fixes' for the problems caused by cars. As outlined in chapter 7, while technological changes in the designs of cars, the fuels they use and so on occur, they are likely themselves to be insufficient in the face of growing demand for, and use of, cars. More importantly, as chapter 7 shows, they are also unlikely to be fully realisable principally because of political/economic and cultural constraints. Even if they could deal with the specific problems – principally concerning resource use and a specific range of pollutants – they would be unable to address the broader critiques of car-dominated societies discussed in chapter 2. Part of the point of the more 'systemic' critiques discussed there is precisely that the 'narrow' environmental problems – of climate change and the like – are intimately connected to the more socio-political

problems of atomistic individualism, sprawl, etc. which the technological approach to 'greening cars' tends to ignore. A serious considera-
tion of the car's problematic politics thus leads logically towards
pushing for futures not dependent on the car, the more radical end of
the arguments developed in chapters 2 and 7.

But this claim has many detractors. I have thus also tried to show that
those who raise the objection that 'resistance is useless' in the face of
the car's economic, social and cultural importance (as does Dunn,
discussed in chapter 3) or that there is a moral value in the car as
an autonomy-enhancing object (as does Lomasky, also in chapter 3)
are mistaken. They mistake specific cultural expressions of powerful
values – autonomy or freedom, in particular – for their general appeal.
They miss, if you like, the properly hegemonic nature of cars – that
they express the interests and visions of particular groups within societies in terms of universal motifs. A world where cars represented
individual freedom in a more or less unambiguous way had still to be
made; it did not and does not exist 'naturally'. The world can be
remade without the car at its socio-technical heart. That such a remaking (or, perhaps more appropriately, *remakings*) has entailed, does
entail and will entail political and cultural struggle is not the same
thing as saying that it is impossible; were that the case, all sorts of social
change would be rendered theoretically impossible even while it
empirically occurs. I have thus tried to show that the arguments of
those who say that to resist cars is both useless and/or immoral are
thoroughly unpersuasive, leaving open the door for the various critiques of car culture outlined in chapter 2 and the more concrete
arguments concerning the possibilities of 'greening automobility' in
chapter 7.

At a second level, I have tried to provide a framework for understanding the complexities underpinning the strategies to 'green the car'.
First and foremost this entails a conceptual shift from thinking about
'the car' as a particular object, to 'automobility', as a system, or regime,
integrating that object with all of its conditions of possibility, unintended consequences and systemic dynamics. To think purely in terms
of the individualist account of 'the car' is to overlook most of the
reasons why individual cars are highly prized commodities, objects of
profound political significance and enormously ecologically problematic. It is the systemic nature of automobility which produces all of
these effects: cultural/economic discourses surrounding the importance

of mobility and flexibility within which cars historically arose; shifts in industrial organisation which made the car industry and the consumption of cars (and allied goods and services) the 'engine' of growth for much of the twentieth century, even after 'Fordism'; and the aggregate, mass, constantly growing, consumption of cars which generates a wide range of environmental consequences and undermines narrowly technical solutions.

In order to understand both these constraints and possibilities I have argued that it is necessary to move beyond an observation and elaboration of the systemic character of automobility and its problems (as in the analyses of John Urry) to an attempt to explain what drives how automobility has become dominant and thus what shapes how it might be transformed or overcome. For me, this involves an emphasis on the political economy of cars, on the one hand, and their cultural politics, on the other. Automobility has played a central role in the various transformations of capitalism from the beginning of the twentieth century onwards, as discussed in chapter 4, and at the same time has been a crucial element in the ways that people have been governed precisely *through* the identities which have been built successfully around cars, as analysed in chapter 5. There are two important conclusions. First, it is necessary to recognise that the role of cars in reproducing contemporary capitalism confers *structural* power on car firms that enables them to resist developments that threaten their interests and shape social development to further them. Opposition to cars thus needs to find political strategies that act as countervailing power against that of the car firms, and/or to find alliances with other important economic sectors to split the interests of 'capital in general'. Second, within the context of capitalist society, the pursuit of a post-car world needs to be articulated as an accumulation strategy; if a significant element of contemporary economic life is to witness 'de-growth' then critics need to suggest what will take its place if capitalism, as a growth-dependent system, is not to collapse.

Automobility was central to the regime of accumulation which emerged in the first half of the twentieth century; it was also central to the shaping of individual subjectivities by governments, and thus to the legitimising of contemporary rule. Chapter 5 drew on literature that showed the centrality of movement as a *problem* for governors since at least the seventeenth century. On the one hand, governors need to control how people move about to prevent political unrest. On the other hand, and increasingly, they need to mobilise people and to accelerate and flexibilise their movements, to meet other goals of governance – be they fighting wars or pursuing growth. But movement is paradoxical in this context; it can be presented as an expression of individual freedom but this potential can be unrealised if movement is experienced as forced (through political coercion) or constrained (by external logistics such as train timetables). Automobiles entered this discursive field in the early twentieth century able (apparently) to reconcile this paradox and again to present movement as freedom. The chapter then goes on to show that this paradox nevertheless remains – automobile subjects, celebrating their movement as freedom, had to be made, and right from the start this 'freedom' of the driver was immediately and increasingly attenuated – from traffic lights and licensing through to GPS systems and surveillance. 'Autonomously mobile' car drivers have been constantly, and increasingly, managed by various systems of governance, at the same time as they have come to understand the car as central to their sense of who they are and who they want to be.

The upshot of these arguments, and especially when they are combined, is that moving beyond automobility is neither (simply) a technical matter of the 'right' policies to be adopted by states to shift patterns of behaviour, nor (solely) a revolutionary resistance which can produce a post-automobile and at the same time post-capitalist society. Rather, it requires a 'both/and' politics which both works with *and* against the dominant logics of political economy, on the one hand, and cultural politics, on the other. It requires a pragmatism which enables an articulation of transport policy and urban development policy, which are at the heart (in the technical sense) of the policy shifts to reduce car dependence, with both a strategy for economic growth and a focus on shifting meanings and identities around mobility. At the same time it requires a radicalism which attempts to de-link growth from visions of the 'good life' or of 'progress'. While this latter strategy, favoured by many anti-car activists (and to which my own instincts are drawn) could deal head-on with the political economy of cars through direct resistance, it cannot reasonably be understood to escape fully the logic of governmentality or of dromocratic politics; as the development of the car remade modern subjects, so resistance to the car is at the same time a similar governing strategy to remake those subjects again, both through a project to disconnect mobility from the modern subject itself and through a rearticulation of the specific forms that modern, mobile, subjects, take. An anti-dromocratic rhetoric that 'the faster you move, the more you are policed', works to an extent, but it escapes neither the logic of governmentality itself – cyclists or pedestrians nevertheless have to be *made* as subjects – nor of dromocracy – politics still works in a field of contestations where governors seek to mobilise people's energy and will to move for particular purposes.

Cycling is a useful practice through which to explore this complex and paradoxical politics. Within environmental discourses, cycling is routinely valorised as an environmentally benign form of transport (Lowe 1989; Sachs 1992; Morisette 1994; Carlsson 2002; Horton 2003, 2006). In technical terms, it is difficult to envisage a post-automobile society in which bicycles do not become one of the core transport technologies. But while its environmental benefits in narrow terms are difficult to dispute, its complexities are less well explored; we know little in detail about how bicycles have been in the past or might become a central part of an economic development process. We do have a sense that it lowers consumption, in terms of the money and in physical resources involved in the production, distribution and use of the vehicle, compared to the car. But this raises the possibility of a basic contradiction to a growth-oriented world: a cycle-oriented strategy might well be a problem from a political/economic point of view. Roberts (1995), for example, is clear that a bike-based economic strategy is very different from a conventional growth strategy. It redistributes real wealth as it enhances the mobility of the poor, it focuses on enhanced quality of life rather than consumption of goods, it enables a reduction in working hours because of the reduced need for income to sustain a car and so on. None of these fit conventional accumulation-oriented models. But, on the other hand, a lot depends on what happens to the significant amounts of money freed up in switching from cars to bikes. If this is used for extra consumption elsewhere – extra overseas holidays, home appliances or electronic gadgets and the like – then there may well be a growth strategy possible but hardly one without ecological implications.[1]

---

[1] One important qualification would be to think of this in relation to developing countries. According to Alvord (2000: 146), Ghana during the 1990s made bikes a central part of their development strategy. Having spent considerable sums on car-based infrastructure but without the car-owning population to make it

Focusing on cycling creates more complicated possibilities in terms
of its cultural/political logics – many elements of the forms of subjectivity and thus value in cars are also present in cycling: 'Are cyclists not
masters of their mobility . . .?' Sachs asks rhetorically (1992: 199).
Much of the narrative through which cars are routinely legitimised –
that they enable a journey directly from *A* to *B*, they enable you to
travel when and where you want, you are in control of the vehicle's
immediate movements, in particular – also apply to bicycles. In other
words, the key elements which enable 'autonomy' to be conjoined with
'mobility' in 'automobile', turn out also to be applicable to bicycles.
For some, it is not even 'equally' applicable; cycling is an act of more
'authentic' auto-mobility, both since cyclists have more direct control
over the vehicle itself, as they provide the power, are more fully able to
survey their surroundings, can stop more quickly, manoeuvre more
flexibly, can actually travel from *A* to *B* (while car drivers have to park
increasing distances from their destinations) and so on. Cyclists are also
less heavily dependent on (or 'more autonomous from') the whole
apparatus of car-based automobility – from oil extraction to insurance
and traffic rules. Cyclists routinely refer to themselves as being 'more
free' than cars and those shifting from cars to bicycles frequently
articulate their gains in terms of freedom (e.g. Sachs 1992: 199–203;
Krämer-Badoni 1994; Morisette 1994). The classic bike manual,
Richard's 21st Century Bicycle Book, mixes its technical know-how
with sheer ideology in exemplary fashion, and its opening passage is
worth quoting at length:

Motion and freedom are synonymous . . . Alone among the creatures of
Earth, humans are transport engineers, designers and builders of devices
and machines that enhance or even completely transform our ability to get
around . . . cars and buses go fast at times, but owing to their size and lack of
manoeuvrability are often at a standstill. Bikes are quicker because they are
able to wiggle through traffic and keep on moving. Moreover, bikes go
straight door to door. Use public transport, and you've got to walk to the
local stop or station, wait for your bus or train to show up (good luck), travel
(possibly in segments . . .), and then walk to your destination. Use a car, and

worthwhile, it started building roads suitable for bikes at 8 per cent of the cost of
those necessary for cars, recognising that the significant majority of their population were unable to afford a car, but able to afford a bike, which would significantly enhance their mobility.

you've got to walk to where it is parked, travel, and then find a parking space ... Go by bike and there's no walking or waiting ...
And a bike is freedom. You can go where you want, when you want. ... A bike gives you time, freedom, and control – your life is truly your own. (Ballantine 2000: 1–2)

Ballantine's rhetoric mirrors more or less exactly that of pro-car ideology, and much of the narrative – 'motion and freedom are synonymous' – could have been written by ideologists such as Lomasky, discussed in chapter 3. Thus, as a cultural politics of subjectivity, cycling is highly individualist. As with the discourses surrounding SUVs noted at the end of chapter 5, highly masculinist and aggressive versions emphasise the rugged, thrill-seeking, macho character of cycling, whether (as with SUVs) off-road mountain biking, or in the 'urban jungle' (e.g. Fincham 2006). Thus in terms of the argument of this book, the cycling subject appears significantly less 'pure' than often presented in environmental discourses. This provides a tactical route through which the powerful symbols underpinning the car's rise can be transformed to legitimise alternative automobilities oriented around the bike. It is *because* the bicycle shares much with the car in terms of the subjectivity of the cyclist/driver that it opens up cultural/political possibilities, that it is possible to imagine strategies to promote cycling as an alternative practice. But, nevertheless, the implications of a mass re-organisation of society around the bicycle is, to use a term in cyclists' movements, *velorutionary*.

What, however, if anything, does this tell us about more general arguments concerning the future of environmental politics? The need for the transformation of automobility and the more general argument about what 'drives' automobility's politics and shapes the possibility of transforming it, force us to think rather differently about the future of environmental politics than the way such a project is presented in works such as Eckersley's *The Green State* (2004), outlined in chapter 1 of this book. In chapter 1 I suggested that a focus on cars arose out of a concern that the approach to the 'greening of the state' Eckersley (and others) develop was rather abstracted from the material, daily practices through which people's lives are organised (physically and symbolically) and that exploring these practices would suggest rather different ways to think about the trajectory of contemporary environmental politics. It seems to me that this exercise has had an effect, although it is perhaps less clear in what substantive manner.

First, this analysis would make us perhaps more sceptical about the transformations of capitalism towards ecological modernisation than is Eckersley,[2] and certainly provides a different set of arguments concerning what might drive such a transformation. Her analysis of the transformation is that globalisation provides a number of pressures, including competitive ones, which favour the transformation of the practices of firms and consumers, and the performance of whole economies, in an ecological direction. While I have given a fair amount of evidence, in particular in chapter 7, which supports elements of this argument it is nevertheless the case that such possibilities are highly contradictory – in many instances globalisation provides pressures to increase throughput of resources. At the same time 'globalisation' does not operate as a single logic determining concrete developments but is rather a term to describe a series of processes. The view of globalisation most consistent with my analysis is one which emphasises that it is driven primarily by the interests of significant elements of the capitalist class in subordinating states and other social forces (labour, environmentalism, etc.) to a single political logic (as emphasised by the IPE writers mentioned in chapter 1 and at times in chapter 4). Secondly, it entails attempts by subordinate forces to resist capital's global reach and/or to 'govern' global capital in novel ways. Seeing the potential for capitalism to be greened in this light gives a rather different image of the possibilities, perhaps a more explicitly 'politicised' one. The key logics of competitiveness and so on in Eckersley's narrative (or that, for example, of Porter discussed in chapter 7) must be seen principally as the discursive means through which globalising capital has been able to secure its rule – the means of driving down the costs of production and playing states, workforces and environments against each other. This may well at times produce results which enable certain sorts of 'ecological' transformations – the emergence of 'smart growth' which may (it is too soon to tell) produce significant shifts in the ecological

---

[2] Indeed, of her three structures and their transformations, the account of that from 'global capitalism' to 'ecological modernisation' is arguably the weakest. With the other two (from international anarchy to environmental multilateralism and from liberal to ecological democracy) Eckersley provides powerful reasoning and evidence to sustain the case concerning their potential transformation; for capitalism, she is much less clear on what might be the core features of capitalism which permit its ecological transformation, and appears reluctant to engage in an argument that capitalism is inherently unsustainable.

performance of cities, the shift to alternative fuels and so on. But this project is certainly contradictory. The shift to alternative fuels has been stimulated, on the one hand, by activist regulation in California (responding precisely to the problem of the unthinkability there of moving beyond cars, as analysed by Rajan 1996) which has global consequences given the world-wide integration of car markets, as well as by strategies by the big oil firms to maintain high oil prices, including supporting (indeed being the principal corporate supporters of) political coalitions to engage in essentially imperialist foreign policy ventures by the US state (Bichler and Nitzan 2004; McQuaig 2004). One specific result is the accelerated development of alternative fuels, from the relatively tame hybrids through to the more transformational fuel cells. Paradoxical indeed, as globalisation produces such 'rebound' effects.

Eckersley's conception of ecological democracy is largely premised on the transformations of identities of abstract individuals, as opposed to the embodied subjects analysed here. One consequence is that this highlights one of the tensions within the 'cosmopolitan' or 'transnational' democratic project defended by Eckersley (and others such as Held (1995), Dryzek (1999), or Archibugi (2003), with varying degrees of explicit ecological content in their arguments).[3] The condition of possibility of these transnational democratic practices is precisely the sorts of large-scale motorised mobility which is ecologically unsustainable. To be able to *act* as a transnational citizen – (to be a 'frequent flyer activist' (Eckersley 2006)) – in this democratic manner presupposes forms of physical movement (including cars but even more specifically and problematically aeroplanes), which cannot be sustained. At the

---

[3] I inevitably gloss over here the differences between these writers. Eckersley's cosmopolitanism is less heroic certainly than that of Held, and she is aware of the need to balance the need for transnational/cosmopolitan forms of decision-making with the continued need to ground democracy in the specificities of place and community. In *The Green State*, this comes out in her discussion of balancing principles of *affectedness* and *belonging* as principles underpinning democratic participation – i.e. whether one gets to participate on account of being affected by a particular decision, or by being a member of a particular political community. Nevertheless, the emphasis in her book, focusing as it does on the transformations in political practice being brought about (and needing to be furthered) by ecological politics, is on the transnational. For a treatment of this question emphasising further the way that such transnational democratic principles need to be underpinned by a rootedness in place, see her more recent article on communitarianism and environmental politics (Eckersley 2006).

very least there is a significant paradox here. One might argue that such forms of mobility are necessary to create a global democracy which then might act to create the conditions of limiting mobility without threatening the emergent global democracy (for example, by the transformation of that mobility into 'virtual' mobility through telecommunications) but this is contestable, arguably untenable and has its own ecological costs. It is certainly the case that, combined with the reinterpretation of globalisation given above, such a project for transnational democracy can be readily co-opted by globalising capital – 'cosmopolitan democracy' as the legitimation of 'new constitutionalism' or even Empire.[4]

Taking into account the physicality of the movements involved, and the particular forms of subjectivity associated with specific means of moving, is perhaps more suggestive of an argument emphasising a 'localist' turn in environmental politics. The bicycle is more readily associated with a democratic politics of place and locality than an explicitly transnational orientation: 'Because the bicycle invites one to take possession of the world near-at-hand, it stands for a postautomotive ideal: the transformation of the immediate vicinity into home' (Sachs 1992: 203). Another way of expressing this point is perhaps that Eckersley's arguments for transnational ecological democracy presuppose the continuation of widespread material practices through which different societies routinely disrupt the ecological conditions of life of others, necessitating institutional and discursive means of negotiating these disruptions. If, conversely, politics is oriented more thoroughly towards the transformation of material practices such that those *widespread* transnational disruptions are not *systematically* produced, the necessity of elaborate transnational mechanisms is less important.

---

[4] 'New constitutionalism' here refers to Stephen Gill's argument (2000, 2002) that the 1990s saw a series of measures designed to lock states into neoliberal policy reforms – that, in effect, such policies became regarded as the 'constitution' of global capitalism. While arguments such as those of Held (1995) are expressly social-democratic and anti-neoliberal in character, there are certain similarities, such as in the way states are conceived in cosmopolitan democracy as 'local agents of the global good', and in the way they are in effect subordinated to individual rights. Concerning arguments about Empire – perhaps especially those of Hardt and Negri (2000) – cosmopolitan democratic tendencies can again be interpreted as a legitimating means through which capital's empire can spread its global reach.

A simple opposition between 'reformism' and 'radicalism' is not a particularly useful way to characterise the strategic choices facing environmental politics. The critique of Eckersley developed above is not that she is overly 'reformist' and that a more 'radical' alternative is 'needed'. Rather, it is the specification of what it is in contemporary politics that presents opportunities for environmentalism to transform politics in ecological directions: indeed, the spirit of Eckersley's 'immanent critique' is one that I would also want to embrace. But I would see the possibilities and constraints in contemporary politics rather differently. Rather than Eckersley's triad of greening interstate politics, ecological modernisation and transnational/ecological democracy, I see the central task as greening the economic strategies of contemporary societies (ecological modernisation, if you like, but understood differently) and greening 'daily life', the sorts of identity which give meaning to daily practices which engender particular sorts of environmental futures. How can we build an economic strategy without the car and to shape people (or more precisely, given the governmentality logic, to work so that people shape themselves) for whom cycling, walking and the train become the 'normal' daily practice?

References

AA, 1999. *Fair Deal for Motorists* (leaflet). London: Automobile Association

AAM, 2001. *America's Automobile Industry: The Engine That Drives the Economy*. Washington, DC: Alliance of Automobile Manufacturers

Adorno, Theodor, 1974. *Minima Moralia: Reflections from Damaged Life*. London: Verso

Agamben, Georgio, 1995. 'We Refugees', *Symposium* 49, 2: 114–19

Aglietta, Michel, 1979. *A Theory of Capitalist Regulation*. London: New Left Books

1998. 'Capitalism at the Turn of the Century: Regulation Theory and the Challenge of Social Change', *New Left Review* 232: 41–90

Agnew, John, 1999. 'Mapping Political Power Beyond State Boundaries: Territory, Identity, and Movement in World Politics', *Millennium* 28, 3: 499–522

Aird, Alisdair, 1972. *The Automotive Nightmare*. London: Hutchinson

AIT/FIA, 1997. 'A Global Strategy to Reduce CO_2 Emissions from Passenger Cars and to Improve Fuel Efficiency', Alliance Internationale de Tourisme/ Fédération Internationale de l'Automobile, http://www.caa.ca/CAAInternet/ governmentadvocacy/frames3.htm, viewed March 2001

Albert, Mathias, David Jacobson and Yosef Lapid (eds.), 2001. *Identities, Borders, Orders: Rethinking International Relations Theory*. Minneapolis: University of Minnesota Press

Allan, Stuart, Barbara Adam and Cynthia Carter (eds.), 2000. *Environmental Risks and the Media*. London: Routledge

Altheide, D., 1976. *Creating Reality: How TV News Distorts Events*. Beverley Hills, CA: Sage

Alvord, Katie, 2000. *Divorce your Car! Ending the Love Affair with the Automobile*. Gabriola Island, BC: New Society Publishers

Amin, Ash (ed.), 1994a. *Post-Fordism: A Reader*. Oxford: Blackwell

1994b. 'Post-Fordism: Models, Fantasies and Phantoms of Transition', in Amin (ed.): 1–39

Anastakis, Dimitry, 2000. 'The Advent of an International Trade Agreement: The Auto Pact at GATT, 1964–1965', *International Journal* 55: 583–602

236

Andersen, Robin, 2000. 'Road to Ruin: The Cultural Mythology of SUVs', in Robin Andersen and Lance Strate (eds.), *Critical Studies in Media Commercialism*. New York: Oxford University Press: 158–72

Anderson, Alison, 1997. *Media, Culture and the Environment*. London: University College London Press

Anson, Mike, 1997. 'Global Warming Treaty Will Curb Our Freedom of Choice', *The Washington Times*, 23 May, http://www.vehiclechoice.org/climate/anson.html

Archibugi, Daniele (ed.), 2003. *Debating Cosmopolitics*. London: Verso

Arp, Henning, 1993. 'Technical Regulation and Politics: The Interplay between Economic Interests and Environmental Policy Goals in EC Car Emission Legislation', in J. D. Liefferink, P. D. Lowe and A. P. J. Mol (eds.), *European Integration and Environmental Policy*. Oxford: Oxford University Press: 140–74

Athanasiou, Tom, 1996. *Divided Planet: The Ecology of Rich and Poor*. Boston: Little, Brown & Co.

Attali, Jacques, 2003. *L'homme nomade*. Paris: Fayard

Baird, Nicola, 1998. *The Estate We're In: Who's Driving Car Culture?* London: Indigo

Baldwin, David, 1993. 'Neoliberalism, Neorealism, and World Politics', in David Baldwin (ed.), *Neorealism and Neoliberalism: The Contemporary Debate*. New York: Columbia University Press: 3–25

Ballantine, Richard, 2000. *Richard's 21st Century Bicycle Book*. London: Pan

Ballard, J. G., 1973. *Crash*. London: Jonathan Cape
        1974. *Concrete Island*. London: Jonathan Cape

Banham, Reyner, 1971. *Los Angeles: The Architecture of Four Ecologies*. London: Allen Lane

Barry, Andrew, 1999. 'Demonstrations: Sites and Sights of Direct Action', *Economy and Society* 28, 1: 75–94

Barry, John and Matthew Paterson, 2003. 'Globalization, Ecological Modernization, and New Labour', *Political Studies* 52: 767–84

Barthes, Roland, 1967. *Elements of Semiology*, trans. Annette Lavers and Colin Smith. London: Jonathan Cape

Baudrillard, Jean, 1988. *America*. London: Verso

Bauman, Zygmunt, 1987. *Legislators and Interpreters*. Cambridge: Polity Press
        1991. *Modernity and Ambivalence*. Cambridge: Polity Press

Bayley, Stephen, 1998. 'Let's Hear it for the Car', *Guardian*, 27 July 1998, G2: 15

Beckmann, Jörg, 2004. 'Mobility and Safety', *Theory, Culture & Society* 21: 81–100

Beder, Sharon, 1997. *Global Spin: The Corporate Assault on Environmentalism*. Dartington: Green Books

Belasco, Warren, 1983. 'Motivatin' with Chuck Berry and Frederick Jackson Turner', in Lewis and Goldstein (eds.): 262–79
1989. *Appetite for Change: How the Counter-Culture Took on the Food Industry, 1966–1988*. New York: Pantheon
Bellanger, François and Bruno Marzloff, 1996. *Transit: les lieux et les temps de la mobilité*. Paris: Editions de l'Aube
Bellos, Alex, 1997. 'Swampy Fever', *Guardian*, 12 May, G2: 4–5
Benedick, Richard Elliot, 1991. *Ozone Diplomacy: New Directions in Safeguarding the Planet*. Cambridge, MA: Harvard University Press
Bennett, Catherine, 1999. 'On the Road to Nowhere', *Guardian*, 15 July, G2: 5
2002. 'Who Dares Stand Up to the Motorists?', *Guardian*, 14 November
Bennett, W. Lance, 2003. 'Lifestyle Politics and Citizen–Consumers: Identity, Communication and Political Action in Late Modern Society', in Corner and Pels (eds.): 137–50
Berger, Michael, 1992. 'The Car's Impact on the American Family', in Wachs and Crawford (eds.): 57–74
Berman, Marshall, 1982. *All That is Solid Melts into Air: The Experience of Modernity*. London: Verso: 290–311
Bernick, M. and R. Cervero, 1997. *Transit Villages in the 21st Century*. New York: McGraw-Hill
Bichler, Shimshon and Jonathan Nitzan, 2004. 'Dominant Capital and New Wars', *Journal of World Systems Research* 102: 255–327
Bigo, Didier, 2002. 'Security and Immigration: Toward a Critique of the Governmentality of Unease', *Alternatives* 27: 63–92
Birmingham City Council, 2000. *Visions: A Transport Strategy for Birmingham*. Birmingham: Birmingham City Council Transportation Department
Black, William R. and Peter Nijkamp, 2002. *Social Change and Sustainable Transport*. Bloomington, IN: Indiana University Press
Boccioni, Umberto, 1913/1973. 'Plastic Dynamism 1913', in Umbro Apollonio (ed.), *Futurist Manifestos*. London: Thames & Hudson: 92–5
Bodeen, Christopher, 2004. '"BMW Affair" Triggers Backlash against China's Wealthy Elite', *Ottawa Citizen*, 7 April: A12
Boehmer-Christiansen, Sonja and Helmut Weidner, 1995. *The Politics of Reducing Vehicle Emissions in Britain and Germany*. London: Pinter
Böhm, Steffen, Campbell Jones, Chris Land and Matthew Paterson (eds.), 2006. *Against Automobility*. Oxford: Blackwell
Bonham, Jennifer, 2006. 'Transport: Disciplining the Body that Travels', in Böhm *et al.* (eds.)
Bottles, Scott, 1987. *Los Angeles and the Automobile*. Berkeley, CA: University of California Press

1992. 'Mass Politics and the Adoption of the Automobile in Los Angeles', in Wachs and Crawford (eds.): 194–203

Bowers, Chris, 1993. 'Europe's Motorways: The Drive for Mobility', *The Ecologist* 23, 4: 125–30

Boyer, Robert, 1986. *La théorie de la régulation: une analyse critique*. Paris: La Découverte

  1996. 'The Seven Paradoxes of Capitalism ... Or is a Theory of Modern Economics Still Possible ?', Seminar given at the University of Madison–Wisconsin, 18–19 November

  2004. *Une théorie du capitalisme est-elle possible?* Paris: Jacob

Bradsher, Keith, 2002. *High and Mighty: The Dangerous Rise of the SUV*. New York: Public Affairs

Braverman, Harry, 1974. *Labor and Monopoly Capital: The Degradation of Work in the Twentieth Century*. New York: Monthly Review Press

Brenner, Robert, 1991. 'Why is the United States at War with Iraq?', *New Left Review* 185: 122–37

BRF, 1999. *Bypasses and Communities: Position Paper*. London: British Roads Federation

Brock, Lothar, 1999. 'Observing Change, "Rewriting" History: A Critical Overview', *Millennium* 28, 3: 483–98

Brooks, Libby, 1997. 'Cradle of the Revolution', *Guardian*, Parents page, 11 June: 6–7

Brown, Colin, 1997. 'Politics: "Bury Swampy" Remark Fuels Gaffe Machine', *Independent*, 15 March

Brown, Lester and Christopher Flavin, 1996. 'China's Challenge to the United States and to the Earth', *World Watch*, September–October

Brown, Lester R., Christopher Flavin and Colin Norman, 1979a. *The Future of the Automobile in an Oil Short World*, Worldwatch Paper 32. Washington, DC: The Worldwatch Institute

  1979b. *Running on Empty: The Future of the Automobile in an Oil-Short World*. New York: W.W. Norton

Bruce-Briggs, B., 1975. *The War Against the Automobile*. New York: E.P. Dutton

Bryson, Bill, 2003. *A Short History of Nearly Everything*. Toronto: Anchor Canada

Buel, Ronald A., 1972. *Dead End: The Automobile in Mass Transportation*. Baltimore, MD: Penguin

Bull, Michael, 2001. 'Soundscapes of the Car: A Critical Ethnography of Automobile Habitation', in Miller (ed.): 185–202

  2004. 'Automobility and the Power of Sound', *Theory, Culture & Society* 21: 243–59

Butler, Judith, 1990. *Gender Trouble: Feminism and the Subversion of Identity*. London: Routledge
  1993. *Bodies That Matter: On the Discursive Construction of 'Sex'*. London: Routledge
Buttel, Frederick, 2000. 'Ecological Modernisation as Social Theory', *Geoforum* 31: 57–65
Byrd–Hagel, 1997. *Byrd–Hagel Resolution*, 105th Congress, 1st Session, S. Res 98, 25 July
CAA, 2001. 'CAA Position on Fuel Economy Standards', Canadian Automobile Association, http://www.caa.ca/CAAInternet/governmentadvocacy/frames3.htm, viewed 29 March
Cadeau, Emile, 1960. *L'homme à l'auto*. Paris: Editions du Cerf
Callenbach, Ernst, 1975. *Ecotopia: The Notebooks and Reports of William Weston*. New York: Bantam
Campbell, David, 2005. 'The Biopolitics of Security: Oil, Empire and the Sports Utility Vehicle', *American Quarterly* 57: 943–72
Carey, Jim, 1998. 'Fresh Flavour in the Media Soup: The Story of *SQUALL* Magazine', in George McKay (ed.), *DiY Culture: Party & Protest in Nineties Britain*. London: Verso
Carlsson, Chris (ed.), 2002. *Critical Mass: Bicycling's Defiant Celebration*. Oakland, CA: AK Press
Castells, Manuel, 2000. *The Rise of the Network Society*, 2nd edn. Oxford: Blackwell
Centre for Sustainable Transportation, 1998. *Sustainable Transportation. Reflections on the Movement of People and of Freight, With Special Attention to the Role of the Private Automobile*. Toronto: Centre for Sustainable Transportation
Cerny, Philip, 2000. 'Structuring the Political Arena', in Ronen Palan (ed.), *Global Political Economy: Contemporary Theories*. London: Routledge: 21–35
Chambers, D., 1987. 'Symbolic Equipment and the Objects of Leisure Images', *Leisure Studies* 2: 301–15
Charlesworth, G., 1984. *A History of British Motorways*. London: Thomas Telford
Chatterjee, Kiron, Mark Beecroft and Glenn Lyons, 2003. *Economy, Finance and Equity: Number Eight in a Series of Eight Reports from the Transport Visions Network*. London: Landor
Chu, Henry, 1998. 'Four Wheels Good, Two Wheels Bad in Busy Beijing', *Guardian*, 31 October: 20
Clark, Andrew, 2002a. 'Poor Children at Greater Risk on Roads', *Guardian*, 24 September: 10

2002b. 'Darling Unveils £5.5bn Road Building "Binge"', *Guardian*, 11 December: 11

2004. 'A Hump Too Far ... Traffic is Contained, but not the Growing Annoyance of Car Users', *Guardian*, 17 May: 11

Clarkson, Jeremy, 1996a. 'Motorway Ballet but Never on a Sunday', *Sunday Times*, 21 April: 20

1996b. *Clarkson on Cars: The Collected Writings of the BBC's Top Motoring Correspondent*. London: Virgin Books

Cobb, Clifford, 1999. 'The Roads Aren't Free', *Challenge* 42, 3: 63–83

Cohan, Steven and Ina Rae Hark (eds.), 1997. *The Road Movie Book*. London: Routledge

Cohen, Nick, 1997. 'Hold on a Minute ... Mondeo Man is the Real Threat to John Major's Arcadia', *Observer*, 27 April

Connell, R. W., 1987. *Gender and Power*. Cambridge: Polity Press

Cordato, Roy E., 1997. *The Central Planning of Lifestyles: Automobility and the Illusion of Full-Cost Pricing*. Washington, DC: Competitive Enterprise Institute

Corner, John and Dick Pels (eds.), 2003. *Media and the Restyling of Politics*. London: Sage

Coward, Ros, 2000. 'Selling out to Mondeo Man', *Guardian*, 21 July, www.guardian.co.uk/columnists/column/0,345551,00.html, viewed 14 November 2006

Cox, Robert W., 1997. 'A Perspective on Globalization', in James H. Mittelman (ed.), *Globalization: Critical Reflections*. Boulder, CO: Lynne Rienner: 21–32

Crick, Bernard, 1997. 'Politics and the English Language', *Guardian*, 29 March: 23

Curran, James and Jean Seaton, 1997. *Power without Responsibility: The Press and Broadcasting in Britain*, 5th edn. London: Routledge

Curtice, J. and R. Jowell, 1997. 'Trust in the Political System', in R. Jowell, J. Curtice, A. Park, L. Brook and K. Thomson (eds.), *British Social Attitudes, the 14th Report: The End of Conservative Values?* Aldershot: Ashgate: 89–109

Dalby, Simon, 2002. *Environmental Security*. Minneapolis: University of Minnesota Press

Dalby, Simon and Matthew Paterson, 2006. 'Over a Barrel: Cultural Political Economy and "Oil Imperialism"', Paper presented to the Studies of Political Economy conference, Toronto, February

Dant, Tim, 2004. 'The Driver-Car', *Theory, Culture & Society* 21: 61–79

Dauvergne, Peter, 2005. 'Dying of Consumption: Accidents or Sacrifices of Global Morality?', *Global Environmental Politics* 5, 3: 35–47

Davies, Matt and Michael Niemann, 2002. 'The Everyday Spaces of Global Politics: Work, Leisure and Family', *New Political Science* 24, 4: 557–77

Davies, Richard O., 1975. *The Age of Asphalt: The Automobile, the Freeway, and the Condition of Metropolitan America*. Philadelphia, PA: J.B. Lippincott & Co.

de Goede, Marieke (ed.), 2006. *International Political Economy and Poststructural Politics*. London: Palgrave

de Vauban, S., 1843. *Oisivetés de M. de Vauban*. Paris: J. Corréeard

Deans, John, 1997. 'I'll Name the Tory Donors Says Hague', *Daily Mail*, 24 July: 19

Debord, Guy, 1959. 'Situationist Theses on Traffic', *Internationale Situationiste* 3, http://library.nothingness.org/articles/SI/en/display/316, viewed 14 June 2005

Department for Transport, 2002. *Transport Ten Year Plan 2000: Delivering Better Transport – Progress Report*, London: Department for Transport, http://www.dft.gov.uk/stellent/groups/dft_transstrat/documents/page/dft_transstrat_023008.hcsp, viewed 16 October 2003

2005. *Focus on Personal Travel*. London: The Stationery Office

Der Derian, James, 1992. *Antidiplomacy: Spies, Terrorism, Speed and War*. Oxford: Blackwell

2001. *Virtuous War: Mapping the Military–Industrial–Media–Entertainment Network*. Boulder, CO: Westview Press

Dery, Mark, 2006. '"Always Crashing in the Same Car": A Head-On Collision with the Technosphere', in Böhm *et al.* (eds.)

Deyo, F. C., 1996. *Social Reconstruction of the World's Automobile Industry*. London: Macmillan

Dicken, Peter, 1998. *Global Shift*, 3rd edn. London: Paul Chapman

Dillon, Michael, 2003. 'Culture, Governance, and Global Biopolitics', in François Debrix and Cynthia Weber (eds.), *Rituals of Mediation: International Politics and Social Meaning*. Minneapolis: University of Minnesota Press: 135–53

Diment, Richard, 1996. 'Why the Road Protestors are Wrong', *Global Transport* 7, Autumn: 18–21

Dimitriou, Harry, 1990. 'Transport Problems of Third World Cities', in Harry Dimitriou (ed.), assisted by George Banjo, *Transport Planning for Third World Cities*. London: Routledge: 50–84

Dobson, Andrew, 2003. *Citizenship and the Environment*. Oxford: Oxford University Press

Dodd, Vikram, 2002. 'Tracking Devices Urged as Drivers Faces Charges to Use Busy Roads', *Guardian*, 25 February, www. guardian.co.uk/guardianpolitics/story/0,656530,00.html, viewed 14 November

DoE/EPA, 2005. *Fuel Economy Guide, Model Year 2005*. Washington, DC: US Department of Energy/Environmental Protection Agency, http://www.fueleconomy.gov/feg/feg2000.htm

Doherty, A. and O. Hoedeman, 1994. 'Misshaping Europe: The European Round Table of Industrialists', *The Ecologist* 24: 135–41

Doherty, Brian, 1997. 'Tactical Innovation in the Radical Ecology Movement in Britain', Paper for the European Sociological Association Conference, Essex University, 27–30 August

  1999. 'Paving the Way: The Rise of Direct Action against Road-Building and the Changing Character of British Environmentalism', *Political Studies* 47: 275–91

  2000. 'Manufactured Vulnerability: Protest Camp Tactics', in Seel, Paterson and Doherty (eds.): 62–78.

Doherty, Brian, Matthew Paterson and Benjamin Seel, 2000. 'Direct Action in British Environmentalism', in Seel, Paterson and Doherty (eds.): 1–24

Doherty, Brian, Alexandra Plows and Derek Wall, 2003. '"The Preferred Way of Doing Things": The British Direct Action Movement', *Parliamentary Affairs* 56, 4: 669–86

Doherty, Brian, Matthew Paterson, Alexandra Plows and Derek Wall, 2002. 'The Fuel Protests of 2000: Implications for the Environmental Movement in Britain', *Environmental Politics* 11, 2: 165–73

  2003. 'Explaining the Fuel Protests,' *British Journal of Politics and International Relations* 5, 1: 1–23

Donaghy, Greg, 1998. 'A Continental Philosophy: Canada, the United States, and the Negotiation of the Auto Pact, 1963–65', *International Journal* 53, Summer: 441–64

Doty, Roxanne Lynn, 1999. 'Racism, Desire, and the Politics of Immigration', *Millennium* 28, 3: 585–606

Douglas, Ian R., 1999. 'Globalization as Governance: Toward an Archaeology of Contemporary Political Reason', in Aseem Prakash and Jeffrey Hart (eds.), *Globalization and Governance*. London: Routledge: 134–60

Downs, Anthony, 1957. *An Economic Theory of Democracy*. New York: Harper

Doyle, Jack, 2000. *Taken for a Ride: Detroit's Big Three and the Politics of Pollution*. New York: Four Walls Eight Windows

Drucker, Peter, 1946. *The Concept of the Corporation*. New York: John Day

Dryzek, John, 1999. 'Transnational Democracy', *Journal of Political Philosophy* 7, 1: 30–51

Du Gay, Paul and Michael Pryke (eds.), 2002. *Cultural Economy*. London: Sage

Dumont, René, 1974. *Utopia or Else ...* London: André Deutsch

Dunford, Michael, 2000. 'Globalization and Theories of Regulation', in Ronen Palan (ed.), *Global Political Economy: Contemporary Theories*. London: Routledge: 143–67

Dunn, James, 1981. *Miles to Go: European and American Transportation Policies*. Cambridge, MA: MIT Press

   1998. *Driving Forces: The Automobile, Its Enemies and the Politics of Mobility*. Washington, DC: Brookings Institution

   1999. 'The Politics of Automobility: Fewer Trips or Better Cars?', *Brookings Review* Winter: 40–3

Dury, Ian and the Blockheads, 1977. 'Billericay Dickie', on *New Boots and Panties*, Stiff Records

Duteurtre, Benoît, 2002. *Le grand embouteillage*. Monaco: Editions du Rocher

Eagar, Charlotte, 1997. 'Have Modem, Won't Travel', *Guardian*, 12 March, G2: 6

Eason, Kevin, 1997. 'Did Sierra Man Know about New Labour's Old Banger?', *The Times*, 3 May, Car Magazine: 97

Eckersley, Robyn, 2004. *The Green State: Rethinking Democracy and Sovereignty*. Cambridge, MA: MIT Press

   2006. 'Communitarianism', in Andrew Dobson and Robyn Eckersley (eds.), *Political Theory and the Ecological Challenge*. Cambridge: Cambridge University Press

Eden, Lorraine and Maureen Molot, 1993. 'Insiders and Outsiders: Defining "Who is Us" in the North American Automobile Industry', *Transnational Corporations* 2, 3: 31–64

Ek, Richard, 2004. 'From Democracy to Dromocracy? European Citizenship in an Age of Mega-Corridors', Paper presented to the ECPR Joint sessions, Uppsala, Sweden, 13–18 April

Ekins, P., 2000. *Economic Growth and Environmental Sustainability: The Prospects for Green Growth*. London: Routledge

Elton, Ben, 1991. *Gridlock*. London: Sphere

Energy Policy, 2000. 'On the Rebound?', Special Issue, ed. Lee Schipper, *Energy Policy* 28, 6–7

Engler, Yves, 2004. 'Car Hegemony', *Dissident Voice*, 19 April, www.dissidentvoice.org/April2004/Engler0419.htm

Engwicht, David, 1993. *Street Reclaiming: Creating Livable Streets and Vibrant Communities*. Gabriola Island, BC: New Society Publishers

Ericson, R. V., P. M. Baranek and J. B. Chan (eds.), 1991. *Representing Order: Crime, Law and Justice and the Mass Media*. Milton Keynes: Open University Press

Evangelical Environmental Network, n.d. 'Peace and Security', http://whatwouldjesusdrive.org/resources/fs_security.php, viewed 13 June 2005

Eyerman, R. and O. Löfgren, 1995. 'Romancing the Road: Road Movies and Images of Mobility', *Theory, Culture & Society* 12: 53–79

Fabre, Julien and Hervé Michael, 1973. *Stop, ou l'automobile en question*. Paris: Mercure de France

Featherstone, Mike, 2004. 'Automobilities: An Introduction', *Theory, Culture & Society* 21: 1–24

Featherstone, Mike, Nigel Thrift and John Urry (eds.), 2004. 'Automobilities', Special Issue, *Theory Culture & Society* 21, 4–5

Field, Patrick, 2002. 'No Particular Place to Go', in Wollen and Kerr (eds.): 9–64

Fincham, Ben, 2006. 'Bicycle Messengers and the Road to Freedom' in Böhm *et al.* (eds.)

Flavin, Christopher, 1985. *World Oil: Coping with the Dangers of Success*, Worldwatch Paper 66. Washington, DC: The Worldwatch Institute

Flink, James, 1972. 'Three Stages of American Automobile Consciousness', *American Quarterly* 24: 451–73
  1975. *The Car Culture*. Cambridge, MA: MIT Press
  1988. *The Automobile Age*. Cambridge, MA, MIT Press

Foster, Mark, 1981. *From Streetcar to Superhighway*. Philadelphia, PA: Temple University Press

Foucault, Michel, 1967. *Madness and Civilization*. London: Tavistock
  1977. *Discipline and Punish*. London: Allen Lane.
  1980. *Power/Knowledge: Selected Interviews and Other Writings, 1972–1977*. New York: Pantheon Books
  1988. 'The Political Technology of Individuals', in Luther H. Martin, Huck Gutman and Patrick H. Hutton (eds.), *Technologies of the Self: A Seminar with Michel Foucault*. London: Tavistock: 16–49

Freund, Peter and George Martin, 1993. *The Ecology of the Automobile*. Montreal: Black Rose Books
  1996. 'The Commodity That is Eating the World: The Automobile, the Environment, and Capitalism', *Capitalism, Nature, Socialism* 7, 4: 3–29
  1999. 'Driving South: The Globalization of Auto Consumption and its Social Organization of Space', 2nd draft, June, www.chss.montclair.edu/~hadisb/drivsout.htm, viewed 10 December 2002

Freyssenet M., K. Shmizu and G. Volpato (eds.), 2003. *Globalization or Regionalization of the European Car Industry?*, London and New York, Palgrave Macmillan

Friedman, Thomas, 2000. *The Lexus and the Olive Tree*. London: HarperCollins

Gamble, Nick, 1998. 'My Day with the Road Builders', *TransMission* 5, 1: 8–9

Gamson, William A. and Gadi Wolfsfeld, 1993. 'Movements and Media as Interacting Systems', *Annals of the American Academy of Political and Social Sciences* 528: 114–25

Gartman, David, 1994. *Auto Opium: A Social History of American Automobile Design*. London: Routledge

2004. 'Three Ages of the Automobile: The Cultural Logics of the Car', *Theory, Culture & Society* 21, 4–5: 169–95

Garvey, Pauline, 2001. 'Drinking, Driving and Daring in Norway', in Miller (ed.): 133–52

Gayle, Dennis, 1993. 'Regulating the American Automobile Industry: Sources and Consequences of US Air Pollution Standards', in Molot (ed.): 181–208

GCC, n.d. 'Climate Economics: Kyoto Protocol Would Drive Up Gasoline Prices', http://www.globalclimate.org/Heartland.htm, viewed 18 April 2005

Gelbspan, Ross, 1997. *The Heat is On: The High Stakes over Earth's Threatened Climate*. Reading, MA: Addison-Wesley,

Gibbs, Geoffrey, 1997. 'Swampy the Star Returns to his Hole', *Guardian*, 4 March: 5

Gibbs, Geoffrey and Mark Milner, 2003. 'Happy Motoring as Car Prices Fall', *Guardian*, 28 August, www.business.guardian.co.uk/story/0,103055,11.html, viewed 14 November 2006

Giedion, Siegfried, 1949. *Space, Time and Architecture: The Growth of a New Tradition*. Cambridge, MA: Harvard University Press

Gill, Stephen, 1995. 'The Global Panopticon? The Neoliberal State, Economic Life and Democratic Surveillance', *Alternatives* 20, 1: 1–49

1997. 'Globalization, Democratization and the Politics of Indifference', in James H. Mittelman (ed.), *Globalization: Critical Reflections*. Boulder, CO: Lynne Rienner: 205–28

2000. 'The Constitution of Global Capitalism', Paper presented to the International Studies Association Annual Convention, http://www.theglobalsite.ac.uk/press/010gill.pdf

2002. 'Constitutionalizing Inequality and the Clash of Globalizations', *International Studies Review* 4, 2: 47–66

Gilroy, Paul, 2001. 'Driving While Black', in Miller (ed.): 81–104

Gitlin, T., 1980. *The Whole World is Watching: Mass Media in the Making and Unmaking of the New Left*. Berkeley, CA: University of California Press

Goddard, Stephen, 1994. *Getting There: The Epic Struggle between Road and Rail in the American Century*. New York: Basic Books

Gökay, Bülent, 2002. 'Introduction: Oil, War and Geopolitics from Kosovo to Afghanistan. *Journal of Southern Europe and the Balkans* 4, 1: 5–13

Gordon, Deborah, 1991. *Steering a New Course: Transportation, Energy and the Environment*. Washington, DC: Union of Concerned Scientists/ Island Press

Gore, Albert, 1993. *Earth in the Balance: Ecology and the Human Spirit.* New York: Plume

Gorz, André, 1980. 'The Social Ideology of the Motor Car', in André Gorz, *Ecology as Politics.* London: Pluto: 69–77

Graedel, Thomas E. and Braden R. Allenby, 1998. *Industrial Ecology and the Automobile.* Upper Saddle River, NJ: Prentice Hall

Graham, Stephen and Simon Marvin, 2001. *Splintering Urbanism: Networked Infrastructures, Technological Mobilities and the Urban Condition.* London: Routledge

Grahame, Kenneth, 1908. *The Wind in the Willows.* New York: Grossett & Dunlop

Greene, David and Steven Plotkin, 2001. 'Energy Futures for the US Transport Sector', *Energy Policy* 29: 1255–70

Greenman, Catherine, 2001. 'Connecticut Takes Action Against Rental-Car Tracker', *New York Times*, 5 July

Greenpeace International, 1991. *The Environmental Impacts of the Car.* Amsterdam: Greenpeace International

Gregory, J. W., 1931. *The Story of the Road: From the Beginning down to AD 1931.* London: Alexander Maclehose & Co.

Grice, Andrew, 1997. 'Blair Refuses to Get into a Spin as Poll Temperature Rises', *Sunday Times*, 13 April: 14

Griffiths, Jay, 1997a. 'Swampy: He Went Down the Tunnel a Nobody, and Came Back Up a National Hero', *Guardian*, 2 February: 10

  1997b. 'Swampy's Subterranean Homesick Blues', *Guardian*, 9 February 1997: 1

Groupe Lyonnais d'études médicales, philosophiques et biologiques, 1968. *L'automobile et l'homme.* Paris: SPES

Gunster, Shane, 2004. '"You Belong Outside": Advertising, Nature, and the SUV', *Ethics and the Environment*, 9, 2: 4–32

Gwynne, Robert, 1991. 'New Horizons? The Third World Motor Vehicle Industry in an International Framework', in Law (ed.): 61–87

Hall, Stuart and Martin Jacques (eds.), 1989. *New Times.* London: Lawrence & Wishart

Hamer, Mick, 1987. *Wheels within Wheels: A Study of the Road Lobby.* London: Routledge & Kegan Paul

Hanasz, Waldemar, n.d. *Engines of Liberty: Cars and the Collapse of Communism in Eastern Europe. A Personal Essay.* Washington, DC: Competitive Enterprise Institute

Hannigan, John A., 1995. *Environmental Sociology: A Social Constructionist Perspective.* London: Routledge

Hansen, Anders (ed.), 1993. *The Mass Media and Environmental Issues.* Leicester: Leicester University Press

Haraway, Donna, 1991. *Simians, Cyborgs and Women: The Reinvention of Nature*. New York: Routledge

Hardt, Michael and Antonio Negri, 2000. *Empire*. Cambridge, MA: Harvard University Press

Harvey, David, 1990. *The Condition of Postmodernity*. Oxford: Blackwell
    2003. *The New Imperialism*. Oxford: Oxford University Press

Hastings, Chris, 1997. 'Taxi Man Ranks Hague a No-Hoper', *Sunday Times*, 27 July: 10

Haugestad, Anne K., and J. D. Wulfhorst (eds.), 2004. *Future As Fairness: Ecological Justice and Global Citizenship*. Amsterdam and New York: Rodopi

Hawken, Paul, Amory Lovins and Hunter Lovins, 1999. *Natural Capitalism: The Next Industrial Revolution*. London: Earthscan

Hay, Colin, 1994. 'Environmental Security and State Legitimacy', in M. O'Connor (ed.), *Is Capitalism Sustainable? Political Economy and the Politics of Ecology*. New York: Guilford Press: 217–31
    1996. 'From Crisis to Catastrophe? The Ecological Pathologies of the Liberal-Democratic State Form', *Innovation* 9, 4: 421–34
    1999. *The Political Economy of New Labour*. Manchester: Manchester University Press

Haynes, Steve and Jonathan Leake, 1996. 'How Blair Stared Defeat in the Face', *Sunday Times*, 13 October: 5

Heartland Institute, 1999. *The Instant Expert Guide to Global Warming*. Chicago: Heartland Institute

Held, David, 1987. *Models of Democracy*. Cambridge: Polity Press
    1995. *Democracy and the Global Order*. Cambridge: Polity Press

Held, David, Anthony McGrew, David Goldblatt and Jonathan Perraton, 1999. *Global Transformations: Politics, Economics, Culture*. Cambridge: Polity Press

Helleiner, Eric, 1994. *States and the Reemergence of Global Finance: From Bretton Woods to the 1990s*. Ithaca, NY: Cornell University Press

Hey, Kenneth, 1983. 'Cars and Film in American Culture, 1929–1959', in Lewis and Goldstein (eds.): 193–205

Hillman, Mayer, John Adams and John Whitelegg, 1990. *One False Move: A Study of Children's Independent Mobility*. London: Institute for Policy Studies

Hobbes, Thomas, 1651/1968. *Leviathan*. London: Penguin

Holloway, Julian, 1998. '"Undercurrent Affairs": Radical Environmentalism and Alternative News', *Environment and Planning A* 30, 7: 1197–1217

Holmes, John, 1993. 'From Three Industries to One: Towards an Integrated North American Industry', in Molot (ed.): 23–62

Holtz Kay, Jane, 1997. *Asphalt Nation: How the Automobile Took over America and How We Can Take it Back*. Berkeley, CA: University of California Press

Hooper, Charlotte, 2001. *Manly States: Masculinities, International Relations, and Gender Politics*. New York: Columbia University Press

Horton, Dave, 2003. 'Computers, Cars and Televisions: The Role of Objects in Cultivating Sustainable Lifestyles', Paper presented to Environmental Thought – Environmental Practice, Manchester Environmental Forum Postgraduate Conference, School of Geography, University of Manchester, 31 January

2006. 'Environmentalism and the Bicycle', *Environmental Politics* 15, 1: 41–58

Houghton, J. T., G. J. Jenkins and J. J. Ephraums, 1990. *Climate Change: The IPCC Scientific Assessment*. Cambridge: Cambridge University Press

Howe, John, 2002. 'Vehicle of Desire', *New Left Review* 15: 105–17

Hoyle, Brian and Richard Knowles, 1998. 'Transport Geography: An Introduction', in Brian Hoyle and Richard Knowles (eds.), *Modern Transport Geography, Edition 2*. Chichester: John Wiley: 1–12

Hoyle, Brian and José Smith, 1998. 'Transport and Development: Conceptual Frameworks', in Brian Hoyle and Richard Knowles (eds.), *Modern Transport Geography, Edition 2*. Chichester: John Wiley: 13–40

IEA, 1989. *Energy and the Environment: An Overview*. Paris: International Energy Agency/OECD

1993. *Cars and Climate Change*. Paris: International Energy Agency/OECD

2004. *Energy Technology for a Sustainable Future*. Paris, International Energy Agency

Ihde, D., 1974. 'The Experience of Technology: Human–Machine Relations', *Cultural Hermeneutics* 2: 267–79

Illich, Ivan, 1974. *Energy and Equity*. London: Calder & Boyars

Imbs, Paul (ed.), 1974. *Trésor de la langue française*. Paris: Editions du CNRS

Institute of Labor and Industrial Relations, University of Michigan, Office for the Study of Automotive Transportation, University of Michigan Transportation Research Institute, Center for Automotive Research, Environmental Research Institute of Michigan, 2001. *Contribution of the Automotive Industry to the US Economy in 1998: The Nation and its Fifty States*, A Study Prepared for The Alliance of Automobile Manufacturers, Inc. and The Association of International Automobile Manufacturers, Inc. Ann Arbor: University of Michigan

IPCC, 2001. *Climate Change 2001 Synthesis Report: Summary for Policymakers*. Geneva: Intergovernmental Panel on Climate Change

Ironside, Virginia, 1997. 'Dilemmas: My Daughter Wants to be with Swampy', *Independent*, 20 March

IRTAD/OECD, 2003. 'Fatalities by Road Location', International Road Traffic Accident Database, http://www.bast.de/htdocs/fachthemen/irtad/english/we32.html, viewed 6 October 2003

Jackson, Tim, 1996. *Material Concerns: Pollution, Profit and Quality of Life*. London: Routledge

Jacobs, Jane, 1961. *The Death and Life of Great American Cities*. New York: The Modern Library

Jacobs, Michael, 1997. 'Sustainability and Markets: On the Neo-Classical Model of Environmental Economics', *New Political Economy* 2, 3: 365–85

Jaffe, Hosea, 2005. *Automobile, pétrole et impérialisme*. Paris: Paragon

Jakle, J. A., 2001. *City Light: Illuminating the American Night*. Baltimore, MD: Johns Hopkins University Press

Jerome, John, 1972. *The Death of the Automobile: The Fatal Effect of the Golden Era, 1955–1970*. New York: Norton

Jessop, Bob, 1990. *State Theory: Putting Capitalist States in their Place*. Cambridge: Polity Press

Johnson, Elmer W., 1993. *Avoiding the Collision of Cities and Cars: Urban Transportation Policy for the Twenty-First Century*. Chicago: American Academy of Arts and Sciences

Johnson, R. J., Peter J. Taylor and Michael J. Watts, 1995. *Geographies of Global Change: Remapping the World in the Late Twentieth Century*. Oxford: Blackwell

Jordan, Andrew, 2000. 'Environmental Policy', in Patrick Dunleavy, Andrew Gamble, Ian Holliday and Gillian Peele (eds.), *Developments in British Politics 6*. London: Palgrave: 257–75

Jürgens, Ulrich, Thomas Malsch and Knuth Dohse, 1993. *Breaking from Taylorism: Changing Forms of Work in the Automobile Industry*. Cambridge: Cambridge University Press

Jury, Louise, 1997. 'One Week On, Swampy Comes Out Blinking into the Television Lights', *Independent*, 31 January

Kalawsky, Keith, 2001. 'Car Trouble: The Big Three Automakers Face Overflowing Inventories and Dwindling Sales. And Those Aren't the Only Problems on the Horizon', *Canadian Business*, 8 January: 26–9

Karliner, Joshua, 1997. *The Corporate Planet: Ecology and Politics in the Age of Globalization*. San Francisco: Sierra Club Books

Kawahara, A., 1997. *The Origin of Competitive Strength: 50 Years of the Auto Industry in Japan and the US*. Kyoto: Kyoto University Press

Kazman, Sam, 2001. 'Automobility and Freedom: Kazman Remarks at The Objectivist Center', 1 September, http://www.cei.org/gencon/027,02162.cfm, viewed 22 March 2005

Keats, John, 1958. *The Insolent Chariots*. Philadelphia, PA: Lippincott

Kelly, Scott and Greg Clark, for the Conservative Policy Unit, n.d. *Free to Travel*. London: Conservative Party

Kenyon, Susan, Glenn Lyons and Jane Austin, n.d. *Public Transport Information Web Sites: How to Get It Right. A Best Practice Guide*, London: Institute of Logistics and Transport, http://www.trg.soton.ac.uk/bpg/

Kenyon, Susan, Glenn Lyons and J. Rafferty, 2002. 'Transport and Social Exclusion: Investigating the Possibility of Promoting Inclusion Through Virtual Mobility', *Journal of Transport Geography* 10, 3: 207–19

Keohane Robert O., 1984. *After Hegemony: Cooperation and Discord in the World Political Economy*. Princeton, NJ: Princeton University Press

Kindleberger, Charles P., 1973. *The World in Depression, 1929–1939*. London: Allen Lane

Kinnock, Neil, 1996. 'Keynote Address to Conference on "Creating Successful Public/Private Partnerships in Trans-European Transport Networks"', Brussels, 27 February

Kirton, John, 1998. 'The Impact of Environmental Regulation on the North American Auto Industry since NAFTA', in Sidney Weintraub and Christopher Sands, *The North American Auto Industry Under NAFTA*. Washington, DC: Center for Strategic and International Studies: 184–220.

Klare, Michael T., 2001. *Resource Wars*, London: Palgrave Macmillan
   2004. *Blood and Oil: The Dangers and Consequences of America's Growing Petroleum Dependency*. New York: Metropolitan Books

Koppel, T., 1999. *Powering the Future: The Ballard Fuel Cell and the Race to Change the World*. Toronto: John Wiley

Kramarae, C. (ed.), 1988. *Technology and Women's Voices: Keeping in Touch*. London: Routledge

Krämer-Badoni, Thomas, 1994. 'Life without the Car: An Experiment and a Plan', *International Journal of Urban and Regional Research* 18, 2: 347–58

Krier, James E. and Edmund Ursin, 1977. *Pollution and Policy: A Case Essay On California and Federal Experience with Motor Vehicle Air Pollution, 1940–1975*. Berkeley, CA: University of California Press

Kuehls, Thom, 1996. *Beyond Sovereign Territory: The Space of Ecopolitics*. Minneapolis: University of Minnesota Press

Kunstler, James Howard, 1994. *The Geography of Nowhere: The Rise and Decline of America's Man-Made Landscape*. New York: Simon & Schuster

 1996. *Home From Nowhere: Remaking our Everyday World for the Twenty-First Century*. New York: Simon & Schuster

Laclau, Ernesto and Chantal Mouffe, 1985. *Hegemony and Socialist Strategy*. London: Verso

Lacy, Mark, 2005. *Security and Climate Change*. London: Routledge

Laird, David, 1983. 'Versions of Eden: the Automobile and the American Novel', in Lewis and Goldstein (eds.): 224–43

Langley, Paul, 2003. 'The Everyday Life of Global Finance', IPEG Papers in Global Political Economy 5, British International Studies Association, International Political Economy Group, www.bisa.ac.uk/groups/ipeg/papers/PaulLangley.pdf, viewed 21 July 2005

Lash, Scott and John Urry, 1987. *The End of Organized Capitalism*. Cambridge: Polity Press

Lattimore, Owen, 1962. *Studies in Frontier History: Collected Papers, 1928–1958*. London: Oxford University Press

Law, C. M. (ed.), 1991. *Restructuring the Global Automobile Industry*. London: Routledge

Leavitt, Helen, 1970. *Superhighway – Superhoax*. New York: Doubleday

LeBillon, Philippe and Fouad El Khatib, 2004. 'From Free Oil to "Freedom Oil": Terrorism, War and US Geopolitics in the Persian Gulf', *Geopolitics* 9, 1: 109–37

Lefebvre, Henri, 1971. *Everyday Life in the Modern World*. New York: Harper & Row

Lehrer, Ute Angelika and Richard Milgrom, 1996. 'New (Sub)Urbanism: Countersprawl or Repackaging the Product', *Capitalism, Nature, Socialism* 7, 2: 49–63

Leonard, Tom and Sandra Barwick, 1997. 'I'm proud of Him, Says Mother of Swampy, the Master Tunneller', *Telegraph*, 1 February: 4

Levinson, Paul, 2004. *Cellphone: The Story of the World's Most Mobile Medium and How it Has Transformed Everything*. London: Palgrave

Levy, David L. and Peter Newell (eds.), 2005. *The Business of Global Environmental Governance*. Cambridge, MA: MIT Press

Levy, David L. and Sandra Rothenberg, 2002. 'Heterogeneity and Change in Environmental Strategy: Technological and Political Responses to Climate Change in the Automobile Industry', in Andrew Hoffman and Marc Ventresca (eds.), *Organizations, Policy and the Natural Environment: Institutional and Strategic Perspectives*. Stanford, CA: Stanford University Press: 173–93

Lewis, David L. and Laurence Goldstein (eds.), 1983. *The Automobile and American Culture*. Ann Arbor: University of Michigan Press

Lex Service, 1999. *The 1999 Lex Report on Motoring*. Bourne End: Lex Service plc

Leyshon, Andrew and Nigel Thrift, 1997. *Money/Space: Geographies of Monetary Transformation*. London: Routledge

Ling, Peter J., 1990. *America and the Automobile: Technology, Reform and Social Change*. Manchester: Manchester University Press

Lipietz, Alain, 1987. *Mirages and Miracles: The Crisis of Global Fordism*. London: Verso
  1992. *Towards a New Economic Order: Postfordism, Ecology, and Democracy*. Cambridge: Polity Press

Lipschutz, Ronnie with James K. Rowe, 2005. *Regulation for the Rest of Us? Globalization, Governmentality, and Global Politics*. London: Routledge

Litfin, Karen, 1994. *Ozone Discourses: Science and Politics in Global Environmental Cooperation*. New York: Columbia University Press

Litman, Todd, 2002. *The Costs of Automobile Dependency and the Benefits of Balanced Transportation*. Victoria, BC: Victoria Transport Policy Institute

Lomasky, Loren, 1997. 'Autonomy and Automobility', *The Independent Review* 2, 1: 5–28

Longrigg, Clare, 1997. 'Swampy the Subterranean Star Buries Politicians in Fame Name Poll', *Guardian*, 24 February: 4

Lovins, Amory B., 1977. *Soft Energy Paths: Toward a Durable Peace*. San Francisco, CA: Friends of the Earth International

Lovins, Amory B. and J. Barnett, 1993. 'Advanced Ultralight Hybrid-Electric Vehicles', in *Proceedings of the International Symposium on Automotive Technology and Automation*, Aachen, 13–17 September

Lovins, Amory B. and L. Hunter Lovins, 1982. *Brittle Power: Energy for National Security*. Andover, MA: Brick House Publishing
  1990. 'Make Fuel Efficiency our Gulf Strategy', *New York Times*, 13 December: A15.

Low, Nicholas and Brendan Gleeson, 2001. 'Ecosocialization or Countermodernization? Reviewing the Shifting "Storylines" of Transport Planning', *International Journal of Urban and Regional Research*, 25, 4: 784–803
  (eds.) 2003. *Making Urban Transport Sustainable*. London: Palgrave Macmillan

Lowe, Marcia, 1989. *The Bicycle: Vehicle for a Small Planet*, Worldwatch Paper 90. Washington, DC: The Worldwatch Institute

1990. *Alternatives to the Automobile: Transport for Livable Cities*, Worldwatch Paper 98. Washington, DC: The Worldwatch Institute

1994. *Back on Track: The Global Rail Revival*, Worldwatch Paper 118. Washington, DC: The Worldwatch Institute

Luger, Stan, 2000. *Corporate Power, American Democracy and the Automobile Industry*. Cambridge: Cambridge University Press

Luke, Timothy W., 1996. 'Liberal Society and Cyborg Subjectivity: The Politics of Environments, Bodies, and Nature', *Alternatives* 21, 1: 1–30

1997. *Ecocritique*. Minneapolis: University of Minnesota Press

2001. 'SUVs and the Greening of Ford: Reimagining Industrial Ecology as an Environmental Corporate Strategy in Action', *Organization and Environment* 14, 3: 311–35

2002. 'Braking with Bytes: Telematics as a New Mode of Automobility', Paper presented to conference on Automobility, Keele University, September

Lupton, Deborah, 1999. 'Monsters in Metal Cocoons: "Road Rage" and Cyborg Bodies', *Body and Society* 51: 57–72

Macnaghten, Phil and John Urry, 1998. *Contested Natures*. London: Sage

MAD, 2002. 'Fleecing not Policing!', Press release, Motorists Against Detection, http://www.speedcam.co.uk/welcome.htm, viewed 21 March 2005

Mandaville, Peter, 1999. 'Territory and Translocality: Discrepant Idioms of Political Identity', *Millennium* 28, 3: 653–74

Maples, Wendy, 2000. '"It's Just not Natural"'?: Queer Insights on Eco-Action', in Seel, Paterson and Doherty (eds.): 133–50

Marchand, Roland, 1998. 'Customer Relations and Public Relations: General Motors in the 1930s', in Susan Strasser, Charles McGovern and Matthias Judt (eds.), *Getting and Spending: European and American Consumer Societies in the Twentieth Century*. Cambridge: Cambridge University Press: 85–109

Margolis, Jonathan, 1997. 'Theme of the Week: Twaddle', *Guardian*, 15 March: 2

Marinetti, Filippo Tommaso, 1909/1973. 'The Founding and Manifesto of Futurism', *Le Figaro*, 20 February 1909, in Umbro Apollonio (ed.), *Futurist Manifestos*. London: Thames & Hudson: 19–24

Marsh, Peter and Peter Collett, 1986. *Driving Passion: The Psychology of the Car*. London: Jonathan Cape

Marshall, Emma and Nerys Thomas, 2000. *Traffic Calming: The Reality of Road Rage*, Home Office Briefing Note 12/00. London: Home Office Research, Policing and Reducing Crime Unit

Martin-Jones, David, 2006. 'No Literal Connection: Images of Mass Commodification, US Militarism, and the Oil Industry, in *The Big Lebowski*', in Böhm *et al.* (eds.)

Marx, Karl and Friedrich Engels, 1848/1967. *The Communist Manifesto.* London: Pelican

Maryland State Highway Administration, 2002. *Smart Growth and Transportation: Issues and Lessons Learned: Report of a Conference, September 8–10, 2002, Baltimore, Maryland.* Washington, DC: Transportation Research Board of the National Academies

Massey, Ray, 1996. 'Mondeo Man Makes his Home Up North: Prestige Cars on the Road to Extinction', *Daily Mail*, 1 November: 29

Mattelart, Armand, 1996. *The Invention of Communication.* Minneapolis: University of Minnesota Press

  2000. *Networking the World, 1794–2000.* Minneapolis: University of Minnesota Press

Matthews, Karine and Matthew Paterson, 2005. 'Boom or Bust? The Political–Economic Engine Behind the Drive for Climate Change Policy', *Global Change, Peace and Security*, 17: 59–75

Maxton, Graeme and John Wormald, 1995. *Driving Over a Cliff? Business Lessons from the World's Car Industry.* Reading, MA:Addison-Wesley: 132–41

Mayer, Donald, 2002. 'Corporate Governance in the Cause of Peace: An Environmental Perspective', *Vanderbilt Journal of Transnational Law* 35: 585–653

McCormick, John, 1989. *Acid Earth.* London: Earthscan

McKay, George, 1996. 'Direct Action of the New Protest: Eco-Rads on the Road', in George McKay, *Senseless Acts of Beauty: Cultures of Resistance Since the Sixties.* London: Verso: 127–58

  1998. 'DiY Culture: Notes towards an Intro', in George McKay (ed.), *DiY Culture: Party & Protest in Nineties Britain.* London: Verso: 1–53

McKibben, Bill, 1995. 'Not So Fast: The Environmental Optimists are Wrong: There is no Market-Oriented Technological Fix. Simply, and Radically, People Have to Change their Lives', *New York Times Magazine*, 23 July: 24–5

McQuaig, Linda, 2004. *It's the Crude, Dude: War, Big Oil, and the Fight for the Planet.* Toronto: Doubleday

McShane, Clay, 1994. *Down the Asphalt Path: The Automobile and the American City.* New York: Columbia University Press

Meadows, Donella, Dennis Meadows, Jorgen Randers and William Behrens, 1972. *The Limits to Growth.* London: Pan

Meaton, Julia and David Morrice, 1996. 'The Ethics and Politics of Private Automobile Use', *Environmental Ethics* 18: 39–54

Meikle, James, 2001. 'Children's Safety Bought at a Price', *Guardian*, 6 February: 6

Melucci, Alberto, 1989. *Nomads of the Present: Social Movements and Individual Needs in Contemporary Society*. London: Century Hutchinson

Merriman, Peter, 2006. '"Mirror, Signal, Manoeuvre": Assembling and Governing the Motorway Driver in Late Fifties Britain', in Böhm *et al.* (eds.)

Meyer, John M., 2001. *Political Nature: Environmentalism and the Interpretation of Western Thought*. Cambridge, MA: MIT Press

Michael, Mike, 2001. 'The Invisible Car: The Cultural Purification of Road Rage', in Miller (ed.): 59–80

Millennium, 1999. Special Issue on 'Territorialities, Identities and Movement in International Relations', *Millennium* 28, 3

Miller, Daniel (ed.), 2001. *Car Cultures*. London: Berg

Miller, Hillis, 2006. 'Virtual Automobility: Two Ways to Get a Life', in Böhm *et al.* (eds.)

Milton, Terence, 1991. *Car Wars*. Lewes: The Book Guild

Mishan, E. J., 1977. *The Costs of Economic Growth*. London: Allen & Unwin

Mitchell, William J., 1995. *City of Bits: Space, Place, and the Infobahn*. Cambridge, MA: MIT Press

Mittelman, James H., 1998. 'Globalisation and Environmental Resistance Politics', *Third World Quarterly* 19, 5: 847–72

Mol, Arthur, 2001. *Globalization and Environmental Reform: The Ecological Modernization of the Global Economy*. Cambridge, MA: MIT Press

Mollard, Angela, 1997. 'At 16, the Rebellious Road of a Girl They Call Animal', *Daily Mail*, 29 January: 12

Molot, Maureen 1993a. 'Introduction', in Molot (ed.): 1–22

   (ed.) 1993b. *Driving Continentally: National Policies and the North American Auto Industry*. Ottawa: Carleton University Press

   (ed.) 2003. *The Auto Industry in the 21st Century: Challenges and Prospects*. Proceedings of a Conference, Ottowa, 10–11 April

Monbiot, George, 2004. 'Fallen Fruit', *Guardian*, 30 October, www.guardian.co.uk/food/story/0,1338349,00.html, viewed 14 November 2006

Moncur, Andrew, 1997. 'And Another Thing ... Name of the Game', *Guardian*, 3 February, G2: 6

Mooney, Bel, 1997. 'Right or Wrong, the Young at Least Show Some Guts', *Daily Express*, 1 February: 10

Morisette, Claire, 1994. *Deux roues, un avenir: le vélo en ville*. Montréal: Ecosociété

Morse, Edward L., 1999. 'A New Political Economy of Oil?', *Journal of International Affairs* 53, 1: 1–29

Möser, Kurt, 1998. 'World War I and the Creation of Desire for Automobiles in Germany', in Susan Strasser, Charles McGovern and Matthias Judt (eds.), *Getting and Spending: European and American Consumer Societies in the Twentieth Century*. Cambridge: Cambridge University Press: 195–222

Mottram, Eric, 2002. 'Blood on the Nash Ambassador: Cars in American Films', in Wollen and Kerr (eds.): 95–114

Mowbray, A. Q., 1969. *Road to Ruin*. Philadelphia, PA: Lippincott

Mumford, Lewis, 1934. *Technics and Civilization*. New York: Harcourt
    1963. *The Highway and the City*. New York: Harcourt, Brace & World

Munkis, John with David Braunfeld, Spencer Carter, Barbara Kuester and Charles Myart, 1993. 'The Automobile Industry, Political Economy, and a New World Order', *Journal of Economic Issues* 27, 2: 627–38

Mytelka, Lynn, 2003. 'New Wave Technologies: How Soon?', Paper presented at the AUTO21 Conference, Ottawa, 10–11 April

Nader, Ralph, 1965. *Unsafe at Any Speed*. New York: Grossman
    1972. *Unsafe at Any Speed: The Designed-In Dangers of the American Automobile*, 2nd edn. New York: Grossman

Neale, Alan, 1999. '"Take My Breath Away": Can Technical Fixes Make Cars Environmentally Friendly?', in Ben Fairweather, Sue Elworthy, Matt Stroh and Piers Stephens (eds.), *Environmental Futures*. London: Macmillan: 185–98

Nederveen Pieterse, Jan, 2004. *Globalization or Empire?* London: Routledge

Negrine, Ralph, 1989. *Politics and the Mass Media in Britain*. London: Routledge

Newell, Peter, 2000. *Climate for Change; Non-State Actors and the Global Politics of the Greenhouse*. Cambridge: Cambridge University Press

Newman, Peter and Jeffrey Kenworthy, 1999. *Sustainability and Cities: Overcoming Automobile Dependence*. Washington, DC: Island Press

Nitzan, Jonathan and Shimshon Bichler, 1995. 'Bringing Capital Accumulation Back In: The Weapondollar–Petrodollar Coalition – Military Contractors, Oil Companies and Middle-East "Energy Conflicts"', *Review of International Political Economy* 2, 3: 446–515

O'Connell, Sean, 1998. *The Car and British Society: Class, Gender and Motoring 1896–1939*. Manchester: Manchester University Press

O'Dell, Tom, 2001. 'Raggare and the Panic of Mobility: Modernity and Hybridity in Sweden', in Miller (ed.): 105–33

O'Neill, Sean, 1997. 'Police Raid Camp as Bypass Protestors Spend Dole at Pub', *Telegraph*, 25 January: 6

O'Neill, Sean and Caroline Davies, 1997. 'Girl Called Animal Tells of Four Days in Protest Tunnel', *Telegraph*, 29 January: 5

O'Toole, Randal, 2000. *The Vanishing Automobile and Other Myths: How Smart Growth Will Harm American Cities*. Bandon, OR: Thoreau Institute

OECD, 2003. *Analysis of the Links Between Transport and Economic Growth*. Project on Decoupling Transport Impacts and Economic Growth, OECD Environment Directorate, document ENV/EPOC/WPNEP/T(2003)4/FINAL. Paris: Organisation for Economic Cooperation and Development

Offe, Claus, 1985. *Disorganized Capitalism*. Cambridge: Polity Press

Office of Technology Policy, 2003. *Fuel Cell Vehicles: Race to a New Automotive Future*. Washington, DC: US Department of Commerce

Orecchini, F. and D. Sabatini, 2003. 'Cars and the Environment: A New Approach to Assessment Through ISO14001 Certification of the Car Process', *Proceedings of the Institution of Mechanical Engineers, Part D: Journal of Automobile Engineering* 217, 1: 31–40

Osborn, Andrew, 2001. 'Cars Cost "Up to Double in Britain"', *Guardian*, 20 February: 10

Overy, Richard, 1990. 'Heralds of Modernity: Cars and Planes from Invention to Necessity', in Mikulas Teich and Roy Porter (eds.), *Fin de Siècle and its Legacy*. Cambridge: Cambridge University Press: 54–79

Owen, Wilfrid, 1972. *The Accessible City*. Washington, DC: Brookings Institution

Palad, Isabelle, 2004. 'Landscapes of Fear and the Demand for Armoured Automobility', Research Paper for Masters Course, The Political Economy of the Automobile, Carleton University, Ottawa, April

Palan, Ronen and Jason Abbott with Phil Deans, 1999. *State Strategies in the Global Political Economy*. London: Pinter

Parker, Andrew and Eve Kosofsky Sedgwick, 1995. 'Introduction: Performativity and Performance', in Andrew Parker and Eve Kosofsky Sedgwick (eds.), *Performativity and Performance*. London: Routledge

Pascoe, David, 2002. 'Vanishing Points', in Wollen and Kerr (eds.): 75–82

Paterson, Matthew, 1996. *Global Warming and Global Politics*. London: Routledge

1999. 'Understanding the Green Backlash', *Environmental Politics* 8, 2: 183–7

2000. 'Car Trouble', in Matthew Paterson, *Understanding Global Environmental Politics*. London: Macmillan: 95–117

2001. 'Climate Policy as Accumulation Strategy: The Failure of COP6 and Emerging Trends in Climate Politics', *Global Environmental Politics* 1, 2: 10–17

Paterson, Matthew and Simon Dalby, 2006. 'Empire's Ecological Tyreprints', *Environmental Politics* 15, 1: 1–22

Patterson, Jeffrey, 1995. *Green City Views: Public Opinion and Urban Environments in Ten Canadian Cities*, Research Working Paper 39, Institute of Urban Studies, University of Winnipeg

Peluso, Nancy Lee, 1993. 'Coercing Conservation: The Politics of State Resource Control', in Ronnie D. Lipschutz and Ken Conca (eds.), *The State and Social Power in Global Environmental Politics*. New York: Columbia University Press: 343–52

Penman, Danny, 1997. 'Swampy™: Been There, Dug That . . . Now Buy The T-Shirt', *Independent*, 10 August: 4

Pinkney, David, 1972. *Napoleon III and the Rebuilding of Paris*. Princeton, NJ: Princeton University Press

Piore, M. and C. Sabel, 1984. *The Second Industrial Divide: Possibilities for Prosperity*. New York: Basic Books

Pisarski, Alan E., 1999. *Cars, Women, and Minorities: The Democratization of Mobility in America*. Washington, DC: Competitive Enterprise Institute

Plotkin, Steven, 2001. 'European and Japanese Fuel Economy Initiatives: What They Are, Their Prospects for Success, Their Usefulness as a Guide for US Action', *Energy Policy* 29: 1073–84

Plumstead, Janice, Brian Russell and David Stuewe, 1993. 'The North American Automotive Industry: State Government Response to a Changing International Environment', in Molot (ed.): 163–80

Porter, M., 1990. *The Competitive Advantage of Nations*. New York: Free Press

Pruett, Barbara, 1990. *Marty Robbins: Fast Cars and Country Music*. Metuchen, NJ: Scarecrow Press, Inc.

Putnam, Robert D., 2000. *Bowling Alone: The Collapse and Revival of American Community*. New York: Simon & Schuster

Rae, John, 1971. *The Road and the Car in American Life*. Cambridge, MA: MIT Press

Rajan, Sudhir Chella, 1996. *The Enigma of Automobility: Democratic Politics and Pollution Control*. Pittsburgh, PA: University of Pittsburgh Press

2006. 'Automobility and the Liberal Disposition', in Böhm *et al.* (eds.)

Raven, Charlotte, 1997. 'New Lads Out, New Man Swampy In', *Guardian*, 22 April, G2: 5

Ray, Larry and Andrew Sayer (eds.), 1999, *Culture and Economy: After the Cultural Turn*. London: Sage

Rees, A. L., 2002. 'Moving Spaces', in Wollen and Kerr (eds.): 83–94

Rees, Alun, 1997. 'Raid Police Dole Out a Surprise', *Daily Express*, 25 January

Reich, Simon, 1989. 'Roads to Follow: Regulating Direct Foreign Investment', *International Organization* 43: 543–84

1993. 'NAFTA, Foreign Direct Investment, and the Auto Industry: A Comparative Perspective', in Molot (ed.): 63–100

Renaud, Hubert, 1967. *L'automobiliste et la morale chrétienne*. Gembloux: Edition J. Duculot

Renner, Michael, 1988. *Rethinking the Role of the Automobile*, Worldwatch Paper 84. Washington, DC: The Worldwatch Institute

Richardson, Tim, 1997. 'The Trans-European Transport Network: Environmental Policy Integration in the European Union', *European Urban and Regional Studies* 4, 4: 333–46

Robert, 1985. *Le grand Robert de la langue française*, 2nd edn. Paris: Le Robert

Roberts, Wayne, 1995. 'Blazing Saddles and Appropriate Technology: The Bike Path to a Green Economy', in Zielinski and Laird (eds.): 102–4

Robinson, Nick, 2000. 'The Politics of the Car: The Limits of Actor-Centred Models of Agenda Setting', in Seel *et al.* (eds.): 199–217

2002. 'The Politics of the Fuel Protests: Towards a Multi-Dimensional Explanation', *Political Quarterly* 73, 1: 58–66

Ronson, Jon, 2002. *Them: Adventures with Extremists*. London: Picador

Rosenbloom, Sandra, 1992. 'Why Working Families Need a Car', in Wachs and Crawford (eds.): 38–56

Ross, Kristin, 1995. *Fast Cars, Clean Bodies: Decolonization and the Reordering of French Culture*. Cambridge, MA: MIT Press

Rothschild, Emma, 1973. *Paradise Lost: The Decline of the Auto-Industrial Age*. New York: Random House

Rowell, Andrew, 1996. *Green Backlash: Global Subversion of the Environmental Movement*. London: Routledge

Rucht, D., 1990. 'The Strategies and Action Repertoires of New Movements', in R. J. Dalton and M. Kuechler (eds.), *Challenging the Political Order: New Social and Political Movements in Western Democracies*. Cambridge: Polity Press: 156–75

Ruggie, John Gerrard, 1983. 'International Regimes, Transactions, and Change: Embedded Liberalism in the Postwar Economic Order', in Stephen Krasner (ed.), *International Regimes*. Ithaca, NY: Cornell University Press: 195–232

Rupert, Mark, 1995. *Producing Hegemony: The Politics of Mass Production and American Global Power*. Cambridge: Cambridge University Press

2000. *Ideologies of Globalization: Contending Visions of a New World Order*. London: Routledge

Rupert, Mark and Hazel Smith (eds.), 2002. *Historical Materialism and Globalization: Essays on Continuity and Change*. New York: Routledge

Ruth, Matthias, 2006. *Smart Growth and Climate Change: Regional Development, Infrastructure and Adaptation.* Cheltenham: Edward Elgar

Sabatier, Paul and Hank Jenkins-Smith (eds.), 1993. *Policy Change and Learning: An Advocacy Coalition Approach.* Boulder, CO: Westview Press

Sachs, Wolfgang, 1992. *For the Love of the Automobile.* Berkeley, CA: University of California Press

SACTRA, 1994. *Trunk Roads and the Generation of Traffic,* Standing Advisory Committee on Trunk Roads Assessment. London: HMSO

 1999. *Transport and the Economy.* Standing Advisory Committee on Trunk Roads Assessment, London, http://www.dft.gov.uk/stellent/ groups/dft_econappr/documents/pdf/dft_econappr_pdf_022512.pdf, viewed 7 April 2005

SAFE Alliance, 1994. *The Food Miles Report: The Dangers of Long Distance Food Transport.* London: SAFE

Salter, Mark, 2004. 'And Yet it Moves: The Global Mobility Regime', in Libby Assassi, Duncan Wigan and Kees van der Pijl (eds.), *Global Regulation: Managing Crises after the Imperial Turn,* London: Palgrave: 177–90

Sampson, Anthony, 1975. *The Seven Sisters: The Great Oil Companies and the World They Made.* New York: Viking Press

Samuels, Allen, 2002. 'Accidents: The Car and Literature', in Wollen and Kerr (eds.): 50–8.

Sauvy, Alfred, 1968. *Les quatre roues de la fortune.* Paris: Flammarion

Scammell, Margaret, 2000. 'The Internet and Civic Engagement: the Age of the Citizen–Consumer', *Political Communication.* 17: 351–5

 2003. 'Citizen Consumers: Towards a New Marketing of Politics?', in Corner and Pels (eds.): 117–36

Scharff, Virginia, 1991. *Taking the Wheel: Women and the Coming of the Motor Age.* New York: Free Press

 1992. 'Gender, Electricity and Automobility', in Wachs and Crawford (eds.): 75–85

Schneider, Kenneth, 1971. *Autokind vs. Mankind.* New York: Norton

Schneider, William, 2002. 'America Keeps On Trucking', *National Journal,* 23 March, http://www.aei.org/ra/raschn020323.htm, viewed 12 September 2002

Schumpeter, Joseph, 1943. *Capitalism, Socialism, Democracy.* London: George Allen & Unwin

Seel, Benjamin, 1997. 'Strategies of Resistance at the Pollok Free State Road Protest Camp', *Environmental Politics* 6, 4: 102–33

Seel, Benjamin and Alex Plows, 2000. 'Coming Live and Direct: Strategies of Earth First!', in Seel *et al.* (eds.): 112–32

Seel, Benjamin, Matthew Paterson and Brian Doherty (eds.), 2000. *Direct Action in British Environmentalism*. London: Routledge

Shapiro, Michael and Hayward Alker (eds.), 1996. *Challenging Boundaries: Global Flows, Territorial Identities*. Minneapolis: University of Minnesota Press

Sharpe, Tom, 1977. *Blott on the Landscape*. London: Pan

Sheehan, Molly O'Meara, 2001. *City Limits: Putting the Brakes on Sprawl*, Worldwatch Paper 156. Washington, DC: The Worldwatch Institute

Shove, Elizabeth, 1998. 'Consuming Automobility'. Discussion Paper for Project SceneSusTech, Employment Research Centre, Department of Sociology, Trinity College, Dublin

Shukin, Nicole, 2006. 'The Mimetics of Mobile Capital', in Böhm *et al.* (eds.)

Silk, Gerald, 1983. 'The Image of the Automobile in American Art', in Lewis and Goldstein (eds.): 206–21

Simon, David, 1996. *Transport and Development in the Third World*. London: Routledge

Sklair, Leslie, 2000. *The Transnational Capitalist Class*. Oxford: Blackwell

Slater, Cliff, 1997. 'General Motors and the Demise of Streetcars', *Transportation Quarterly* 51, 3: 45–66

Smith, Giles, 2000. 'Berth of a Salesman', *Guardian*, 4 December, www.guardian.co.uk/wheels/story/0,406361,00.html, viewed 14 November 2006

Smith, Joe (ed.), 2000. *The Daily Globe: Environmental Change, the Public and the Media*. London: Earthscan

Smith, Julian, 1983. '*The Automobile in the American Film, 1900–1920*', in Lewis and Goldstein (eds.): 179–92

Smith, Mick, 1997. 'Against the Enclosure of the Ethical Commons: Radical Environmentalism as an "Ethics of Place"', *Environmental Ethics* 19, 4: 339–53

Smith, Richard, 1997. 'Creative Destruction: Capitalist Development and China's Environment', *New Left Review* 222: 3–41

Smith, S. E., 1999. *Dancing in the Street: Motown and the Cultural Politics of Detroit*. Cambridge, MA: Harvard University Press

SMMT, 1993. *Road Transport and Climate Change*. London: Society of Motor Manufacturers and Traders

    1998. *New Deal for Transport: Better for Everyone. The Government's White Paper on the Future of Transport, the Motor Industry Response*. London: Society of Motor Manufacturers and Traders

Sofoulis, Zöe, 2002. 'The Open Road', Paper presented at the Automobility Conference, Keele University, 8–10 September

Soguk, Nevgat and Geoffrey Whitehall, 1999. 'Wandering Grounds: Transversality, Identity, Territoriality, and Movement', *Millennium* 28, 3: 675–98

St Clair, David J., 1988. *The Motorization of American Cities*. New York: Praeger

Stanford, Peter, 1997. 'Second Front: Jesus Christ's Smarter Brother', *Guardian*, 25 February, G2: 2

Sutter, Paul S., 2002. *Driven Wild: How the Fight Against Automobiles Launched the Modern Wilderness Movement*. Seattle: University of Washington Press

Switzer, Jacqueline Vaughn, 1997. *Green Backlash: The History and Politics of Environmental Opposition in the US*. Boulder, CO: Lynne Rienner

Szerszynski, Bronislaw, 2002. 'Ecological Rites: Ritual Action in Environmental Protest Events', *Theory, Culture & Society* 19, 3: 51–69
2003. '*Marked Bodies: Environmental Activism and Political Semiotics*', in Corner and Pels (eds.): 190–206

Tarrow, Sidney, 1994. *Power in Movement: Social Movements, Collective Action and Politics*. Cambridge: Cambridge University Press

Taylor, A. J. P., 1969. *War by Timetable: How the First World War Began*. London: Purnell

Thacker, Andrew, 2006. '*Traffic, Gender, Modernism*', in Böhm *et al.* (eds.)

The iWalk Club, n.d. iWalk Club – Backgrounder, Toronto: iWalk Club, http://www.saferoutestoschool.ca/index.php?page=iwalkclub, viewed 10 June 2005

Thrift, Nigel, 1996. 'Inhuman Geographies: Landscapes of Speed, Light and Power', in Nigel Thrift, *Spatial Formations*. London: Sage: 256–309
2004. 'Driving in the City', *Theory, Culture & Society* 21: 41–59

TI, 2003. 'Preserving the American Dream of Mobility and Homeownership', Conference agenda, http://www.ti.org/amdream.html, viewed 27 March 2005

Tickell, Oliver, 1998. 'Death Duties', *Guardian*, 24 June, G2: 4–5

Tiles, Mary and Hans Oberdiek, 1995. *Living in a Technological Culture: Human Tools and Human Values*. London: Routledge

Tolley, Rodney and Brian Turton, 1995. *Transport Systems, Policy and Planning: A Geographical Approach*. Harlow: Longman

Tolliday, Steven and Jonathan Zeitlin (eds.), 1986. *The Automobile Industry and its Workers*. Cambridge: Polity

Trainer, F. E., 1985. *Abandon Affluence!* London: Zed

Transnet, 1990. *Energy, Transport and the Environment*. London: Transnet

Tunali, Odil, 1996. 'A Billion Cars: The Road Ahead', *World Watch*, January–February: 24–34

Tyme, John, 1978. *Motorways versus Democracy: Public Enquiries Into Road Proposals and Their Political Significance*. London: Macmillan

UNCTC, 1992. *Climate Change and Transnational Corporations: Analysis and Trends*. New York: United Nations Center on Transnational Corporations

Urban Land Institute, 1998. *Smart Growth: Economy, Community, Environment*. Washington, DC: Urban Land Institute

Urry, John, 2000. *Sociology Beyond Societies: Mobilities for the Twenty-First Century*. London: Routledge

   2004. 'The "System" of Automobility', *Theory, Culture & Society*, 21, 4: 25–39.

   2006. 'Inhabiting the Car', in Böhm *et al.* (eds.)

van der Pijl, Kees, 1998. *Transnational Classes and International Relations*. London: Routledge

Vanderheiden, Steven, 2006. 'The Case Against the SUV', *Environmental Politics* 15, 1: 23–40

Vidal, John 1996. 'Bogotà and the Bypass', *Guardian* 22 May, G2: 4

   1997a. 'Gone to Ground', *Guardian*, 22 February: 4

   1997b. 'The Scum also Rises', *Guardian*, 29 January: 17

   1998. 'Swampy Goes to Ground', *Guardian*, 1 April, G2: 2–3

Vigar, Geoff, 2001. *The Politics of Mobility: Transport, the Environment and Public Policy*. London: Spon

Virilio, Paul, 1978. 'L'Empire de l'emprise', *Traverses* 13

   1983. *Pure War*. New York: Semiotexte

   1986. *Speed and Politics*. New York: Semiotexte

Vogel, David, 1995. *Trading Up: Consumer and Environmental Regulation in a Global Economy*. Cambridge, MA: Harvard University Press

Volti, Rudi, 1996. 'A Century of Automobility', *Technology and Culture* 37, 4: 663–85

Von Vegesack, Alexander and Mateo Kries (eds.), 1999. *Automobility: was uns bewegt*. Weil am Rhein: Vitra Design Museum

Von Weiszäcker, Ernst, Amory Lovins and Hunter Lovins, 1998. *Factor Four: Doubling Wealth, Halving Resource Use*. London: Earthscan

Wachs, Martin and Margaret Crawford (eds.), 1992. *The Car and the City*. Ann Arbor: University of Michigan Press

Wagner, Fritz W., 2005. *Revitalizing the City: Strategies to Contain Sprawl and Revive the Core*. Armonk, NY: M.E. Sharpe

Wainwright, Martin, 2004. 'The Phoney War', *Guardian*, 27 November

Wajcman, Judy, 1991. *Feminism Confronts Technology*. Cambridge: Polity Press

Wall, Derek, 1999. *Earth First! and the Anti-Roads Movement*. London: Routledge

2000. 'Snowballs, Elves and Skimmingtons?: Genealogies of Environmental Direct Action', in Seel et al. (eds.): 79–92

Wallace, Jennifer, 1997. 'Swampy's Smart Set', *Times Higher*, July 4: 15

Walsh, Michael P., 1993. 'Highway Vehicle Activity Trends and their Implications for Global Warming: The United States in an International Context', in David Greene and Danilo Santini (eds.), *Transportation and Global Climate Change*. Washington, DC: American Council for an Energy Efficient Economy: 1–50

Walters, William, 2002. 'Mapping Schengenland: Denaturalizing the Border', *Environment & Planning D: Society & Space* 20, 5: 561–80

Ward, Colin, 1991. *Freedom to Go: After the Motor Age*. London: Freedom Press.

Weber, Cynthia, 1998. 'Performative States', *Millennium: Journal of International Studies* 27, 1: 97–118

Weintraub, Sidney and Christopher Sands, 1998. *The North American Auto Industry Under NAFTA*. Washington, DC: Center for Strategic and International Studies

Welsh, Ian and Phil McLeish, 1996. 'The European Road to Nowhere', *Anarchist Studies* 4, 1: 27–44

Wendt, Alexander, 1992. 'Anarchy is What States Make of It: The Social Construction of Power Politics', *International Organization* 46, 2: 391–425

Wernick, Andrew, 1991. *Promotional Culture: Advertising, Ideology and Symbolic Expression*. London: Sage

While, Aidan, Andrew E. G. Jonas and David Gibbs, 2004. 'The Environment and the Entrepreneurial City: Searching for the Urban "Sustainability Fix" in Manchester and Leeds', *International Journal of Urban and Regional Research* 28, 3: 549–69

White, Daman Finbar, 2002. 'A Green Industrial Revolution? Sustainable Technological Innovation in a Global Age', *Environmental Politics* 11, 2: 1–26

Whitelegg, John, 1997. *Critical Mass: Transport, Environment and Society in the Twenty-First Century*. London: Pluto

Widmer, E. L., 2002. 'Crossroads: The Automobile, Rock and Roll, and Democracy', in Wollen and Kerr (eds.): 65–74

Wilson, James Q., 1997. 'Cars and their Enemies', *Commentary*, July: 17–23

Winner, Langdon, 1980. 'Do Artifacts have Politics?', *Daedalus* 109: 121–36

Wolf, Winfried, 1996. *Car Mania: A Critical History of Transport*. London: Pluto

Wollen, Peter, 2002. 'Automobiles and Art', in Wollen and Kerr (eds.): 25–49

Wollen, Peter and Joe Kerr (eds.), 2002. *Autopia: Cars and Culture*. London: Reaktion Books

Wolmar, Christian, 2001. 'How Labour Failed its MOT Test', *Guardian*, 18 May, www.guardian.co.uk/analysis/story/0,492753,00.html

Womack, James, David Jones and Daniel Roos, 1990. *The Machine that Changed the World*. New York: Macmillan

Wood, Dennis, 1992. *The Power of Maps*. New York: Guilford Press

Woods, Richard and Paul Nuki, 1997. 'PM gets Upwardly Mobile by Trading in Sierra for Galaxy Man', *Sunday Times*, 4 May: 1

World Bank, 1986. *Urban Transport: A World Bank Policy Study*. Washington, DC: World Bank

World Council of Churches (WCC), 2000. *Motorised Mobility, Climate Change and Globalisation*, Memorandum of the Project team to the World Council of Churches, www.wcc-coe.org/wcc/what/jpc/motorized.pdf, viewed 9 May 2006

World Health Organisation (WHO) and World Bank, 2004. *World Report on Road Traffic Injury and Prevention*. Geneva: World Health Organisation

Wykes, Maggie, 2000. 'The Burrowers: News about Bodies, Tunnels and Green Guerrillas', in Allan, Adam and Carter (eds.): 73–89

Yergin, Daniel, 1993. *The Prize: The Epic Quest for Oil, Money, and Power*. New York: Touchstone

Younge, Gary and Jonathan Glancey, 1999. 'Hot under the Bonnet', *Guardian*, 13 July, G2: 2–3

Zielinski, Sue and Gavin Laird (eds.), 1995. *Beyond the Car: Essays on the Auto Culture*. Toronto: Steel Rail Publishing

Zinsmeister, Karl, 1996. 'Are Today's Suburbs really Family Friendly?', *American Enterprise*, November–December, http://www.taemag.com/issues/articleid.16262/article_detail.asp, viewed 17 June 2005

Zuckermann, Wolfgang, 1991. *End of the Road: The World Car Crisis and How We Can Solve It*. Cambridge: Lutterworth Press

Index

acid rain 8, 37, 39
advertising 147–62
  animals in 152–3
  communications technologies in
    155–9
  environmental images in 148–9,
    152–3, 160
  environmental protest and 149
  gender in 47–8, 147
  military images in 157–8
  nostalgia and 153–5
Aglietta, Michel 105–9, 112, 113
alternative fuels 196–9, 210, 211, 233
Alvord, Katie 13, 34, 35, 223
anti-car politics 32–60
  as anti-freedom 70, 77
  as doomed 71, 78–80
  as elitist 72, 77–8
  backlash against, 61–90
Association of British Drivers (ABD)
  61, 62, 67, 68
Australia 36, 44, 68, 202
automobile subject, the 121–65,
  221–4, 228
  as constraint on greening cars 221–3
  as consumer–citizen 166, 184–91
  as hybrid 139–40, 161–2
  as violent 163–5
automobiles *see* cars
automobility 7, 24–7, 91, 94, 97,
  123–5, 132–6, 226–9
  ambiguity of 87–8, 139–40
  ambivalence towards 89, 145–6, 163
  and Fordism 107–11
  and post-Fordism 112–14
  as contradictory 87–9
  as system 25, 88, 124–5, 193
  greening of 192–224
  individualist account of 81–2
  John Urry on, 25–6, 88, 124–5, 193

autonomy
  Lomasky on 80–7

backlash against anti-car sentiments
  61–90
Ballard, J.G. 143, 164
Bauman, Zygmunt 89, 126, 163
Berman, Marshall 11, 14, 32, 43, 44,
  50, 123, 133, 163, 192
bicycles *see* cycling
Blair, Tony 185–6, 189–90
BMW 4, 100
Boyer, Robert 105–6
Bretton Woods system 6, 107, 109

Cadillac 113, 144, 146, 186
CAFÉ standards 25, 65, 67, 194, 212, 222
California zero emissions legislation 65,
  196, 205, 209
capitalism 7, 15, 19, 22, 48, 91–120
car industry 92–3
  globalisation of 98–101
  problems for in 1970s 34–5
cars
  ambivalence towards 33, 89
  disenchantment with 35
  in art 143
  in literature 143
  in popular music 143–7
  'greening' of 194–200
  people killed by 40
  pollution produced by 9, 26, 36–8
  protests about 9–11
  rates of ownership 49–50, 94–5
  reducing use of 201–4
  resource use of 9, 26, 38
  romance with 35
  safety and 40–1
  urban planning and 12–14, 39, 45,
    87–8

267

cars and economic growth 91–8
  flexible mobility 96
  forward/backward linkages 96–7
  size of industry 92–3
  technical innovation 95–6
cars, growth of 29, 124–5
  as 'natural' 72–6, 92
  as inevitable 72–6, 78–9
  systems-theory account of 124–5
China 1–4
Chrysler 100, 164
circulation metaphors 12, 42, 46, 127–9
citizenship
  consumerism and 184–91
  environmental conception of
    16–17, 233
Clarkson, Jeremy 68, 164
class 19, 48–50, 103–4, 106–7, 113–14,
    122, 136, 171–2, 173
climate change 3, 5, 8, 9, 10, 36–7, 39,
    54, 61, 63, 67, 72, 75, 189
Competitive Enterprise Institute 65–6,
    77, 81
congestion 52, 141, 189–90, 200, 201
Conservative Party (UK) 68, 181, 182,
    187, 190
cultural politics 8, 15, 121–65, 166–91,
    227–8, 234–5
cycling 3, 13, 39, 45, 50, 53, 115,
    163–4, 201, 202, 203, 213,
    229–31, 234
  and political economy 229
  and subjectivity 184, 223, 230–1

democracy
  car as democratic 46–7, 66
  ecological 17–18, 233
Dicken, Peter 93, 95, 98–9, 100, 112
disorganised capitalism *see*
    post-Fordism
Doherty, Brian 50, 59, 69–70,
    180–2, 184
Douglas, Ian 126–30
dromocracy 5–6, 60, 138, 228–9
Dunn, James 28, 47, 59, 63, 70–80, 86,
    185, 202, 226

Eckersley, Robyn 17–19, 192, 231–5
ecological modernisation 17, 18, 192,
    204, 212, 214, 216–17, 232, 235

European Union 69, 117–18, 138,
    214–15
everyday life 11, 18, 22–3, 235

false consciousness 75–6, 122–3
flexible accumulation *see* post-Fordism
Flink, James 34, 35, 38, 72, 78, 94,
    96–7, 102–3, 140
Ford, Henry 46–7
Ford Motor Company 73, 93, 95, 97,
    98, 100, 134, 152, 197, 208, 211
Fordism 106–14, 122, 209, 227
  consumption and 106–7, 108–9
  crisis of, 1970s 109–13
Foucault, Michel 19, 23, 126–30, 180
France 69, 115, 127–30
freedom 51–2, 80–9, 130, 132, 134,
    142 *see also* autonomy
  positive and negative accounts of 84–5
Freund, Peter 11, 38, 42, 46, 47, 49, 58,
    73, 108, 116, 132
fuel cells 198, 210, 233
fuel economy *see* fuel efficiency
fuel efficiency 25, 54, 57, 65, 67 194–7,
    212, 222
  limits to 38, 198–9
  possible gains in 196
  rebound effects 199
fuel protests (UK, 2000) 69–70, 191
fuel taxation 25, 69, 194, 206, 210
Futurists, Italian 121, 163–4

Gartman, David 122–3
  on shifts in car consumption 113–14
gender 47–9, 146, 147, 149, 155, 171,
    173–5, 188
General Motors 64, 73–5, 93, 98, 101,
    113, 210
Germany 46, 49, 102, 118, 135, 215
Global Climate Coalition (GCC) 64,
    72, 205–8
global warming *see* climate change
globalisation 4, 6–7, 8–9, 19,
    232–3, 234
  of car industry 98–101
  relation to the greening of cars
    213–17
Gorz, André 43, 45, 51, 122
governmentality 19, 126–32, 135–42,
    217–21, 223–4, 228

Harvey, David 54, 104, 110, 112–14
Hitler, Adolf 46, 117, 119, 133, 186
Holtz Kay, Jane 34, 72, 78, 221
Honda 152, 159–60, 197
hybrid engines 195, 197, 222, 233

identity 20–1, 122–3, 142–62,
    221–2, 235
  and roads protests 11, 182–4
  cars as false consciousness, 122–3
Illich, Ivan 43, 50, 53, 60
information and communications
    technologies
  environmental performance of cars
    and 199–200
  in car advertising 155–9
  in cars 140–2
International Energy Agency (IEA) 36,
    37, 39
international political economy
    19, 22
  neo-Gramscian perspective 19, 23
  of car industry 98–102
Italy 135, 163–4

Jacobs, Jane 14, 34, 42, 60, 72
Japan 99, 194
Japanese car industry 100, 101,
    110–11, 112
Jeep 146, 149–51
just-in-time (JIT) 95, 110–11

Kenworthy, Jeff 13, 39, 45, 192,
    201–3
Kings Heath, Birmingham 11–14
Kunstler, James Howard 42–3, 52, 72,
    80, 90
Kyoto Protocol, car lobbying against
    67, 205–8

Land Rover 100, 152–3
Le Corbusier 14, 133
lean production 110, 112, 114
liberty *see* autonomy; freedom
Litman, Todd 39, 41, 192
Lomasky, Loren 25, 51–2, 66,
    80–9, 136, 139, 162, 185,
    226, 231
Lovins, Amory 57–8, 196, 201
Luke, Timothy 39, 123, 139

Martin, George 11, 38, 42, 46, 47, 49,
    58, 73, 108, 116, 132
Marx, Karl 3, 32, 103
mass transit *see* public transport
Mattelart, Armand 3, 127–31
McShane, Clay 33, 40, 47, 48, 49, 73,
    115, 132, 134, 135
media
  construction of anti-roads protests
    166–80
  construction of fuel protests 69–70
migration 6, 20–2
Mill, John Stuart 52, 84
mobility *see* movement
modernisation 4, 32, 133
modernity 11, 123, 133, 163, 218, 219
Molot, Maureen 100, 101
Mondeo Man 68, 184–91
  as consumer–citizen 184–5,
    186, 188
  as relegitimation of cars 188–9
  class character of 186–8
  policy consequences of 190–1
Moses, Robert 14, 43, 49–50
Motorists Against Detection (MAD)
    61–2, 63
motorways 34, 46 116–17, 135
  governmentality and 137–8
  military reasons for 117, 135
  roads lobby and 117
movement 1–14
  and capitalism 7
  and modernity 3, 11
  as domination 130
  as freedom 7, 80–9, 130, 132,
    134, 142
  ecology of 7–8
  resistance against 4, 6, 9–11
  to be accelerated 130–1
  to be channelled 127–30
  to be controlled 127
Mumford, Lewis 8, 34, 42, 72

Nader, Ralph 34, 38, 40–1, 64
National City Lines 'conspiracy' 73–5
Newman, Peter 13, 39, 45, 192,
    201–3
Nissan 147–9, 154–5, 160
North American Free Trade Agreement
    (NAFTA) 101–2, 214–15

oil
  and geopolitics 54–8, 116
  consumption of 9, 38–9
  OPEC 39, 54, 57
Organisation for Economic
    Cooperation and Development
    (OECD) 36, 37, 40, 93, 94
organised capitalism *see* Fordism

Partnership for a New Generation of
    Vehicles 212, 214
pedestrians 136–7, 229
planning 12–14, 39, 45, 82–3, 86–7,
    130–1, 202–3
political economy 8, 91–120, 128–9,
    204–17, 227, 232–3
  and poststructuralism 19–23
  and resistance to pollution control
    205–9
  Marxist account of 103–4
  state–economy relationship 104,
    114–15
  structural power of capital 204–9
post-Fordism 109–14, 209
poststructuralism 19–23
progress 3, 11, 76, 92, 123, 147, 152,
    155–7, 160, 179, 228
public transport 12–13, 43, 45, 50, 118,
    189, 190, 201–3, 213, 230

race, racism 6, 20–2, 49–50, 136
railways 76, 118, 130–2, 189–90
  and First World War 4, 133
  rigidities of 132
  speed and 131
Rajan, Sudhir Chella 18, 25, 51, 64, 87,
    88, 217–21, 224, 233
regime of accumulation 105
  greening cars and 209–13
regulation theory 104–5, 107, 109
Renault 101, 151, 152
road building 42–5, 116–18
  and urban destruction 42–3
  and wilderness destruction 42
  protests against *see* roads protests
  lobby for 117
roads protests (UK) 9–11, 33, 44,
    148, 149
  A30 (Fairmile) 10, 167, 168, 179,
    180, 181

'Animal' in 170–1
anti-capitalism and 10
Carbusters 44–5
critical mass 45, 184
direct action 9–11, 180–4
'manufactured vulnerability' 181
Newbury 10, 169, 172, 181, 183
origins of 10, 181
Reclaim the Streets (RTS) 10, 44,
    169, 184
'Swampy' in 166–80
trajectory of 10
World Carfree Network 44
Rothschild, Emma 35, 38, 60, 78,
    103, 111
Rupert, Mark 19, 23, 74, 99, 108

Sachs, Wolfgang 46, 53, 60, 118–19,
    122, 201, 229, 230, 234
safety 40–1, 140, 144, 195, 208, 212, 214
Scharff, Virginia 19, 48, 64, 134
school run 12, 149–51
Sloan, Alfred 97, 114
Sloanism 113–14
smart growth 45, 66, 203–4, 216,
    223, 232
  as accumulation strategy, 212–13
space 42–5, 135–6, 199, 201
speed 52–3, 115, 131, 132–3, 144, 163
Sport Utility Vehicles (SUVs) 54–7, 158,
    164–5, 231
  anti-SUV campaigns 54–5, 151
sprawl 42–5, 66, 72, 76, 82, 86, 202
state, the
  and capitalism 103–4
  green state 17–19, 231
  interstate system 5, 16
  neglect of public transport by 118
  promotion of cars by 114–19
  road building by 116–18
subjectivity 121–65, 182–4, 223–4,
    228, 231
suburbanisation 42–5, 66, 72, 76, 82,
    86, 97, 108, 135–6, 203, 223
surveillance 61–2, 141–2, 157–8, 199,
    220–1, 228
sustainability 15, 193, 201, 222,
    225, 232
'Swampy' 166–80
systems theory 26–7, 124–5, 193

Thrift, Nigel 107, 111, 123, 131, 139–42
Toad of Toad Hall 33
Toyota 79, 93, 101, 197

United Kingdom 9–11, 32, 40–1, 44, 47, 61–2, 67, 68–70, 93, 100, 102, 117, 118, 147–62, 164, 166–91
United States 32, 34, 35, 38, 42–3, 48, 52, 54, 56, 57, 65–7, 70–80, 93, 101, 106, 111, 115, 117, 118, 204–8
Urry, John 8–9, 25–7, 88, 89, 106, 107, 109, 123–5, 139, 143, 193, 227

Vauxhall 149, 151, 153–4, 195
Virilio, Paul 4, 5–6, 46, 60, 130–1, 133, 134, 225
Volatile Organic Compounds (VOCs) 37, 38, 195

Wall, Derek 33, 34, 115, 168, 169, 180, 182
war 54–8 128, 129–31, 163–4
    First World War 4, 54, 56, 133–4
    Gulf War 1990–1 56, 57
    Iraq War 2003–8, 54, 56
    mobility as key advantage 4–5
    Second World War 5, 40, 46, 56, 107, 108, 132, 135
war on motorists 62, 65, 68
Wernick, Andrew 47, 115, 147, 153–5
Wolf, Winfried 40, 43, 46, 47, 49, 53, 73, 116, 118, 122
women 47–9, 66, 134, 144
Worldwatch Institute 36, 38–9

Zielinski, Sue 34, 213